J(

D0335079

QUANTITY COOKERY

*Menu Planning and Cookery
for Large Numbers*

BY

NOLA TREAT *and* LENORE RICHARDS

The Richards Treat Cafeteria, Coffee Shop and Food Shop

Formerly Assistant Professors of
Institution Management
College of Agriculture
University of Minnesota

Completely Revised Edition

Little, Brown and Company · Boston

1939

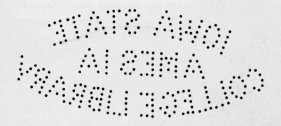

PRINTED IN THE UNITED STATES OF AMERICA

Preface to Revised Edition

This completely revised edition of *Quantity Cookery* is designed to assist managers of food departments in restaurants, schools, colleges and institutions and to serve as a text for teachers of large-quantity cookery.

In this edition that material from *Quantity Cookery* and *Tea-Room Recipes* which has proved most helpful has been revised and brought up to date. To this has been added much that is new, both in recipes and discussions of quantity-cookery problems. The purpose has been to apply the established principles of cookery to large-quantity food production; to set up standards for quantity food production; to give such detailed instructions as to make good cookery easy to accomplish; to standardize the size of servings in amounts acceptable to the eating public; and to offer only those recipes which have been found popular.

The authors wish to acknowledge the work of Mrs. Libby Nessel in the preliminary testing of this material. Special thanks are due to the work done by Mrs. Blanche Wehrend whose care, accuracy and interest in the final checking of these recipes assisted greatly in accomplishing this revision. Acknowledgment is due, also, to the loyalty and interest shown by the staff and employees of the Richards Treat Cafeteria who put these recipes into production to prove their accuracy and who assisted wholeheartedly in the preparation of the manuscript.

Minneapolis, Minnesota   N. T.
March 31, 1939   L. R.

Introduction

The contents of this book have been developed and tested by scientific method and approved by a discriminating clientele. If a cafeteria, restaurant or tearoom maintains and increases its patronage, it must do it by the quality of its food and service and by maintaining prices which customers can afford to pay. It is well known that enough people will pay for good food to justify competent managers to continue with the enterprise.

The authors of this book have placed emphasis where it belongs. They show the importance of accurate recipes or formulæ, the wise use of leftover food, the importance of producing food with excellent flavor and the part that the appearance of food plays in the enjoyment and satisfaction of patrons.

Those who are responsible for the food for school children, or for hotel dining-room and tearoom guests, or for restaurant and cafeteria patrons, will need to put forth every effort to meet their actual responsibility to the public which they serve. The number of people who eat one or more meals away from home is very large at the present time. The number will increase rather than diminish due to the organization of modern society. The age groups vary from the child in the nursery school to the aged in hotels and institutional homes. The nutritional needs of the various age groups must be met at the same time that the expense for food must be kept within such bounds as to allow for a reasonable profit. While home-cooked food has been highly praised and held as the model for commercial enterprises, it is obvious that public eating places can maintain, and some do maintain, a standard for food and service which surpasses the home standard of many families. Public supervision calls for a standard of sanitation not demanded of the home producer of food. Competition keeps the public dispenser of food aware of the necessity of giving excellent food and maintaining the quality from meal to meal and day to day. This is not an easy thing to do; on the other hand, it is a very difficult problem, one calling for constant vigilance on the part of those responsible. The manager of a food enterprise must know good food, must understand how racial differences affect eating habits and how weather and other conditions affect the sale of various foods.

Suggestions have been made by the authors which will help to solve such problems. They have been successful in providing, within the covers of this book, a very large variety of recipes illustrating the use of fruits, vegetables, dairy products, cereals and meats of practically all sorts. This has been accomplished as the result of experimentation and years of successful experience in university cafeterias and dining-rooms, and public business. Travel in this country and foreign countries has added to the authors' knowledge of what constitutes the best in food and service.

One can predict ready acceptance of this fine material, and gratifying results for those who use it. These statements are the result of my interest in the improvement of the quality of food served the public, in the education of young women for the field of institution management, and my respect and appreciation for the high standards maintained by two home economists in the field of public food service.

Wylle B. McNeal
University of Minnesota

Contents

QUANTITY COOKERY

CHAPTER I

Principles Underlying the Planning of Menus for Large Numbers

Well-Balanced and Appropriate Menus Are Necessary to the Success of Any Establishment Serving Food. Given the best of raw materials and the most competent cooks, the institutional manager will fail to please his patrons if his menus show lack of careful planning.

On the other hand, successful menu planning is not especially difficult. Like any other art it requires careful study and observance of a few simple rules.

Of course, it is impossible to formulate one set of rules that will apply to all situations. Each manager must make his own rules based on the conditions he has to meet. There are, however, certain basic principles to be recognized and followed. The ensuing discussion explains these principles and their importance.

In Planning Menus for the Institution There Are Certain Points to Be Kept in Mind:

1. The nature of the institution; its purpose; the character of its patronage.

2. Dietetic principles.

3. The necessity for constant variety in the food choices offered.

4. Temperature, weather, season and holidays.

5. The limitations imposed by equipment, the number and skill of the employees, the range of cost, the leftovers and the speed of service.

The First Point to Consider in Planning a Menu Is the Type of Institution to Be Served. For reasons that are obvious, the purpose of the high-school cafeteria is very different from that of the metropolitan hotel, while neither of these has the same object as the sanitarium.

The Age, Sex, Nationality, Economic Condition and Occupation of the Patrons Must Be Kept in Mind. The adult demands a freedom of choice which may be denied children. For this reason the content of the grade-school lunch may be fixed in an arbitrary way, while this is not possible when one is dealing with adults. For instance, grade-school children are satisfied with the morning bowl of bread and milk and a simple luncheon of soup and sweet. Adults, even in a charitable home, would undoubtedly complain of the simplicity of such meals. The high-school lunchroom may eliminate coffee from its menu and have frequent "pieless" days. Any such attempt to regulate the diet of adults, except from the standpoint of health or for patriotic reasons such as were the incentive to denial during the World War, are highly inadvisable.

As far as the food values are concerned, the same kinds of food may be served to boys and girls or to men and women. But, practically, they will not eat the same foods with equal satisfaction, and this should influence the planning of menus in different institutions.

School-lunch managers and social-service workers have found that in order to accomplish their aims they must recognize racial food tastes.

The economic condition of the group to be served determines the variety in the menu. While the old eight-page menu of the fashionable tearoom has been succeeded by a simpler form and fewer choices, it still reflects the ability of the patrons to pay for and to demand variety in rarer foods and in out-of-season delicacies. On the other hand, the menu offered in the basement-store lunchroom must be governed, ordinarily, by what the customers there can or are willing to pay.

The occupation of the patrons, whether active or sedentary, determines to a large extent the kind of food served to them, from the dietetic standpoint as well as that of their personal likes and dislikes. The lumberjacks of the north woods require and enjoy a diet very different in quality and quantity from that of the telephone operators in a city exchange.

When Serving Set Menus, with Little or No Choice, Special Attention Should Be Given to Dietetic Principles. Examples of such institutions are college dining-halls or dormitories, hospitals, benevolent "homes," boarding houses, fraternities, clubs and restaurants serving table d'hôte or "club" meals.

For those who have had little or no training in dietetics and yet who have the responsibility for planning menus it may be said that if a good variety is provided, with some meat each day and ample fresh vegetables, fruit and milk, the dietetic requirements will probably be met.*

The sequence of foods in the menu is important. Where several courses are to be served, and it is the aim of those planning the menu to keep the appetite stimulated, acids, meat extractives and warm foods should be served first. Cloying foods such as sweets, very cold foods and foods which are satisfying tend to depress the appetite and hence have no place in the first course of a meal, except for luncheon where the menu may be very simple. In institutions which have fixed menus, it is especially desirable that the meal, no matter how simple, be so planned that it may be served in courses. Children especially are likely to hurry through their meals, and the serving of food in courses prevents too rapid eating.

* References on Nutrition Problems:
   Feeding the Family, Mary Swartz Rose, The Macmillan Company.
   Food and Health, Henry C. Sherman, The Macmillan Company.
   Nutrition, Chaney and Ahlborn, Houghton Mifflin Company.

It is true, of course, that extra service requires more labor, and so may not prove possible, even though desirable.

The One Who Is Responsible for the Menu Must Maintain a Constant Variety in Food. This calls for the continued exercise of initiative, the determination to avoid monotonous repetition, a mind open to new foods and new methods of preparation and systematic marketing trips in order to keep in touch with seasonal changes. Perhaps the most frequent criticism of restaurants and institutions serving groups is the lack of variety in meals. Hotels, clubs and tearooms can draw trade by serving out-of-season foods when they first appear in the market. Institutions whose purchases are limited by a budget should make the most of seasonal foods when the market is at its height and the food is cheapest. Such institutions should avoid serving foods that are not actually in season. Serving berries or melons before the height of the season dulls the appetite of the patron for these foods so that by the time they have become economical to serve he has tired of them.

Variety should be introduced not only in the kinds of food but in the preparation, garnish and service. Even in institutions on limited budgets the menus may be made attractive through variety in preparation. For example, corn meal and cottage cheese, two of the least expensive foods we have, can be utilized in a wide variety of ways. There should be no hesitation about serving new dishes, for maximum variety is essential to a happy patronage whether in the tearoom or elsewhere. The point to be kept in mind, where the guest has the privilege of selection, is that all the variety should not come within the day or meal but within the week or month. Surprise always helps to induce appetite and this fact is applicable to all groups.

It Is Good Business Practice As Well As Good Dietetic Practice to Plan Meals According to the Weather and the Time of Year. Hot, heavy foods sell best in cold weather. Cool, crisp, fresh foods sell best on the hottest days. The public is very susceptible to weather conditions. Holidays give a popularity to certain foods which they enjoy at no other time of the year. It is good business to make the most of these foods by serving them on appropriate days.

There Are Definite Relations between the Menu and the Equipment Available for Its Execution. For instance, a menu which calls for oven cooking to the exclusion of the use of the top of the stove or supplementary steamers will be impossible to carry out. The menu should be planned in such a way that the cooking may be divided between all the available equipment, such as ovens, steamers and top space on stoves. In the kitchen, as in the industrial plant, it is good management to give space only to efficient equipment and to use that equipment to its maximum capacity.

Again, inadequate equipment may have to be considered in planning the menu. If there is no power machinery the amount of hand work or heavy physical preparation called for may have to be cut down in accordance with the equipment at hand. In serving large numbers, power machinery will often pay for itself in a few months through the saving in labor. It will not only do the work better and more humanely but will allow a much greater variety of food. In the matter of equipment the institution must get away from the idea that it is a large home, with working conditions as they have been in the average home. It should consider itself an industrial plant where one of the aims is maximum production with minimum labor; and it should realize that proper equipment and proper working conditions are necessary in the accomplishment of this aim. Even though the labor supply may be adequate, efficient planning of menus demands that there be an adjustment between those foods requiring much labor and those requiring little, so that proper balance may be maintained.

In Discussing the Limitations in Menu Making the Element of Cost Has Come Up Again and Again. It becomes a definite restriction in institutions that work on a budget, or where the group to be served demands good, wholesome food at the lowest price. As examples of such institutions there are the factory cafeteria, the school lunch and the college cafeteria, as well as restaurants and hotels whose patrons comprise the lower-income groups. The point to remember in considering cost is that the menu must always be planned for profit. Sometimes the profit aimed for is intangible, such as health and satisfaction, but in the commercial institution it is dollars and cents, and the menu is the "salesman" to bring in this profit.

Though Menus Must Be Made Out in Advance of the Day When They Are to Be Used, They Should Be Sufficiently Elastic to Allow for Proper Utilization of Leftovers. Using leftovers may mean very little change and substitution, or may require complete revision of the day's meals. Leftovers must be used, for it is only by constant care that the food cost can be kept down to a minimum. That this is true of all institutions, whether great or small, is shown by the extreme care exercised in the largest hotels to the end that no food shall be wasted. Where there is family service, rather than plate service from the kitchen, there will probably be a larger amount of leftover food. It requires a good deal of ingenuity to use these leftovers in some other form so as to maintain variety and that element of surprise which is so essential. In restaurants using à la carte service the leftover problem should not be serious, provided the planning is done intelligently. This means that when the menu is planned, the number of servings of each dish likely to be required should be arrived at on the basis of past experience. The required number of servings of each dish is determined by :

1. The popularity of the item.
2. The popularity of the competing items.
3. The amount of the item sold when served last (taking into consideration whether it was served on a day with propitious weather and whether served at a corresponding meal — that is, lunch or dinner).

If records have been kept so that these questions can be answered intelligently, the amount of leftovers will be negligible except when some minor catastrophe such as a heavy rain may descend inopportunely and affect the number of customers.

Menus perfect in themselves are often spoiled by over-production, which is the arch-enemy not only of a proper food cost but of freshness and variety. Overproduction means the carry-over of food from one meal to the next, thereby taking the sparkle and vitality from the best-planned menus because of the need for readjustment to use the leftovers. Quick turnover of food is a prime essential to good food management.

The Speed of Service Required May Affect the Menu. Where especially fast service is demanded the menu should include some pre-dished items. Individual casseroles of stew, chicken pies, jars of beans, while they require more time for preparation, may be worth the effort since they demand no last-minute dishing and hence speed service.

The Question of What Member of the Staff Is to Make Out the Menus Is an Important One. This work calls for a definite aptitude, involving a "feeling" for food and food combinations, creative ability, alertness to all new ideas pertaining to food and service as well as practical business judgment. Too often menu making is turned over to subordinates who lack this ability and interest.

Experience seems to show that the best menus are often made by someone other than the food-production manager. This person is in such close contact with kitchen problems that the tendency is to give too much attention to these problems and to restrict or bias the menu accordingly with the result that the menus drift into routine monotony. The best menus are made by the person who is able to see the public's point of view. Often this is not the person who is in charge of the kitchen and who, as has been said, consequently recognizes all too well the difficulties of production, but one in the merchandising end of the business who better knows what the customer wants, demands and will find satisfaction in finding on the menu.

CHAPTER II

Standards for Judging Meals

Provided the Principles of Good Nutrition Have Not Been Violated, the Main Basis for Judging Any Meal Is Palatability. Palatability depends upon appearance and quality. Appearance in turn depends upon quantity, color, form and service upon the plate. Quality is determined by odor, flavor, temperature, texture and consistency. Reduced to outline form, the elements of palatability are :

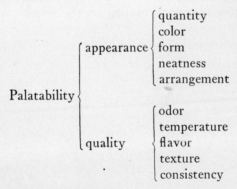

$$\text{Palatability} \begin{cases} \text{appearance} \begin{cases} \text{quantity} \\ \text{color} \\ \text{form} \\ \text{neatness} \\ \text{arrangement} \end{cases} \\ \\ \text{quality} \begin{cases} \text{odor} \\ \text{temperature} \\ \text{flavor} \\ \text{texture} \\ \text{consistency} \end{cases} \end{cases}$$

Commercially and Æsthetically It Is Unwise to Make Servings Too Large. Everyone has had the experience of being served with more food than can be eaten with relish and without waste. The effect is to surfeit the appetite and to limit the variety which a patron may have, unless he is able financially to order the variety ; in which case he is obliged to leave some food uneaten. In any institution which serves à la carte, it is better to adjust portions and prices to the end that the patron may have some variety in his meal without prohibitive expense.

Color Is Important in Inducing Appetite. The cafeteria counter displaying a buff-colored pie, snow pudding, rice custard and yellow cake does not tempt patrons to buy. A basket of fruit, a bright-colored gelatin dessert or attractive garnishes may transform a drab meal into a most interesting one. Particularly in all kinds of plate service, attention must be paid to color, for while clashing color combinations must be avoided, some color must be used to give the food an appetizing appearance. A great deal of our food is very neutral in color and admits of a liberal use of garnishes of one kind or another.

As a Rule Articles of Food Served Together Should Be of Diverse Shapes. One may enjoy a croquette, a stuffed baked potato, peas in timbales and a roll in the same meal, but it is usually uninteresting to serve them on the same plate.

The Necessity for Neatness and Orderly Arrangement of Servings Is Obvious. Where there is plate service, it is wise to make up a sample plate before the time of serving in order to determine the best arrangement of food and in order actually to show those who are to dish up the food how each plate must look when it is placed before the guest. One who is inexperienced in planning menus, especially for table d'hôte service, should accustom himself to visualizing the meal as it will appear when written upon the menu card and as it will appear upon the plate. A menu which has seemed very good when planned will often be unsatisfactory when actually served because some of the above points have been overlooked.

Odor and Temperature Are Important Factors in Quality. It would seem superfluous to say that hot things must be served hot, and cold things must be served cold, yet in serving large numbers the strict observance of these rules is one of the difficult problems to be solved. It can be solved, however, with efficient equipment properly arranged, a carefully-thought-out organization of service and unceasing care.

Repetition of Texture and Consistency Should Also Be Avoided. That is to say, there should be the maximum variety in preparation of food in order that no meal, to give a few examples, shall contain two or more creamed dishes, fried foods, foods with custard basis or foods with bread foundation.

If a Score Card Were Made Out for Judging a Meal, Flavor Would Perhaps Be Given the Most Importance. Here again care must be taken to avoid duplicating flavors. Too many strong flavors or too many bland flavors are undesirable. While strong flavors stimulate the appetite it is unwise to employ them continually, especially where the same group of people is being served day after day. A more blandly flavored diet is likely to be less palling and more constantly inviting.

In Serving the Public the Aim Should Always Be to Have the Food Better Than That to Which the Patrons Are Accustomed. As an aid to accomplishing this aim, visiting trips to the best hotels, tearooms, inns, cafeterias and restaurants are invaluable. These trips impart a knowledge of the way things are done, which in turn creates a confidence and assurance that nothing else can give.

CHAPTER III

Examples of Good Menus

The menus of successful commercial restaurants may well be studied with the idea of noting what these restaurants have found in greatest demand in food as well as in the number of choices offered. It is interesting to note that in contrast to the almost unlimited choice of some years ago, restaurants and institutions everywhere are endeavoring to reduce the number of items on their menu to the minimum that will satisfy their patrons.

The authors feel especially privileged to be able to reprint here examples of menus from three of the outstanding restaurants in the country. These menus represent a cafeteria; an organization of restaurants with branches in several cities; and a tearoom. They admirably illustrate what is best in present-day menu making.

SAMPLE CAFETERIA MENU *

(In Order of Arrangement Approaching Counter)

SALADS, JUICES AND COCKTAILS

Head Lettuce with Choice of Dressing
Water Cress with Choice of Dressing
Section Fruit Salad
Diet (Chopped Cabbage, Carrots, Pickles)
Tossed Green Salad Bowl
Endive with Choice of Dressing
Tomato Stuffed with Tuna Fish Salad
Blackstone (Pineapple, Orange, Cottage Cheese)

* Reproduced through courtesy of the Grace E. Smith Company, Toledo, Ohio.

APPETIZERS
Chicken Fresh Vegetable Soup
Frosted Fruit Cup
Chilled Tomato Juice

SALAD PLATES
Cinnamon Roll, Raised or Hard Roll
For 20c additional Choice of a 15c Dessert and Coffee, Tea or Milk
Chilled Fresh Fruit Salad with
English Walnuts, Cinnamon Roll

Salad Bowl of Tossed Fresh
Vegetables, French Dressing .

Old Fashioned Potato Salad with
Buttered Green Peas . .

Chicken and Fresh Vegetable Salad
with Dressing, Cinnamon Roll .

VEGETABLES
Corn on the Cob . . . .
Waffle Potatoes . . . . .
Fresh Green Beans . . . .
Buttered Green Peas . . .
Creamed Mushrooms a la King .
Whipped Potatoes . . . .

Saturday, August 20

A SUMMER SUGGESTION
Fresh Crabmeat Salad with
Waffle Potatoes and Fresh Tomato Slice
Blueberry Pie
Choice of Freshly Baked Rolls   Coffee, Tea or Milk

LUNCHEON PLATES
Cinnamon Roll, Raised or Hard Roll
For 20c additional Choice of a 15c Dessert and Coffee, Tea or Milk
Chicken and Gravy with Toasted Noodles, Broiled
Fresh Peach, Green Peas . . . .   .

Cold Baked Ham with Fresh Mushrooms a la King
on Toast, Sliced Tomato Salad . . .   .

Cheese Souffle with Tomato Sauce, Chilled Fresh Fruit Salad

Individual Beef Steak Pie with Whipped Potato Top,
Fresh Green Peas . . . .   .

Fresh Vegetable Plate .
Corn on the Cob, Fresh Green Beans,
Whipped Potatoes and Gravy

Fresh Crabmeat Salad with Waffle Potatoes and
Fresh Tomato Slice . . . .   .

SANDWICHES
For 20c additional Choice of a 15c Dessert and Coffee, Tea or Milk
Sardine, American Cheese and Chili Sauce on Toast . . .
Toasted Bacon and Tomato with Crisp Lettuce . . .
Roast Fresh Ham with Spiced New Apple Sauce . . .
Sliced Tomato and Egg with Crisp Lettuce and
Thousand Island Dressing . . .
Salmon Salad with Watercress on White Bread . . .
Sliced Chicken and Crisp Bacon on Toast with Jelly . .

DESSERTS AND ICE CREAMS
Ice Cream Puff with Fresh Peaches
New Apple Pie with Cheese
Chocolate Chiffon Pudding with
Whipped Cream and Pecans
Silver Coconut Cream Cake
Chilled Melon Cup with Frosted
Cake Square
Dutch Fresh Peach Pie
Double Chocolate Sundae
Ice Cream with Frosted
Cake Square
Vanilla, Chocolate, Special Ice Creams
or Sherbet

FRESH FRUITS
Chilled Melon
Fresh Peaches and Cream
Stewed Fresh Pears with
Whipped Cream

BEVERAGES AND SODAS
Fresh Lime Orangeade
Ice Tea or Coffee
Choco Milk   Coca Cola
Malted Milk (all flavors)
Coffee   (second cup if desired)
Milk, bottle   Buttermilk
Pineapple, Fresh Lemon or Chocolate
Soda

APPETIZERS
Fresh Vegetable Soup
Chilled Tomato Juice
New Apple Cider

SALAD PLATES
Currant Muffin, Raised or Hard Roll
Sardine, Head Lettuce and Sliced
Tomato Salad with Thousand
Island Dressing . . . .

Peach, Pear and Pineapple Salad
with Cream Dressing, Currant
Muffin . . . .

Fresh Vegetable Salad, Thousand
Island Dressing . . . .

Fruit Salad Plate with Cream
Dressing, Currant Muffin . .

VEGETABLES
Fresh Green Peas . . .
New Brussels Sprouts . . .
Glazed Sweet Potatoes . . .
French Fried Eggplant . . .
Parsley New Potatoes . . .

Saturday, October 22

A SUGGESTION
Chicken and Gravy on Hot Biscuit
Fresh Cranberry Relish, New Brussels Sprouts
Fresh Lemon Meringue Pie
Currant Muffin   Coffee, Tea or Milk

LUNCHEON PLATES
Currant Muffin, Raised or Hard Roll
For 20c additional Choice of a 15c Dessert and Coffee, Tea or Milk
Chicken and Gravy on Hot Biscuit, Fresh Cranberry Relish,
New Brussels Sprouts . . . .

Roast Round of Beef au jus with Parsley Potatoes,
Carrot and Celery Salad . . . . . .

Broiled Bacon and Sliced Tomatoes on Toast with
Rarebit Sauce, Crispy Pickles . . . . .

Fresh Vegetable Plate .
French Fried Eggplant, Carrot and Celery Salad, Fresh Green Peas

Pork Chop Baked in Tomato Sauce, New Brussels Sprouts,
Glazed Sweet Potatoes . . . .

Crabmeat, Egg and Fresh Mushrooms en Casserole,
Fresh Green Peas . . . .

SANDWICHES
For 20c additional Choice of a 15c Dessert and Coffee, Tea or Milk
Toasted York State Cheese and Pineapple Ring . . . .
Sardine and Tartar Sauce on Rye Bread . . . . . .
Junior Club . . .
Sliced Chicken, Broiled Bacon and Tomato on Toast
Roast Fresh Ham and Tomato Relish . . . . . .
Egg Salad and Fresh Chives on Whole Wheat Bread . .
Roast Beef and Chopped Mustard Pickles on Toast . . .

DESSERTS AND FRUITS
Steamed Chocolate Pudding with Hard
and Supreme Sauce
Mincemeat Pie
English Walnut Layer Cake
Fresh Lemon Meringue Pie
Orange and Banana Cup with
Cookie
Huckleberry Pie
Tapioca Cream Pudding
Sherbet and Ice Cream with Cookie
Dutch Apple Pie with Cheese

ICE CREAMS AND SUNDAES
Fruit Salad Sundae
Chocolate Fudge Sundae
Pecan Ice Cream Roll with Hot Rum
Toffee Sauce
Cherry 'Mallow Sundae
Chocolate Toasted Almond Sundae
Vanilla, Chocolate, Special Ice Creams
or Sherbet

BEVERAGES AND SODAS
Coffee   (second cup if desired)
Tea, per Pot   Choco' Milk
Hot Chocolate
Chocolate or Pineapple Soda
Milk, bottle   Buttermilk
Beer, per bottle

Fresh Shrimp Cocktail
Orange, Prune, Tomato and Pineapple Juice

ENTREES

Roast Prime Ribs of Beef
Baked Whitefish with Butter Sauce
Casserole Sea Food au Gratin
Roast Leg of Lamb with Mintlade
Veal Bird with Mushroom Sauce
Pork Chop with Apple Sauce
Stuffed Baked Pepper with Tomato Sauce

SOUPS

French Onion; Cream of Vegetable

VEGETABLES AND HOT BREADS

Mashed Potatoes
Lyonnaise Potatoes
Green Beans
Baked Creole Tomato
Brussels Sprouts
Harvard Beets
Fresh Buttered Peas
Creamed Celery
Corn O'Brien
Buttered Fresh Spinach
Spaghetti and Cheese
Boston Baked Beans
Smith's Special Rolls and Bran Muffins

DESSERTS

PUDDINGS AND FRUITS

Tapioca Cream Pudding; Chocolate Cream Pudding
Boysen Berries; Stewed Pears; Stewed Apricots
Spanish Cream Mold with Cherry Sauce
Ohio Steamed Pudding with Date Nut Sauce

PIES AND CAKES

Chocolate Layer Cake with Chocolate Filling
Yellow Layer Cake with Fresh Cocoanut Icing

DESSERTS (*Continued*)

PIES

Apple, Cherry, Peach Pie
Lemon Meringue Pie; Fresh Pumpkin Pie

BREAD, ROLLS AND BUTTER

White, Rye, Whole Wheat and Oatmeal Bread
Hard and Sweet Rolls

BEVERAGES

Tea, Coffee, Cocoa, Sanka
Milk or Chocolate Milk

SPECIAL LUNCHEON
$1.00

*Maramor Salad Bowl
of
Fresh Crab, Fresh Shrimp or Chicken*

Toasted English Muffins

Frozen Fresh Cocoanut Ball with Chocolate Sauce

Coffee, Tea or Milk

WE CANNOT SUBSTITUTE

Reproduced through the courtesy of The Maramor,
Columbus, Ohio.

Appetizers

Orange and Avocado Cocktail

Fresh Crab Cocktail   Chilled Fruit Cocktail
Fresh Lobster Cocktail   Chilled Tomato Juice with Canapés

New Orleans Fresh Shrimp Appetizer

Soups

Oyster Stew   Fresh Mushroom Bisque   Chicken Noodle Soup

Luncheon Plates

MARAMOR ASSORTED MUFFINS AND BREADS ARE PASSED WITH THESE ORDERS

Turkey Hash with Poached Egg Center, Grape Preserves and Toasted Rolls
Devilled Fresh Crab Served with Orange, Avocado and Grapefruit Salad
Broiled Calves' Sweetbreads on Toast with Fresh Green Peas and Stuffed Blue Plums
Pot Roast of Beef with Assorted Vegetables
Old Favorite—Fresh Mushrooms Chantilly on Sauted Egg Plant with Preserved Orange and Toasted English Muffins
Broiled Tenderloin Steak (Luncheon Size) with Assorted Vegetables

A Plate of Assorted Vegetables

Fruits ~ Sweets

Imported Crème de Menthe Parfait   Angel Pudding with Fruit   Custard Pie
Butterscotch Pecan Sundae   Frozen Pecan Cake Ball with Chocolate Sauce   Cherry Pie
Chocolate Mint Meringue   Frozen Raspberry Macaroon Glacé   Blueberry Pie a la Mode
Compote of Fruit with Cheese   Individual Buttercream Cakes   Lady Baltimore Cake

maramor made ice creams   (Coffee   Mint   Orange Delicious)

maramor made ices   (Raspberry   Pineapple   Mint)

Camembert or Roquefort Cheese with Toasted Wafers

October The Twenty Sixth

CHAPTER IV

Suggestive Lists To Be Used in Menu Planning

LIST OF FOODS

SOUPS

CREAM SOUPS

Cream of Asparagus
Cream of Lima Bean
Cream of Navy Bean
Cream of Fresh Carrot
Cream of Celery
Cream of Chicken
Cream of Corn
Cream of Fresh Mushroom
Cream of Browned Onion
Cream of Pea
Cream of Split Pea
Cream of Peanut Butter
Cream of Potato
Cream of Potato and Onion
Cream of Spinach
Cream of Tomato
Cream of Tomato and Celery
Cream of Tomato and Corn
Cream of Tomato and Water Cress
Cream of Fresh Vegetable
Corn Chowder
Fish Chowder
New England Clam Chowder
Oyster Stew
Swedish Rice

SOUPS (*Continued*)

CREAM SOUPS

_____

_____

_____

_____

_____

STOCK SOUPS

Bean Soup
Beef Noodle
Bouillon
Chicken Broth
Chicken Giblet
Chicken Mushroom
Chicken Noodle
Chicken Okra
Chicken Rice
Chicken Rice Soup with Fresh Vegetables
Clam Bisque
Clam Bisque with Mushrooms
Consommé
Creole
Italian Minestrone
Lentil
Manhattan Clam Chowder
Mutton Broth
Paris Market Onion
Split Pea
Scotch Broth with Barley
Tomato Bouillon
Tomato Rice
Vegetable

_____

_____

_____

MEATS

BEEF

Beef à la Mode
German Pot Roast (*Sauerbraten*)
Hot Roast Beef Sandwich
Mock Duck
Pot Roast of Beef
Rib Roast of Beef
Broiled Steaks: Sirloin, Tenderloin, Porterhouse, Club
Chopped Steaks
Cubed Steaks
Swiss Steak, with Brown Gravy
Swiss Steak, with Tomato Sauce
Braised Ox-Joints
Braised Short Ribs and Noodles
Braised Short Ribs and Browned Potatoes
Corned Beef and Cabbage
New England Boiled Dinner
Baked Meat Pie
Baked Meat Pie with Dressing
Meat Stew with Dumpling
Meat Stew with Fresh Vegetables
Creamed Dried Beef on Toast
Creamed Dried Beef on Toast with Buttered Green Beans
Creamed Dried Beef with Noodles en Casserole
Baked Roast Beef Hash
Beef Biscuit Roll, Mushroom Sauce
Beef Loaf, Mushroom Sauce
Chopped Beef and Macaroni au Gratin

MEATS (*Continued*)

BEEF

Corned Beef Hash
Corned Beef Hash with Poached Egg
Hamburg Balls
Hamburg Balls with French Fried Onions
Hamburg Balls with Pan Fried Onions
Hamburg Balls with Spaghetti au Gratin
Hungarian Goulash with Homemade Noodles
Meat Croquettes with Mushroom Sauce
Meat Croquettes with Creole Sauce
Spanish Spaghetti
Baked Beef Heart with Sage Dressing
Frankfurters with Mustard Sauce
Neapolitan Macaroni
Fresh Tongue with Mustard Sauce
Pickled Tongue with Fresh Spinach

PORK

Roast Pork and Dressing
Roast Pork, Dressing and Apple Sauce
Broiled Pork Tenderloin
Pork Chops with Red Apple Rings
Stuffed Pork Chops
Stuffed Pork Chops with Wild Rice
Baked Ham
Baked Ham with Raisin Sauce
Broiled Ham with Fresh Asparagus and Cheese Sauce
Broiled Ham with Pineapple Rings
Ham à la King in Noodle Ring

Ham Baked in Milk
Ham and Corn Baked in Green Pepper
Ham and Eggs
Ham Fondue with Parsley Cream Sauce
Ham Hocks and Sauerkraut
Ham Loaf; Horse-Radish Sauce
Ham Patties and Baked Lima Beans
Ham Pies
Ham and Potatoes au Gratin
Ham Rarebit on Toasted Rolls
Scalloped Ham with Mushrooms and Celery
Bacon with Glazed Sweet Potatoes and Pineapple
Creamed Fried Salt Pork on Corn Bread
Country Sausage and Cream Gravy
Country Sausage and Fried Apples
Barbecued Spare Ribs
Spare Ribs and Dressing; Sauerkraut; Fried Apples
Thuringer Sausages Baked with Sauerkraut

LAMB AND MUTTON
Roast Lamb, Mint Sauce
Stuffed Lamb Shoulder
Roast Mutton
Broiled Lamb Chops
Mutton Chops
Lamb Croquettes with Fresh Peas
Lamb Curry with Rice Mounds
Lamb Hash à la George Rector
Lamb Stew with Dumplings
Lamb Stew with Fresh Vegetables

MEATS (*Continued*)

LAMB AND MUTTON

Mutton Stew

_____

_____

_____

_____

_____

VEAL

Roast Veal and Dressing
Breaded Veal Cutlets
Paprika Schnitzel
Veal Birds, with Mushroom Gravy
Veal Cutlet with Buttered Noodles
Baked Veal Pie with Fresh Vegetables
Liver Patties in Bacon Ring
Scalloped Veal with Rice
Veal Croquette with Creamed Pea Sauce
Veal Curry on Rice
Veal Loaf with Mushroom Sauce
Veal Rosettes with Jelly
Veal Stew with Dumplings
Veal Stew with Fresh Vegetables
Braised Veal Hearts
Broiled Calves' Liver and Bacon
Creamed Sweetbreads and Mushrooms
Creamed Sweetbreads in Patty Shells
Creamed Sweetbreads and Peas with Parsleyed
    Biscuit Rings
Sweetbreads à la King
Veal Hearts en Casserole

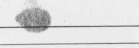

_____

_____

_____

CHICKEN

Roast Chicken
Chicken and Dumplings; Biscuits
Chicken Fricassee
Fried Chicken
Chicken Maryland
Chicken Pie
New England Chicken Pot Pie
Chicken à la King
Creamed Chicken with Hot Biscuits
Creamed Chicken in Bread Cases
Creamed Chicken and Corn Bread
Creamed Chicken in Patty Shells
Creamed Chicken and Peas with Biscuit Rings
Creamed Chicken on Toast
Creamed Chicken and Waffles
Baked Chicken and Ham Pie
Chicken Biscuit Roll, Mushroom Gravy
Chicken and Cheese Croquettes
Chicken Croquettes with Peas
Chicken and Ham Croquettes
Chicken Hash
Chicken and Noodles
Chicken and Potatoes au Gratin
Chicken and Rice, Cuban Style
Chicken Shortcake
Chicken and Spaghetti
Curried Chicken and Rice
Hot Chicken Sandwich
Hot Chopped Chicken Sandwich
Jellied Chicken Loaf
Macaroni Ring with Creamed Chicken

MEATS (*Continued*)

CHICKEN

Scalloped Chicken and Rice
Scalloped Chicken, Mushrooms and Almonds
Chicken Giblet and Bacon Sandwich
Chicken Giblets on Corn Bread
Chicken Giblets, Cuban Style
Chicken Giblets and Noodles
Creamed Chicken Giblets on Rice Molds
Creamed Chicken Giblets on Toast
Scalloped Eggplant, Mushrooms and Giblets

_____

_____

_____

_____

FISH

Baked Bluefish
Clams, Steamed
Codfish
    Creamed Codfish on Boiled Potato
    Creamed Codfish and Egg on Boiled Potato
    Codfish Balls, Parsley Cream Sauce
Crabmeat
    Scalloped Crabmeat with Noodles and Almonds
    Creamed Crabmeat on Toast
Finnan Haddie
    Creamed Finnan Haddie on Toast
    Creamed Finnan Haddie on Boiled Potato
Fish à la King
Fish Cakes
Fish Chowder
Baked Fish Fillets with Dressing and Egg Sauce
Fish Ring with Egg Sauce

Scalloped Fish and Egg
Fish Soufflé with Crabmeat Sauce
Fish Soufflé with Fresh Shrimp Sauce
Haddock
   Broiled Fillet of Haddock
   Fried Fillet of Haddock
Halibut
   Baked Halibut with Creamed Shrimp Sauce
   Baked Halibut with Dressing
   Fried Halibut
Lobster
   Broiled African Lobster Tails
   Broiled Lobster
   Creamed Lobster
   Lobster, Farci (Stuffed)
   Lobster Newburg
   Lobster, Noodles and Almonds en Casserole
Broiled Pompano
Mackerel
   Broiled Mackerel
   Baked in Cream
Salmon
   Creamed Salmon on Toast
   Salmon Croquettes
   Baked Salmon
   Salmon Loaf, Pea Sauce
   Scalloped Salmon
   Salmon Steak, Broiled
   Salmon Steak, Fried
   Scallops, Fried, with Tartare Sauce
Shrimp
   Shrimp Cocktail
   Creamed Shrimp on Toast
   Curried Shrimp with Rice
   French Fried Shrimp

MEATS (*Continued*)

FISH

Smelts, Fried, with Tartare Sauce
Sole, Baked Fillet of Sole; Fried
Trout: Fried; Baked; Broiled
Tuna Fish Loaf, Rarebit Sauce
Whitefish
  Steamed; Baked; Planked with Dressing
Oysters
  Creamed Oysters on Toast
  Fried Oysters
  Oyster Cocktail
  Oyster Pie
  Oyster Stew
  Pigs in Blanket
  Scalloped Oysters

_____

_____

_____

_____

_____

EGGS

Eggs à la Goldenrod
Eggs à la King
Eggs à la King in Spinach Ring
Baked Eggs in Ramekin
Baked Eggs in Potato Nest
Creamed Eggs on Toast
Creamed Stuffed Eggs on Toast
Egg Croquettes, Tomato Sauce
Egg Cutlets, Parsley Cream Sauce
Fried Eggs with Bacon
Fried Eggs with Ham
Omelet with Creamed Chicken Giblets
Omelet with Jelly

Omelet with Chopped Parsley
Poached Eggs
Poached Eggs on Toast
Scrambled Eggs with Bacon
Scrambled Eggs with Chicken Giblets
Scrambled Eggs with Cubed Ham
Scrambled Eggs with Jelly
Scrambled Eggs with Marmalade
Scrambled Eggs with Fried Green Tomatoes

_____

_____

_____

_____

_____

CHEESE DISHES

Asparagus Tips with Rarebit Sauce on Toast
Asparagus Tips on Broiled Ham with Rarebit Sauce
Cottage Cheese and Nut Croquettes
Cottage Cheese Loaf with Nuts and Green Peppers,
    Cheese Sauce
Cheese Fondue
Cheese Fondue with Creole Sauce
Hominy and Cheese
Macaroni and Cheese
Macaroni and Cheese with Grilled Tomato and Bacon
Scalloped Rice and Cheese
Scotch Woodcock on Toast
Cheese Soufflé
Spaghetti and Cheese
Welsh Rarebit on Toast

_____

_____

_____

_____

_____

MEATS (*Continued*)

MEAT SUBSTITUTES

Macaroni Loaf, Cheese Sauce
Macaroni Loaf, Mushroom Sauce
Broiled Fresh Mushrooms
Creamed Mushrooms on Toast
Creamed Fresh Mushrooms with Rice Mounds
Creamed Fresh Mushrooms with Wild Rice
Toasted Mushroom Sandwich
Peanut and Rice Loaf, Cheese Sauce
Rice Croquettes, Syrup
Rice and Nut Loaf, Cheese Sauce
Rice Omelet
Spanish Rice
Spaghetti and Mushrooms
Spaghetti and Tomatoes

_____

_____

_____

_____

_____

PANCAKES AND WAFFLES

Buckwheat Cakes
Corn Cakes
Crumb Griddle Cakes
Wheat Cakes
Waffles
Chocolate Waffles
Ginger-Cake Waffles
Pecan Waffles

_____

_____

_____

_____

_____

VEGETABLES

ASPARAGUS

Buttered Asparagus
Buttered Asparagus on Toast
Creamed Asparagus
Creamed Asparagus on Toast

_____

_____

_____

_____

_____

BEANS

Buttered Green Beans with Carrots and Celery
Buttered Green Beans with Carrots and Peas
Creamed Green Beans
Green Beans, French Style
Kidney Beans
Baked Lima Beans
Buttered Lima Beans
Green Lima Beans in Cream
Boston Baked Beans
Boiled Navy Beans
Succotash
Buttered Wax Beans

_____

_____

_____

_____

_____

BEETS

Buttered Beets
Beet Greens with Bacon
Harvard Beets

VEGETABLES (*Continued*)

BEETS
Pickled Beets
Beets Stuffed with Spinach
Beets in Vinegar

BROCCOLI
Buttered Broccoli
Creamed Broccoli
Broccoli with Hollandaise Sauce
Broccoli Soufflé

BRUSSELS SPROUTS
Buttered Brussels Sprouts
Creamed Brussels Sprouts
Brussels Sprouts with Hollandaise Sauce

CABBAGE
Cabbage au Gratin
Buttered Cabbage

Creamed Cabbage
Fried Cabbage
Hot Slaw
Red Cabbage and Apples
Sauerkraut
Scalloped Cabbage

CARROTS
Buttered Carrots
Buttered Carrots and Onion Rings
Buttered Carrots and Peas
Creamed Carrots
Creamed Carrots and Peas
Creamed Carrots in Spinach Ring
Minted Carrots
Parsleyed Carrots

CAULIFLOWER
Buttered Cauliflower
Cauliflower with Buttered Crumbs
Cauliflower with Cheese Sauce
Cauliflower with Hollandaise Sauce
Creamed Cauliflower
French Fried Cauliflower
Scalloped Cauliflower in Ramekins

VEGETABLES (*Continued*)

CAULIFLOWER
Scalloped Cauliflower au Gratin

_____

_____

_____

_____

_____

CELERY
Buttered Celery
Buttered Celery with Peas and Carrots
Creamed Celery

_____

_____

_____

_____

_____

CELERY CABBAGE
Buttered Celery Cabbage
Celery Cabbage in Cream

_____

_____

_____

_____

_____

CORN
Corn on the Cob
Corn in Cream
Fried Corn
Corn Fritters
Corn with Green and Red Peppers
Corn Pudding

Scalloped Corn
Succotash

_____

_____

_____

_____

_____

EGGPLANT

Broiled Eggplant
Fried Eggplant
Scalloped Eggplant
Eggplant Fritters with Orange Marmalade

_____

_____

_____

_____

HOMINY

Buttered Hominy
Creamed Hominy
Fried Hominy

_____

_____

_____

_____

LETTUCE

Wilted Lettuce with Bacon

_____

_____

MACARONI

Macaroni and Cheese
Macaroni Croquettes

VEGETABLES (*Continued*)

MACARONI
Macaroni and Tomatoes

_____

_____

_____

_____

_____

MUSHROOMS
Creamed Mushrooms

_____

_____

NOODLES
Buttered Noodles
Creamed Noodles
Scalloped Noodles and Fresh Vegetables
Noodles and Mushrooms

_____

_____

_____

_____

ONIONS
Onions au Gratin
Baked Stuffed Onions
Buttered Onions
Creamed Onions
French Fried Onions
Pan Fried Onions
Onion Rings with Green Peas
Scalloped Onions

_____

_____

_____

_____

_____

PARSNIPS
  Buttered Parsnips
  Fried Parsnips

_____

_____

_____

_____

_____

PEAS
  Buttered Peas
  Buttered Peas and Carrots
  Buttered Peas with Small Green Onions
  Creamed Peas
  Creamed Peas and Carrots
  Scalloped Peas, Eggs and Celery
  Creamed Peas with Dumplings

_____

_____

_____

_____

_____

PEPPERS
  Peppers Stuffed with Corn
  Peppers Stuffed with Meat

_____

_____

_____

_____

_____

VEGETABLES (*Continued*)

POTATOES

Potatoes au Gratin
Baked Potatoes
Stuffed Baked Potatoes
Browned Potatoes
Hashed Browned Potatoes
Potato Cakes
Potato Cones
Creamed Potatoes
Creamed Potatoes with Carrots and Peas
Potato Croquettes
American Fried Potatoes
French Fried Potatoes
Lyonnaise Potatoes
Mashed Potatoes
Parsley Buttered Potatoes
Potato Chips
Potatoes O'Brien
Potato Pancakes with Apple Sauce
Potato Puffs
Riced Potatoes
Hot Potato Salad
Scalloped Potatoes
Shoestring Potatoes
Sweet Potatoes, Baked
Boiled Sweet Potatoes
Almond and Sweet Potato Croquettes
Sweet Potato Croquettes
Fried Sweet Potatoes
Glazed Sweet Potatoes
Baked Mashed Sweet Potatoes with Marshmallows
Scalloped Sweet Potatoes with Apples; Oranges; Pineapple

RICE
  Buttered Rice
  Buttered Brown Rice
  Rice in Cream
  Rice Croquettes
  Scalloped Rice and Cheese
  Spanish Rice
  Wild Rice, Creamed Mushrooms

RUTABAGAS
  Buttered Rutabagas
  Mashed Rutabagas

SPAGHETTI
  Spaghetti Croquettes
  Spaghetti and Tomatoes
  Spaghetti and Tomatoes with Bacon Strips

VEGETABLES (*Continued*)

SPINACH

Spinach and Egg
Spinach and Lemon
Spinach with Broiled Mushrooms
Spinach Ring and Creamed Carrots
Spinach Soufflé, Cheese Sauce

_____

_____

_____

_____

_____

SQUASH

Baked Squash
Mashed Squash
Buttered Summer Squash
Summer Squash in Cream

_____

_____

_____

_____

TOMATOES

Baked Stuffed Tomatoes
Grilled Tomatoes
Scalloped Tomatoes
Scalloped Tomatoes with Hominy
Stewed Tomatoes
Stewed Tomatoes with Corn

_____

_____

_____

_____

_____

TURNIPS
  Buttered Diced Turnips
  Creamed Turnips
  Mashed Turnips

_____

_____

_____

_____

_____

_____

FRUITS USED AS ACCOMPANIMENTS TO MEATS
  Apples
    Fried Apples
    Baked Apples
  Apricots
    Hot Spiced Apricots
  Bananas
    Baked
    French Fried
  Pears
    Hot Gingered Pears
  Pineapple
    Glazed
  Prunes
    Hot Spiced Prunes
  Raisins
    Hot Spiced Raisins

_____

_____

_____

_____

_____

_____

BREADS
QUICK BREADS
Biscuit Type
Baking Powder Biscuits
Biscuit Cinnamon Rolls with Frosting
Cheese Biscuits
Drop Biscuits
Graham Biscuits
Orange Biscuits
Peanut Butter Biscuits
Scotch Scones

_____

_____

_____

_____

_____

Loaf Breads
Banana Bread
Brown Bread
Cherry Nut Bread
Date Bread
Gingerbread
Nut Bread
Nut and Raisin Bread
Orange Bread

_____

_____

_____

_____

_____

Muffins
Bacon Muffins
Blueberry Muffins
Bran Muffins

Corn Muffins
Cranberry Muffins
Crumb Muffins
Date Muffins
Date and Nut Muffins
Ginger Muffins
Graham Muffins
Grapenut Muffins
Honey Muffins
Orange Muffins
Pineapple Muffins
Prune Bran Muffins
Raisin Graham Muffins
Rice Muffins
Rye Muffins
White Muffins

Miscellaneous
Popovers
Corn Bread
Spoon Bread

YEAST BREADS
Breads
Cheese Bread
Chocolate Bread

BREADS (*Continued*)

YEAST BREADS

Cracked-Wheat Bread
Graham Bread
Nut Bread
Oatmeal Bread
Raisin Bread
Raisin Spice Bread
Old-fashioned Rye Bread
Salt Rising Bread
Sweet Rye Bread
White Bread

_____

_____

_____

_____

_____

Coffee Cakes

Almond Coffee Cake
Dutch Apple Coffee Cake
German Coffee Cake
Fruit Coffee Cake
Swedish Cardamon Coffee Cake
Tea Rings

_____

_____

_____

_____

_____

Rolls

Bran Rolls
Brioches
Butterfluff Rolls

Caramel Rolls
Cinnamon Rolls
Cloverleaf Rolls
Cottage Rolls
Crescent Rolls
Currant Buns
Dinnerette Rolls
Finger Rolls
French Rolls
Graham Rolls
Graham Parkerhouse Rolls
Hot Cross Buns
Orange Rolls
Parkerhouse Rolls
Pecan Rolls
Poppy Seed Rolls
Raisin Twists
Sesame Rolls
Twin Rolls

_____

_____

_____

_____

_____

Muffins
English Muffins
Raised Muffins
Squash Muffins

_____

_____

_____

_____

_____

_____

SALADS

FRUIT SALADS

Apple, Banana and Date
Apple and Cabbage
Apple, Celery and Nut
Apple, Date and Celery
Apple and Pineapple
Apple, White Grape and Almond
Shredded Apple, Stuffed Prune and Celery
Apricot, Raisin and Marshmallow
Avocado
Avocado, Orange and Water Cress
Banana, Pecan and Red Cherry
Bing Cherry
All Fresh Fruit
Frozen Fruit
Malaga Grapes and Orange
Grapefruit
Grapefruit and Avocado
Grapefruit and Stuffed Celery
Grapefruit, Orange and Pineapple
Grapefruit and Pear with Cream Cheese
Grapefruit and Romaine
Orange and Bermuda Onion
Orange and Nut
Peach Stuffed with Cream Cheese
Pear and Cream Cheese
Fresh Bartlett Pear and Roquefort Cheese
Fresh Pineapple and Apricot with English Chutney
    Dressing
Pineapple, Cream Cheese and Date
Pineapple and Grated Cheese
Stuffed Prune with Cream Cheese
Stuffed Prune with Orange Sections

GELATIN SALADS
Jellied Apricot
Jellied Carrot and Pineapple
Cider
Jellied Cranberry
Lime Jelly with Cottage Cheese and Candied Orange
    Peel
Mexican Gelatin
Jellied Pear
Perfection Salad
Tomato Aspic
Tomato Aspic with Cottage Cheese Layer
Tomato Aspic with Vegetable
Jellied Vegetable

PROTEIN SALADS
Chicken Salad
Jellied Chicken, Cottage Cheese, Asparagus and
    Tomato Salad
Cottage Cheese Loaf with Celery and Pimentos
Cottage Cheese and Chopped Chives
Cottage Cheese Mold with Green Peppers and Nuts
Cottage Cheese with Chopped Cucumber
Crabmeat Salad
Deviled Eggs with Sardine Stuffing
Stuffed Deviled Eggs
Stuffed Egg, Anchovy
Ham Salad
Lobster Salad

SALADS (*Continued*)

PROTEIN SALADS

    Peas, Cheese and Pickle Salad
    Stuffed Pepper Ring
    Salmon and Celery Salad with Ripe Olives
    Shrimp Salad
    Sweetbread Salad
    Tomato Filled with Sea Food
    Tomato Stuffed with Deviled Eggs
    Tomato Surprise (with Chicken Salad)
    Tuna Fish Salad
    Tuna Fish and Apple Salad

VEGETABLE SALADS

    Hearts of Artichokes, French Dressing
    Asparagus and Tomato Salad
    Beet and Egg Salad
    String Beans and Shallot Salad
    Bowl Salad
    Cabbage Salad
    Cabbage, Marshmallow and Almond Salad
    Cabbage Relish
    Sour Cream Slaw
    Yankee Slaw
    Carrot and Peanut Salad
    Carrot and Raisin Salad
    Celery and Apple Salad
    Hearts of Celery
    Celery Stuffed with Cream Cheese Salad
    Celery Stuffed with Cream Cheese and Pimento Salad
    German Cucumbers
    Hearts of Lettuce with Tomato, Beet and Egg

Hearts of Lettuce with Thousand-Island Dressing;
    Roquefort Cheese Dressing
Wilted Lettuce with Chopped Bacon
Kidney Beans with Chopped Egg Salad
Peas, Cauliflower and Beet Salad
Potato Salad
Tomato Sliced with Hard-Cooked Egg and Green
    Pepper Ring
Tomato Stuffed with Cottage Cheese, Cucumber and
    Celery
Tomato and Cucumber
Tomato and Water Cress
Water Cress with French Dressing

SANDWICHES

CHEESE SANDWICHES

American Cheese
American Cheese on Rye Bread
Brown Bread and Cream Cheese
Cream Cheese and Pineapple
Cream Cheese and Nut
Cheese Dreams
Cottage Cheese and Strawberry Jam on Nut Bread
Date and Cream Cheese with Chutney Sauce on Nut
    Bread
Swiss Club Sandwich
Swiss Cheese on Rye

SANDWICHES (*Continued*)

MEAT SANDWICHES

Chopped Beef and Horse-Radish
Sliced Cold Roast Beef
Chopped Corned Beef and Horse-Radish on Rye
  Bread
Sliced Cold Corned Beef
Ham Salad
Minced Ham
Sliced Ham on Rye
Toasted Sweetbread and Bacon
Minced Tongue with Horse-Radish
Sliced Tongue
Sliced Tongue and Horse-Radish
Veal Loaf Sandwich

_____

_____

_____

CHICKEN SANDWICHES

Chicken Giblet and Chopped Bacon Sandwich
Chicken Loaf Sandwich
Chicken Salad Sandwich
Chicken Salad Roll
Club Sandwich
Minced Chicken Sandwich
Minced Chicken and Ripe Olive Sandwich
Sliced Chicken Sandwich
Toasted Chicken Liver and Bacon Sandwich

_____

_____

_____

FISH SANDWICHES

Crabmeat and Mayonnaise Sandwich
Lobster Salad Sandwich

Fresh Lobster Salad Roll
Salmon Salad Sandwich
Salmon and Cucumber Sandwich
Fresh Shrimp Salad Roll
Tuna Fish Salad Sandwich

SWEET SANDWICHES
Date Nut Sandwich
Toasted Chocolate Sandwich
Toasted Orange Sandwich
Orange Marmalade on Nut Bread
Orange Marmalade and Candied Ginger Sandwich
Peanut Butter and Jelly or Marmalade

VEGETABLE SANDWICHES
Cucumber
Lettuce and Mayonnaise
Tomato and Bacon
Tomato and Chopped Egg
Tomato, Cucumber and Lettuce with Mayonnaise
Tomato, Cucumber and Lettuce with Russian Dress-
ing
Water Cress and Thousand-Island Dressing

MISCELLANEOUS SANDWICHES
Egg and Olive
Chopped Olive

SANDWICHES (*Continued*)

MISCELLANEOUS SANDWICHES

Peanut Butter and Bacon

DESSERTS

HOT DESSERTS

Dumplings

Apple Dumpling; Lemon Sauce; Hard Sauce;
with Cream

Fruit Dumpling; Lemon Sauce; Hard Sauce;
with Cream

Bread and Bread-Crumb Puddings

Apple Brown Betty; Lemon Sauce

Apple Scallop

Bread Pudding with Raisins and Vanilla Sauce

Bread Pudding à la Mode

Bread Pudding with Jelly and Meringue

Bread Pudding with Fruit Sauce

Caramel Bread Pudding with Marshmallows

Chocolate Bread Pudding; Whipped Cream

Cocoanut Bread Pudding; Fruit Sauce

Orange Bread Pudding; Orange Sauce

Cake Type Puddings

Apple Batter Pudding; Whipped Cream

Cottage Pudding; Lemon Sauce; Fruit Sauce;
Strawberry Hard Sauce

Fruit Rolls with Fruit Sauce

Gingerbread with Apple Sauce and Cheese

Ginger Muffins with Butterscotch Sauce

Orange Shortcake; Hard Sauce

Peach Shortcake; Whipped Cream
Prunecot Shortcake
Strawberry Shortcake; Brown Sugar Hard Sauce
Mixed Fruit Upside-Down Cake
Pineapple Upside-Down Cake
Prune and Apricot Upside-Down Cake

Cobblers

Apple Cobbler; Nutmeg Sauce
Apricot Cobbler; Foamy Sauce
Blueberry Cobbler; with Cream
Cherry Cobbler; Hard Sauce
Peach Cobbler; Nutmeg-Flavored Whipped Cream
Raspberry Cobbler; Hard Sauce

Fritters

Apple Fritters with Syrup
Banana Fritters with Powdered Sugar and Fruit
   Sauce
Corn Fritters with Maple Syrup
Orange Fritters with Orange Sauce
Pineapple Fritters with Lemon Sauce
Plain Fritters with Maple Syrup

Rice Puddings

Baked Rice Pudding
Chocolate Rice Pudding with Meringue
Individual Baked Rice Custard
Lemon Rice Pudding
Rice Compote with Peaches; Prunes; Raspberries
Rice and Raisins with Cream
Rice and Raisins with Hard Sauce

DESSERTS (*Continued*)

HOT DESSERTS

Steamed Puddings
Steamed Carrot Pudding; Foamy Sauce
Steamed Cherry Pudding; Hard Sauce
Steamed Cranberry Pudding; Hard Sauce
Steamed Date Pudding; Vanilla Sauce
Steamed Fig Pudding; Foamy Sauce
Steamed Suet Pudding; Rum Sauce
Christmas Pudding; Brandy Sauce

Miscellaneous Hot Puddings
Apple Tapioca with Whipped Cream
Apple Tapioca Custard with Meringue
Chocolate Soufflé
Fruit Pudding; Custard Sauce
Grapenut Pudding; Lemon Sauce
Indian Pudding; Whipped Cream
Prune Pudding with Meringue

COLD DESSERTS

Bavarians
Caramel Bavarian Cream
Chocolate Bavarian
Cocoanut Bavarian
Fruit Bavarian
Grape Bavarian
Orange Bavarian
Rice Bavarian with Maple Sauce

Blancmange Type Puddings
Chocolate Blancmange with Nuts
Date Nut Blancmange; Custard Sauce

Maple Nut Mold with Custard Sauce
Norwegian Prune Pudding
Orange and Cocoanut Blancmange
Pineapple Pudding
Peanut Brittle Blancmange
Praline Pudding
Vanilla Blancmange, Fresh Berry Sauce; Chocolate
   Sauce; Custard Sauce

Cake Desserts
Angel Food à la Mode with Butterscotch Sauce
Angel Food with Chocolate Sauce, Whipped Cream
Angel Food with Sliced Peaches and Whipped
   Cream
Angel Food with Peppermint Chocolate Sauce and
   Whipped Cream
Angel Food with Peppermint Stick Ice Cream and
   Chocolate Sauce
Angel Food with Fresh Strawberries
Angel Food with Strawberry Jam, Whipped Cream
Angel Food with Whipped Cream and Pistachio
   Nuts
Chocolate Marshmallow Roll with Chocolate Sauce
Chocolate Luxuro
Sponge Cake à la Mode with Fudge Sauce

Custards
Baked Custard
Caramel Custard
Chocolate Custard
Floating Island
Grapenut Custard
Orange Custard

DESSERTS (*Continued*)

Custards
Prune Cream Custard
Rice Custard

Fruits Used as Dessert
Uncooked Fruits
Apples
Apricots
Bananas
Blackberries
Blueberries
Cherries
Figs
Grapefruit
Grapes
Oranges
Peaches
Pears
Pineapple
Plums
Raspberries
Strawberries

Cooked Fruits
Baked Apples
Apples, Stewed with Sliced Lemon
Apple Sauce
Apricot Sauce
Apricot and Prune Sauce
Apricot and Fig Sauce
Apricot and Raisin Sauce

Baked Bananas
Fresh Blackberry Sauce
California Fruit Sauce (Dried Apricots, Prunes,
    Pears and Peaches)
Fresh Cooked Cherries
Cranberry Sauce
Stewed Figs
Fresh Cooked Concord Grapes
Stewed Fresh Peaches
Baked Pears; Spiced
Baked Quince
Baked Rhubarb
Fresh Plum Sauce
Stewed Prunes

Gelatins
Apricot Mold with Almonds
Jellied Apricots
Burnt Almond Sponge
Charlotte Russe
Fruit Gelatin
Fruit Gelatin with Marshmallows
Ginger Cream with Ginger Syrup
Grape Sponge
Lemon Sponge
Snow Pudding; Custard Sauce
Spanish Cream

Ices and Sherbets
Apricot
Cranberry
Grape
Green Gage Plum

DESSERTS (*Continued*)

COLD DESSERTS

Ices and Sherbets
Lemon
Lime
Orange
Raspberry
Peppermint
Pineapple

Icecreams, Parfaits and Mousses
Banana
Black Walnut
Chocolate
Chocolate Chip
Chocolate Peppermint
Coffee
Maple Nut
New York
Fresh Peach
Peppermint Stick
Pineapple
Pistachio
Fresh Strawberry
Toffee
Tutti-frutti
Vanilla

Melons
Canteloupe
Casaba
Honey Dew
Persian
Watermelon

Tapiocas
Apple
Caramel
Fresh Cherry
Tapioca Cream
Fig and Nut
Orange
Pineapple
Raisin
Raspberry
Rhubarb

Tortes
Date
Graham Cracker
Schaum

Whips
Apricot Whip with Whipped Cream and Chopped
   Almonds
Banana Whip Parfait with Chocolate Sauce
Peach Whip with Whipped Cream and Nutmeg
Plum Whip with Cinnamon Whipped Cream
Prune Whip with Custard Sauce
Strawberry Whip, Whipped Cream

Miscellaneous
Cream Puffs with Chocolate Filling and Chocolate
   Sauce
Fruit Cocktail with Fresh Fruit; with Cooked
   Fruit
Mary's Chocolate Pudding

CAKES

ANGEL FOODS
Almond Cream Filled Angel Food
Angel Food de Luxe (White Frosting; Glacé Fruit and Nuts)
Black Walnut Angel Food
Cherry Angel Food
Chocolate Angel Food
Tutti-frutti Angel Food

SPONGE
Almond Cream Filled Sponge Cake
Jelly Rolls
Lemon Filled Sponge Cake
Sponge Cake with Orange Frosting
Sponge Rolls with Chocolate Filling; Almond Custard Filling; Jelly Filling

---

CAKES FROM BASIC WHITE CAKE DOUGH
Banana Cream Filled Cake
Blueberry Cake
Burnt Sugar Cake
Chocolate Frosted Cake
Cocoanut Cake
Fresh Cocoanut Cake
Toasted Cocoanut Cake
Fig Cake with Orange Frosting
Florida Fruit Cake (Orange, Pineapple and Cocoanut Frosting)
Lady Baltimore
Lemon Cream Filled Layer Cake
Maple Nut Cake
Orange Cream Filled Layer Cake
Peppermint Stick Candy Cake

Pineapple Cream Cake
Poppy-Seed Cake
Praline Cake
Fresh Strawberry Marble Cake
Tangerine Cake
Tutti-frutti Cake

CAKES FROM BASIC CHOCOLATE CAKE DOUGH

Chocolate Boston Cream Pie with Banana Filling
Chocolate Layer Cake
Chocolate Roll
Devil's Food
Devil's Food with Black Walnut Icing
Devil's Food with Cocoanut Frosting
Devil's Food with White Frosting and Melted Chocolate (Allegretti Style)
Devil's Food with White Frosting and Whole Red Cherries
Fudge Cake
Wellesley Fudge Cake

CAKES FROM YELLOW CAKE DOUGH

Almond Cream Filled Yellow Cake
Banana Cream Filled Yellow Layer Cake
Boston Cream Pie
Cocoanut Cake
Lord Baltimore
Old-fashioned Jelly Layer Cake
Orange Layer Cake
Tangerine Cake
Yellow Layer Cake with Apricot Filling
Yellow and White Marble Cake

CAKES (*Continued*)

MISCELLANEOUS

Apple Sauce Cake
Banana Cake
Caramel Cake with Caramel Fudge Icing
Caramel and Chocolate Marble Cake
Caramel Nut Cake
Chocolate Frosted Gingerbread
Date Cake
Fruit Cake
Gingerbread Allegretti
Gingerbread Filled with Apple Sauce or Bananas and Whipped Cream
Jam Cake
Martha Washington Pie
Mocha Nut Cake
Old-fashioned White and Chocolate Marble Cake
Old-fashioned Caramel and Chocolate Marble Cake
Orange and Raisin Cake
Pound Cake
Pumpkin Cake
Spice Cake

DOUGHNUTS

Chocolate Coated
Plain
Raised
Sugared

COOKIES

BROWNIE TYPE COOKIES

Black Walnut Brownies
Butterscotch Brownies

Chocolate Brownies
Cocoanut Butterscotch Brownies
Cocoanut Date Brownies
Indians

_____

_____

_____

CHRISTMAS COOKIES *

Bell Cookies ** (bell-shaped sugar cookies, iced or plain, with red and green sugar or "100's and 1000's" candies)

Berlinerkrantz (a rich loop-shaped cooky, sprinkled with red or green sugar)

Christmas Trees (small, plain, undecorated, and larger ones frosted with white or light green frosting and covered with "100's and 1000's" candies)

Christmas Wreaths (sugar-cooky dough cut with doughnut cutter and decorated with pieces of red and green cherries or iced with white icing and dipped in green colored macaroon cocoanut)

Pfeffernüsse (dark and light varieties)

Sand Tarts with crystal sugar decorations

Santa Claus Cookies (plain and iced)

Scandinavian Christmas Cookies
    Fattigmand
    Sandbakkels

Short Breads

Springerle

Sprits

* Since tasteful decoration of Christmas Cookies, like decoration of all food, is achieved by following certain art principles, the following book outlining such principles may prove helpful: *Art in Everyday Life*, Harriet and Vetta Goldstein, The Macmillan Company.

** Cooky cutters, made to one's own design, may be made very reasonably by almost any hardware store and are distinctive. In designing cutters, avoid sharp or slender parts which break easily in the finished cookies.

COOKIES (*Continued*)

CHRISTMAS COOKIES

Star Cookies (stars of various doughs, plain and
decorated)

DROP COOKIES

Cashew Drops
Chocolate Filbert Cookies
Chocolate Frosted Drop Cookies
Chocolate Rocks
Hermits
Molasses Cookies
Oatmeal Rocks
Peanut Butter Cookies
Peanut Drops
Pecan Cookies
Sour Cream Jumbles
Vanilla Wafers

ICEBOX COOKIES

Almond Icebox Cookies
Butterscotch Cookies
Chocolate Nut Cookies
Chocolate Checkers
Chocolate Pinwheels
Date Rolled Cookies

MACAROONS
Almond
Chocolate
Cocoanut
Corn-Flake
Date

_____

_____

_____

ROLLED COOKIES
Bran Cookies
Chocolate Sugar Cookies
Cocoanut Cookies
Filled Cookies
Ginger Cookies
Germantown Cookies
Germantown Spice Cookies
Molasses Cookies
Old-fashioned Sugar Cookies
Orange Cookies
Sand Tarts
Swedish Sugar Cookies

_____

_____

_____

MISCELLANEOUS COOKIES
Date Bars
Date Sandwiches
Date Sponge Bars
Hazelnut Bars
Lady Fingers
Marguerites
Pfeffernüsse

COOKIES (*Continued*)

MISCELLANEOUS COOKIES

    Scotch Short Bread

    Sprits

_____

_____

_____

PIES

TWO-CRUST PIES

    Apple

    Apricot

    Apricot and Prune

    Apricot and Raisin

    Blackberry

    Blueberry

    Cherry

    Cranberry, Latticed

    Cranberry and Raisin

    Gooseberry

    Gooseberry and Raisin

    Grape

    Loganberry

    Mincemeat

    Peach

    Pecan and Raisin

    Pineapple

    Plum

    Prune

    Raisin

    Raspberry

    Raspberry and Currant

    Rhubarb

    Strawberry

ONE-CRUST PIES
  Chiffon Type
    Apricot Chiffon
    Banana Chiffon
    Black Bottom
    Caramel Nut Chiffon
    Chocolate Chiffon
    Eggnog
    Lemon Chiffon
    Orange Chiffon
    Prune Whip
    Pumpkin Chiffon
    Strawberry Whip

  Cream Type
    Almond Cream
    Apricot Cream
    Banana Cream
    Butterscotch
    Butterscotch Nut
    Chocolate Cream
    Cocoanut Cream
    Cream Pie
    Cream Stack Pie
    Graham Cracker Cream
    Lemon
    Orange Cocoanut Cream
    Orange Cream
    Pineapple Cream
    Prune Cream
    Sour Cream
    Strawberry Cream

PIES (*Continued*)

ONE-CRUST PIES

Custard Type

Almond Custard
Caramel Custard
Cheese Cake
Chocolate Custard
Cocoanut Custard
Cottage Cheese
Custard
Hazelnut
Peach Custard
Pecan
Pumpkin

MISCELLANEOUS

Dutch Apple
French Apple

CHAPTER V

Introduction to Recipes

In order to follow these recipes successfully certain explanations may be helpful.

Dry Ingredients Are Given in Weights. This has been done because weighing the dry ingredients saves time and promotes accuracy and hence uniformity of product. Given accurate scales a pound of flour is always a pound, while quarts of flour may vary considerably in weight. However, the restaurant kitchen often does not have the scales to weigh very small amounts, such as fractions of ounces of salt or spices, and in these recipes such amounts are usually given in measures.

Liquids, on the Other Hand, Are Measured. Liquids obviously cannot be packed as can dry ingredients and may, therefore, be measured with little or no error. This reduces the number of kitchen scales necessary, an important consideration when the budget is limited or when, as often happens, the space necessary for a more adequate number of scales is lacking.

Recipes May Be Easily Translated from Weights to Measures or Measures to Weights. For this purpose the list of equivalents in the back of the book and the "Multiple" column in the recipe itself have been provided. This column may also be used for multiplications or divisions of the recipe to such size as fits particular needs.

The Recipes Vary in Number of Servings. No attempt has been made to have each recipe give exactly the same number of portions, but we have for convenience reduced or increased the size of most of them to approximately fifty, or to amounts found practical to prepare.

The Aim Has Been to Make the Recipes Failure-proof. Where the size and number of pans have been given, this has been done in order that the worker may visualize the food in preparation. In this connection employees should be taught to choose the proper utensils for preparing a given dish successfully. Unless a cook selects a kettle or pan the capacity of which is approximately that of the recipe to be produced, there is every probability that the number of servings indicated in the recipe will not be achieved. For instance, if a soup recipe is to be made which will produce two gallons of liquid a ten-gallon or even five-gallon container should not be used. As an example, when two cooks tested the same soup recipe it was found that one produced eight and one half quarts of volume, while the other, by using a kettle of the right size and covering it, produced ten quarts. This meant that in the one case six potential servings of soup had boiled away with a consequent loss of income and alteration of flavor, since the recipe was based on obtaining the larger volume. Other examples might be given, but this is sufficient to make the point that there is a definite relationship between the right-sized utensil and the quality and quantity of food to be prepared.

An Attempt Has Been Made to Set Up Standards for Large Quantity Food Production. As a foreword to the recipes for soups, meats, vegetables and other types of cookery, standards have been set up and some of the relating problems have been discussed from the large quantity viewpoint.

CHAPTER VI

Quantity Soup Making

Standards for Soups Are Probably As Little Defined As Those of Any Branch of American Cookery. This, perhaps, is the reason why good soups are not more frequently found. A soup must, first of all, be suited to the use it is to serve in the meal, whether as a main dish or as a course prior to the main part of the meal. It must be pleasing in taste, the texture right and the flavors well blended. It should be served attractively in bowl or plate, and with appropriate garnish and accompaniments. The effort involved in achieving these standards is worth while, since good soups are popular; they may satisfy those with dietary problems; and may often substitute in the menu for a meat dish which may be less profitable.

There Are Three Main Classes of Soups. These are: (*a*) stock soups, (*b*) cream soups and (*c*) thick soups (chowders and gumbos). The stock soups may be made with white stock of veal, chicken or fish, or with brown stock made from the darker meats such as beef and lamb. A vegetable stock, as the name implies, is made from vegetables. Stocks may or may not be cleared, depending upon the use they are to serve. When the soup is a substantial part of the meal, and a nourishing soup is desired, there is no need to clear it, since clearing removes the coagulated and nourishing particles of protein. These particles, however, detract from appearance, and when a soup is to be served as an appetizer or first course with a meal it should be carefully cleared. Most institutions hit upon a happy medium in clearing by straining to remove all of the coarsest particles but they do not use egg shells to refine the stock to a final degree.

In the institutional kitchen the steam-jacketed stock pot is the modern equivalent of the traditional French *pot au feu* which the housewife kept always on the stove to receive the trimmings from the roast or the odds and ends of vegetables and from which later came steaming, nourishing soup.

The general proportions to use for making stock are one quart of water to each pound of bone, fat and meat. The fat, bone and meat should be provided in the proportion of two thirds meat to one third bone and fat. To this is added vegetables, spices and herbs. The meat may be cut in pieces and browned before starting to cook. The old practice of allowing the meat to soak for a period to draw out the juices is probably without sound basis. When stock has cooked at the simmering point for the required length of time (four to six hours is customary) it should be strained, cooled quickly and placed in jars to be used as needed. The fat will form a seal which helps to prevent spoilage.

When stocks lack an appetizing color a little caramel syrup may be added to enrich the color. This may be used instead of commercial colorings which may be too expensive. This syrup is made by caramelizing the sugar until it has lost its sweetness, then adding water or vegetable stock and cooking down to a heavy syrup which may be kept on hand. It is used to color gravies, as well as stocks.

Cream Soups Vary in Richness and in Thickness. This depends upon the individual taste. A thin white sauce is the conventional base for these soups rather than cream, as the name would imply.

Cream Soups Present Difficulties in Quantity Production. Making cream soups in quantity is complicated by

SUGGESTIVE CHART FOR SOUP MAKING

Base	Thickening Agents	Predominating Flavors	Seasonings	Garnishes	Accompaniments
Brown Stock	Alphabets	Cereals	Allspice	*Stock Soups*	Celery
Beef	Barley	Fish	Basil	Alphabets	Cheese straws
Lamb	Bread crumbs	Legumes	Bay leaf	Carrot	Crackers
White Stock	Corn meal	Meat	Celery salt	Chives	Butter
Veal	Cornstarch	Vegetables	Celery seed	Chopped parsley	Cheese
Chicken	Flour		Chives	Croutons	Toasted
Fish Stock	Noodles		Cloves	Egg custard cubes	Croutons
Vegetable Stock	Rice		Curry	Lemon	Melba toast
White Sauce	Sago		Mace	Okra	Nuts
Milk	Spaghetti		Sweet marjoram	Vermicelli	Olives
Cream	Tapioca		Nutmeg	*Cream Soups*	Radishes
	Vermicelli		Onion	Chives	Raw carrot strips
			Parsley	Chopped pepper	Small sandwiches
			Pepper	Paprika	Toast sticks
			Peppercorns	Parsley sprigs	
			Salt	Pimento	
			Tarragon	Whipped cream	
			Thyme		

the tendency of the soups to separate or curdle on standing any length of time. This is due to several causes, among which may be the maintaining of a high temperature for too long a period; the addition of salt, which hastens separation; or the presence of acids in the soup ingredients, as is the case in tomato soup. For these reasons, it would seem desirable to make cream soups in reasonably small amounts and add the salt just before serving.

Chowders Are Thick Soups with or without Milk. The chief ingredient of chowders may be vegetables or sea food. The thickening agent is usually potatoes, flour or crackers, or a combination of these. Chowders usually serve as the main course of a luncheon, since they are rich, nourishing and satisfying.

CREAM OF CORN SOUP

Ingredients	Amount	Weight	Multiple	Unit Cost	Total Cost
Corn	4 qt.				
Water	1 qt.				
Onion, ground		6 oz.			
Fat		12 oz.			
Flour		5 oz.			
Paprika	$\frac{3}{4}$ tsp.				
Milk	8 qt.				
Salt	6 tbsp.				

Put the corn through a purée sieve. Add the water and bring to a boil. Let simmer. Sauté the onion in the fat until a golden brown. Add the flour and paprika and when well blended add to the scalded milk. Cook from seven to ten minutes. Strain to remove the onion and combine with the corn purée. Add the salt last.

Total Weight: Approximately 25 lb.
Yield: 50 servings, 8 oz. each (approximately 1 c.).
Per Serving: Cost____ Selling Price____ Calories____

CREAM OF MUSHROOM SOUP

Ingredients	Amount	Weight	Multiple	Unit Cost	Total Cost
Mushrooms		1 lb. 8 oz.			
Onion, finely ground . .		4 oz.			
Fat		12 oz.			
Flour		1 lb. 2 oz.			
Chicken stock	6 qt.				
Milk	6 qt.				
Salt	4 tbsp.				

Wash and chop the mushrooms medium fine. Melt the fat and sauté the ground onion and mushrooms in the fat until a golden brown. Add the flour and when well blended add to the boiling chicken stock and milk, stirring vigorously. Cook from seven to ten minutes. Add the salt last.

Total Weight: Approximately 26 lb.
Yield: 52 servings, 8 oz. each (approximately 1 c.).
Per Serving: Cost____ Selling Price____ Calories____

CREAM OF PEA SOUP

Ingredients	Amount	Weight	Multiple	Unit Cost	Total Cost
Milk and juice from peas .	9 qt.				
Bay leaves	1½				
Fat		12 oz.			
Onion, ground		3 oz.			
Flour		6 oz.			
Peas, drained	3 qt.				
Salt	4½ tbsp.				

Measure the juice from the peas and add enough milk to make nine quarts. Add the bay leaves and bring to the boiling point. Melt the fat, add the onion and when a golden brown add the flour. When blended add to the scalded milk. Cook seven to ten minutes. Strain to remove the onion and bay leaves. Add the peas which have been heated in a steamer and run through a purée sieve. Add the salt last.

Total Weight: Approximately 22 lb. 8 oz.
Yield: 45 servings, 8 oz. each (approximately 1 c.).
Per Serving: Cost_____ Selling Price_____ Calories_____

POTATO AND ONION SOUP

Ingredients	Amount	Weight	Multiple	Unit Cost	Total Cost
Potatoes, sliced thin . .		5 lb.			
Celery, cut in ½″ pieces .	1 c.				
Water	2½ qt.				
Onion, sliced thin . . .		2 lb.			
Bacon fat.		7 oz.			
Flour		4 oz.			
Hot milk	5 qt.				
Salt	7 tbsp.				
Parsley, chopped fine . .	2 tbsp.				

Cook the thinly sliced potatoes and cut celery in the water in a covered kettle until well done but not mushy. Cook the onion in the fat until a golden brown. Add the flour and when blended add to the scalded milk, stirring vigorously. Cook from seven to ten minutes. Add the potatoes and celery together with the salt and parsley.

Total Weight: Approximately 20 lb.
Yield: 40 servings, 8 oz. each (approximately 1 c.).
Per Serving: Cost_____ Selling Price_____ Calories_____

CREAM OF SPINACH SOUP

Ingredients	Amount	Weight	Multiple	Unit Cost	Total Cost
Cooked spinach		2 lb.			
Water	2 c.				
Onion, ground		4 oz.			
Fat		12 oz.			
Flour		9 oz.			
Milk	12 qt.				
Salt	6 tbsp.				

Add the water to the spinach.   Heat and put through a purée sieve.   Brown the onion in the fat and stir in the flour.   When blended add to the scalded milk, stirring rapidly.   Cook from seven to ten minutes and strain to remove the onion.   Add the spinach purée and the salt last.

Total Weight: Approximately 27 lb.
Yield: 54 servings, 8 oz. each (approximately 1 c.).
Per Serving: Cost____   Selling Price____   Calories____

CREAM OF TOMATO SOUP

Ingredients	Amount	Weight	Multiple	Unit Cost	Total Cost
Tomatoes	6 qt.				
Soda	1 tbsp.				
Sugar	3 tbsp.				
Bay leaves	3				
Onion, ground		6 oz.			
Fat		12 oz.			
Flour		13 oz.			
Milk	6 qt.				
Salt	4 tbsp.				

Cook the tomatoes, soda, sugar and bay leaves together for fifteen to twenty minutes.   Put through a purée sieve.

Cook the onions in the fat until they are a golden brown. Add the flour and when well blended add to the boiling purée, stirring rapidly. Cook for five minutes. Strain to remove the onion. Stir into the scalded milk, beating vigorously. Add the salt last. It has been found that tomato soup is less apt to curdle if the purée, rather than the milk, is thickened.

Total Weight: Approximately 23 lb.
Yield: 46 servings, 8 oz. each (approximately 1 c.).
Per Serving: Cost_____   Selling Price_____   Calories_____

WHITE BEAN SOUP

INGREDIENTS	AMOUNT	WEIGHT	MULTIPLE	UNIT COST	TOTAL COST
Navy beans		4 lb. 6 oz.			
Ham stock and water . .	2½ gal.				
Ham bones		6 lb. 4 oz.			
Ground onion		5 oz.			
Salt to taste					

Soak the beans overnight in water to cover. Dilute the stock in which the hams have been cooked with water until it is not too salty. Add this to the beans which have been drained. Add the ham bones and ground onion, cover and bring to a boil. Allow to simmer in a covered kettle until the beans are sufficiently broken up to thicken and give body to the soup. Remove the bones and any gristle which may have cooked off the bones. Taste for salt, since the ham stock may not supply a sufficient amount. It has been found that usually one half water and one half stock is a satisfactory proportion of liquid to use.

Total Weight: Approximately 25 lb.
Yield: 50 servings, 8 oz. each (approximately 1 c.).
Per Serving: Cost_____   Selling Price_____   Calories_____

BEEF NOODLE SOUP

Ingredients	Amount	Weight	Multiple	Unit Cost	Total Cost
Beef stock	12 qt.				
Blades of mace	1½				
Bay leaves	1½				
Peppercorns	½ tsp.				
Whole cloves	2				
Ground onion		2 oz.			
Beef fat		2 oz.			
Noodles, uncooked . . .		15 oz.			
Ground cooked beef . .		12 oz.			
Salt to taste	¼–½ c.				

Add the seasonings, except the salt, to the meat stock and bring to a boil. Fry the onion in the beef fat until a golden brown. Add with the broken noodles to the stock and cook covered until the noodles are done. Add the ground beef. Salt to taste and serve.

Total Weight: Approximately 24 lb.
Yield: 48 servings, 8 oz. each (approximately 1 c.).
Per Serving: Cost＿＿ Selling Price＿＿ Calories＿＿

CHICKEN MUSHROOM SOUP

Ingredients	Amount	Weight	Multiple	Unit Cost	Total Cost
Mushrooms		12 oz.			
Onion, ground		4 oz.			
Chicken fat		12 oz.			
Flour		10 oz.			
Chicken stock	3 gal.				
Salt to taste					

Wash and chop the mushrooms. Add with the onion to the chicken fat and sauté until a golden brown. Add the flour and when blended add to the boiling chicken stock, stirring rapidly. Salt to taste. Let simmer fifteen to twenty minutes. The amount of salt will vary depending upon the salt in the chicken stock.

Total Weight: Approximately 25 lb.
Yield: 50 servings, 8 oz. each (approximately 1 c.).
Per Serving: Cost____ Selling Price____ Calories____

CHICKEN NOODLE SOUP

INGREDIENTS	AMOUNT	WEIGHT	MULTIPLE	UNIT COST	TOTAL COST
Chicken stock . . .	3½ gal.				
Onion, ground		1 lb.			
Celery salt	1½ tbsp.				
Cloves	4				
Bay leaves	2				
Mace, blades	2				
Peppercorns	4				
Noodles		1 lb.			
Thickening:					
Fat		4 oz.			
Flour		4 oz.			
Parsley, chopped . . .		1 oz.			
Salt to taste					

Bring the chicken stock to a boil with all the seasonings and let simmer twenty-five to thirty minutes. Strain and add the noodles and cook until tender. Mix the melted fat and flour and add to the soup to thicken. Add the chopped parsley. If a thin soup is preferred the thickening may be omitted.

Total Weight: Approximately 30 lb.
Yield: 60 servings, 8 oz. each (approximately 1 c.).
Per Serving: Cost____ Selling Price____ Calories____

CHICKEN RICE SOUP

Ingredients	Amount	Weight	Multiple	Unit Cost	Total Cost
Chicken stock	14 qt.				
Onion, ground		1 lb.			
Celery salt	1½ tbsp.				
Rice		1 lb.			
Chopped green peppers .		4 oz.			
Salt to taste					

Add the chopped onions, celery salt and rice to the boiling chicken stock and cook until the rice is tender. Add the chopped green pepper during the last ten minutes of cooking. Salt to taste, as the amount needed will depend on the saltiness of the stock. This may be garnished with a thin slice of lemon, sprinkled with paprika or finely chopped parsley.

Total Weight: Approximately 28 lb.
Yield: 56 servings, 8 oz. each (approximately 1 c.).
Per Serving: Cost____ Selling Price____ Calories____

FRENCH ONION SOUP

Ingredients	Amount	Weight	Multiple	Unit Cost	Total Cost
Thinly sliced onion . .		10 lb.			
Beef fat		1 lb.			
Flour		4 oz.			
Meat stock	3 gal.				
Worcestershire sauce . .	¼ c.				
Salt	6 tbsp.				
Pepper, black	1 tsp.				
Toast slices, rye or white	60				
Grated Parmesan cheese .	1¼ c.				

Fry the onion in the beef fat until tender and golden brown. Stir in the flour and add to the boiling stock.

Cook seven to ten minutes.   Add the seasonings.   When serving, place a slice of toast in a soup bowl and pour the soup over it.   Sprinkle one teaspoon (or more) of Parmesan cheese over, as it is served.

Total Weight: Approximately 30 lb.
Yield: 60 servings, 8 oz. each (approximately 1 c.).
Per Serving: Cost____   Selling Price____   Calories____

SPLIT PEA SOUP

INGREDIENTS	AMOUNT	WEIGHT	MULTIPLE	UNIT COST	TOTAL COST
Split peas		3 lb. 10 oz.			
Ham stock and water . .	9½ qt.				
Ham bones		3 lb.			
Onion, ground		10 oz.			
Fat		14 oz.			
Flour		5 oz.			
Milk, hot	2 qt.				
Ground cooked ham or sausage or sliced frankfurters		1 lb.			
Salt to taste					

   Soak the dried peas overnight in water to cover.   Drain. Dilute the stock in which hams have been cooked with water until it is not too salty and add it to the peas.   Add the ham bones and ground onion and cook about three hours until the peas are soft and mushy.   Remove the bones.   Melt the fat, add the flour and when blended add to the hot milk.   Cook seven to ten minutes.   Add to the cooked peas, together with the ground cooked meat.   Salt to taste.   The amount of salt will vary depending on the saltiness of the ham stock.

Total Weight: Approximately 26 lb.
Yield: 52 servings, 8 oz. each (approximately 1 c.).
Per Serving: Cost____   Selling Price____   Calories____

SCOTCH BROTH

Ingredients	Amount	Weight	Multiple	Unit Cost	Total Cost
Lamb bones		24–30 lb.			
Water	7½ gal.				
Salt	5–6 tbsp.				
Barley		1 lb. 8 oz.			
Carrots or turnips, ground		6 oz.			
Onion, ground		9 oz.			
Lamb, cooked and ground		6 oz.			
Lamb fat		4 oz.			
Meat coloring	2 tsp.				

Cook the bones in the seven and one half gallons of water six to eight hours. Drain, cool and remove the fat. Add the barley, vegetables and salt to the stock (there should be about 3¼–3¾ gal.) and cook until tender. Add the cooked lamb which has been browned in the fat. Two teaspoons of meat coloring may be added, if necessary.

Total Weight: Approximately 25 lb.
Yield: 50 servings, 8 oz. each (approximately 1 c.).
Per Serving: Cost____ Selling Price____ Calories____

TOMATO RICE SOUP

Ingredients	Amount	Weight	Multiple	Unit Cost	Total Cost
Tomatoes, #10 can . . .	1				
Onion, ground		8 oz.			
Blades of mace	1½				
Bay leaves	1½				
Peppercorns	½ tsp.				
Whole cloves	2				
Salt to taste					
Beef stock	3 gal.				✓
Uncooked rice		1 lb.			
Fat		6 oz.			
Flour		5 oz.			

Add the tomatoes, onion and seasonings to the stock and boil covered ten minutes. Add the rice and cook until tender. Melt the fat, stir in the flour and add to the above, stirring carefully to avoid breaking up the rice. Add the salt, the amount depending upon whether the stock has been salted or not.

Total Weight: Approximately 29 lb.
Yield: 58 servings, 8 oz. each (approximately 1 c.).
Per Serving: Cost____   Selling Price____   Calories____

VEGETABLE SOUP

Ingredients	Amount	Weight	Multiple	Unit Cost	Total Cost
Meat stock	2½ gal.				
Blades of mace	1½				
Bay leaves	1½				
Peppercorns	½ tsp.				
Whole cloves . . .	2				
Celery		4 oz.			
Cabbage		1 lb.			
Carrots		1 lb.			
Onion, ground		12 oz.			
Tomatoes	1½ qt.				
Rice		4 oz.			
Barley		4 oz.			
Salt	¼ c.				

Add the spices to the meat stock and bring to a boil. Cut the celery and cabbage in one-inch pieces; cut the carrots in slices or in julienne pieces and add with the onion to the boiling stock, together with the whole tomatoes. Cover and let simmer one hour. Add the rice and barley and cook until tender. If desired, the spices may be strained out before adding the vegetables. Add the salt last.

Total Weight: Approximately 24 lb.
Yield: 48 servings, 8 oz. each (approximately 1 c.).
Per Serving: Cost____   Selling Price____   Calories____

FISH CHOWDER

Ingredients	Amount	Weight	Multiple	Unit Cost	Total Cost
Cooked fish, cubed . .		3 lb.			
Sliced raw potatoes . .		6 lb. 4 oz.			
Water or fish stock . .	2¼ qt.				
Onion, ground		15 oz.			
Fat		10 oz.			
Flour		5½ oz.			
Paprika	1¼ tbsp.				
Milk	7½ qt.				
Salt	5 tbsp.				

Cook the fish cubes and the sliced potato in the fish stock or water in a covered kettle until thoroughly done. Fry the onion in fat until a golden brown. Add the flour and paprika and when well blended add to the scalded milk, stirring vigorously. Cook from seven to ten minutes. Add to the fish, potato and stock mixture and simmer twenty to thirty minutes to develop the flavor. Add the salt last.

Total Weight: Approximately 27 lb.

Yield: 54 servings, 8 oz. each (approximately 1 c.).

Per Serving: Cost_____ Selling Price_____ Calories_____

CLAM CHOWDER

Ingredients	Amount	Weight	Multiple	Unit Cost	Total Cost
Potatoes, diced in ⅓″ cubes		4 lb. 8 oz.			
Onion, ground . . .		12 oz.			
Salt	2 tbsp.				
Water	3 c.				
Salt pork, ¼″ cubes . .		12 oz.			
Clams, cut fine		1 lb. 12 oz. to 2 lb.			
Clam juice	6 c.				
Butter		4 oz.			
Cayenne	½ tsp.				
Milk	5 qt.				

Cook the potato, onion and salt in the three cups of water in a covered kettle until done. Cut the salt pork in one-fourth-inch cubes and fry until crisp and brown. Add the pork, with the fat which comes from the pork, to the potato and onion. Add the clams, butter and cayenne and let simmer from one to two hours. Add the hot milk and the clam juice just before serving.

Total Weight: Approximately 20 lb.
Yield: 40 servings, 8 oz. each (approximately 1 c.).
Per Serving: Cost_____ Selling Price_____ Calories_____

SWEDISH RICE SOUP

Ingredients	Amount	Weight	Multiple	Unit Cost	Total Cost
Rice, uncooked		15 oz.			
Coffee cream	2 qt.				
Milk	9 qt				
Salt	2⅓ tbsp.				

Wash the rice and add to the hot milk and cream and cook covered until the rice is tender. Stir frequently to prevent the rice from sticking. Add the salt.

Total Weight: 21 lb.
Yield: 42 servings, 8 oz. each (approximately 1 c.).
Per Serving: Cost_____ Selling Price_____ Calories_____

CHAPTER VII

Meats, Entrées and Sauces

The Aim in Cooking Meats Is to Improve Appearance and Palatability. These two aims must be accomplished with the minimum of shrinkage. Shrinkage is the inevitable result of overcooking and incorrect temperature. For this reason, in roasting, meat thermometers which are inserted to the center of the roast are essential. The use of water around the roast increases shrinkage and should be avoided. It must be remembered that every four to eight ounces of loss in weight means the loss of one or more potential servings.

Tender cuts may be easily cooked by roasting, broiling or pan broiling. For the tougher cuts tenderness is achieved by long, slow cooking; by pre-maceration of the tough fibers, as in Swiss steak; by chopping and grinding, as in meat loaves and chopped steaks; or by cutting, as in stews. In cooking the tougher cuts over a period of time, water is usually added. It is important to remember that even the tougher cuts should be cooked only until tender, as overcooking renders them less palatable and less attractive in appearance.

Meat Menus Should Be Balanced to Give Variety. In planning the menu it is advisable to balance the so-called solid meats with those "made" dishes which give variety and a certain "homelike" quality to the meat menu. To avoid monotony the menu should be so planned that pork, veal, beef or lamb are not repeated in the same meal. It has been the experience of the authors that the public enjoys meats and made dishes which are less obvious than roast, steaks or chops. The National Live Stock and Meat Board, 407 South Dearborn, Chicago, has printed considerable material on meat cuts and how to cook them, which is available and which will be found useful in menu making. Their beef chart and their "Time and Temperature Chart for Beef" are reprinted here.

BEEF — TIME AND TEMPERATURE CHART *

Beef Cut	Method	Cooking Temperature	Approximate Time
Roasts	Roasting	300°–350° F.	
Rare			18–20 min. per pound
Medium			22–25 min. per pound
Well-done			27–30 min. per pound
Boned Roasts	Roasting	300°–350° F.	Add 10–15 min. per pound
Pot Roasts	Braising	Very low	3–4 hours
Steaks	Broiling	350° F. in broiler	
1 inch			15 minutes
2 inches			30–35 minutes
Swiss Steak	Braising	Very low	2–3 hours
Round Steak	Braising	Very low	45 minutes
Stews	Stewing	Below boiling	2–2½ hours
Corned Beef	Simmering	Below boiling	3–4 hours
Beef Pie	Baking	500° F. for 15 min. — reduce to 300° F.	
Uncooked meat			2 hours
Cooked meat			35–40 minutes
Beef Loaf	Baking	300°–350° F.	1½–2 hours
Tongue	Simmering	Below boiling	
Fresh			2–2½ hours
Smoked			3–5 hours
Heart	Braising	Very low	2½–3½ hours
Liver	Braising	300° F. in oven	1 hour
	Broiling	500° F. in broiler	10 minutes
Kidney	Broiling	425° F. in broiler	10 minutes

In the past few years most dietitians have come to believe that some meat is essential to maintaining a satisfactory state of health. This means the institution manager who is fulfilling his obligation to those he serves must provide meat choices in wide enough variety and range of price to appeal to all palates and pocketbooks.

Since Meats Consume from 30 to 40 Per Cent of the Money Spent for Food in the Average Institution, They Should Be Carefully, Wisely and Economically Purchased. Meat should be bought where the amount and cut desired

* Courtesy of the National Live Stock and Meat Board, Chicago, Illinois.

MEAT CUTS and How to Cook Them

BEEF CHART

Retail Cuts   Wholesale Cuts   Retail Cuts

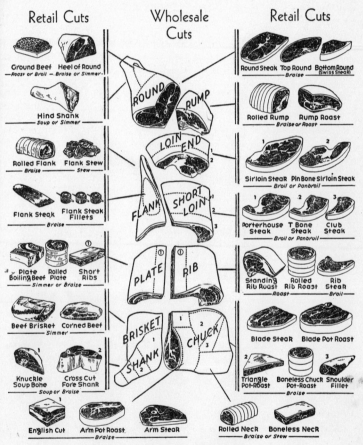

Ground Beef   Heel of Round
— Roast or Broil — Braise or Simmer —

Hind Shank
— Soup or Simmer —

Rolled Flank   Flank Stew
— Braise —   Stew

Flank Steak   Flank Steak Fillets
— Braise —

Plate   Rolled   Short
Boiling Beef   Plate   Ribs
— Simmer or Braise —

Beef Brisket   Corned Beef
— Simmer —

Knuckle Soup Bone   Cross Cut Fore Shank
— Soup or Braise —

English Cut   Arm Pot Roast   Arm Steak
— Braise —

ROUND   RUMP

LOIN END

FLANK   SHORT LOIN

PLATE   RIB

BRISKET   CHUCK

SHANK

Round Steak   Top Round   Bottom Round
— Braise —   (Swiss Steak)

Rolled Rump   Rump Roast
— Braise or Roast —

Sir loin Steak   Pin Bone Sir loin Steak
— Broil or Panbroil —

Porterhouse Steak   T Bone Steak   Club Steak
— Broil or Panbroil —

Standing Rib Roast   Rolled Rib Roast   Rib Steak
— Roast —   Broil

Blade Steak   Blade Pot Roast

Triangle Pot-Roast   Boneless Chuck Pot-Roast   Shoulder Fillet
— Braise —

Rolled Neck   Boneless Neck
— Braise or Stew —

Courtesy of the National Live Stock and Meat Board,
Chicago, Illinois.

may best be obtained.   Few institutions can use meat in wholesale cuts.   Unless a meat cutter is employed it will not be found satisfactory or possible to buy half or quarter carcasses.   Except in so-called original containers such as case lots of ham, bacon or other packaged goods which may be purchased direct from the packer, the small institution finds it more expedient to buy through the middleman who sells in less than quarters but larger cuts than the retail butcher.   The middleman will do the butchering or cutting necessary where women cooks, without meat-cutting strength and experience, are employed. Another advantage is that by this method only such cuts and in such amounts as they are desired need be purchased.

Meat Should Be Bought in Amounts for One or Two Days Only.   Unless the institution is large with adequate storage and temperature-controlled coolers, it is inadvisable to buy meat in advance of the actual need.   Even where such coolers are available, it is not always wise, for there is constant loss of weight by shrinkage and evaporation.   Therefore, the quantity price must be sufficiently low to offset that loss or the need for a certain grade or standard cut must be such as to necessitate keeping an adequate supply of that particular kind of meat on hand.

For the average small institution, therefore, a day-to-day supply of meat is best.   Just enough for a given meal or recipe should be ordered.   This improves the quality of the food, since there will not be leftovers to use up, and permits greater variety in the menu, since no emergencies may arise from overstocked larders demanding immediate use of something the institution is "long on" in order to save it.

BEEF À LA MODE

INGREDIENTS	AMOUNT	WEIGHT	MULTIPLE	UNIT COST	TOTAL COST
Beef round or rump, boned and tied . . .		15 lb			
Water	3¾ qt.				
Carrots, julienne . . .		1 lb. 4 oz.			
Peppers, chopped . . .		2½ oz.			
Onion, chopped		5 oz.			
Tomatoes	1 qt.				
Salt	2½ tbsp.				
Flour		6½ oz.			

Place the meat in a roasting pan in a hot oven to sear. When well browned add the water and continue cooking in a 325–350-degree (F.) oven four to five hours. About an hour and a half before serving add the carrots, peppers, onion, tomatoes and salt. Just before serving, thicken the stock with flour mixed to a paste with water. Serve the vegetables with the meat. The carrots, if small, may be left whole.

Total Weight: 18 lb.
Yield: 48 servings, 3 oz. of meat and 3 oz. of vegetables and gravy (approximately ⅓ c.).
Per Serving: Cost____   Selling Price____   Calories____

BAKED BEEF HASH

INGREDIENTS	AMOUNT	WEIGHT	MULTIPLE	UNIT COST	TOTAL COST
Beef, cooked and chopped		6 lb.			
Potatoes, cooked . . .		8 lb.			
Onion, chopped		1 lb.			
Salt	⅓ c.				
Meat stock	1 qt.				
Fat		1 lb.			

Mix all of the ingredients together lightly and moisten with the stock. Put into four well-greased shallow pans, approximately 9″ × 15″. Allow four pounds and eight ounces per pan. Bake about one hour in a 350–360-degree (F.) oven until brown.

Total Weight: 18 lb., before baking.
Yield: 4 long pans with 12 servings per pan; 48 servings, 6 oz. each.
Per Serving: Cost____   Selling Price____   Calories____

CORNED BEEF HASH

Ingredients	Amount	Weight	Multiple	Unit Cost	Total Cost
Corned beef, cooked . .		4 lb. 8 oz.			
Potatoes, cooked . . .		10 lb. 8 oz.			
Corned beef stock . . .	1¾ c.				
Corned beef fat		1 lb. 11 oz.			
Onion, ground		7 oz.			

Mix the cooked corned beef which has been ground, the chopped potatoes, onion, fat and stock together. Weigh out four and one half pounds of the hash into each of four long shallow baking or steam-table pans, approximately 9″ × 15″. Bake one hour in a moderate oven. Cut into twelve servings. Serve with tartare sauce or poached egg. It will require approximately nine pounds of uncooked corned beef to equal the four and one half pounds of cooked corned beef.

Total Weight: 18 lb.
Yield: 48 servings, 6 oz. each.
Per Serving: Cost____   Selling Price____   Calories____

CREAMED DRIED BEEF ON TOAST

Ingredients	Amount	Weight	Multiple	Unit Cost	Total Cost
Dried beef		2 lb. 8 oz.			
Fat		2 lb.			
Flour		14 oz.			
Milk	2 gal.				
Bread slices	56				

Cut the dried beef into small pieces. Put in a heavy-bottomed kettle large enough to hold the entire volume of the mixture. Add the fat and sauté the beef until crisp. Add the flour and cook to a rich brown with the beef. Scald the milk. Pour all of the milk into the beef mixture, stirring rapidly, and cook until thickened, about seven minutes. Serve on toast or over boiled potatoes. If the dried beef is very salty, it may be necessary to remove some of the salt by pouring hot water over the beef before sautéing. Too salty dried beef may cause the white sauce to curdle.

Total Weight: 21 lb.

Yield: 56 servings, 6 oz. each (approximately $\frac{2}{3}$–$\frac{3}{4}$ c.).

Per Serving: Cost_____ Selling Price_____ Calories_____

GERMAN POT ROAST

Ingredients	Amount	Weight	Multiple	Unit Cost	Total Cost
Rump roast, boned and tied		18 lb.			
Vinegar	1 qt.				
Water	12 qt.				
Mixed pickle spices . .		2 oz.			
Sour cream	1½ qt.				
Buttermilk	3½ qt.				
Salt	½ c.				
Ground onion		12 oz.			
Rye crumbs		1 lb. 3 oz.			
Hot milk	1½ qt.				
Flour	3 tbsp.				
Cold milk	1 c.				

Make a solution of the vinegar and water. Soak the meat for twenty-four hours in the vinegar solution with the spices tied in a bag.

Drain. Put in a hot oven to sear. Mix the sour cream, buttermilk, salt, onion and rye crumbs together. Pour over the meat. Again add the spice bag. Cook covered in a 325–350-degree (F.) oven until tender, approximately four to five hours. Take out the spice bag and the cooked meat. Add the hot milk to the gravy and thicken with the three tablespoons of flour mixed to a paste with one cup of cold milk. Pour around the meat and serve.

Total Weight: Cooked meat — 11 lb. 4 oz.
            Gravy — 13 lb.
Yield: Meat — 48 servings, 3¾ oz. each.
       Gravy — 48 servings, 4⅓ oz. each (approximately ½ c.).
Per Serving: Cost_____   Selling Price_____   Calories_____

HAMBURG STEAKS

Ingredients	Amount	Weight	Multiple	Unit Cost	Total Cost
Ground beef		7 lb. 8 oz.			
Crumbs		2 lb. 3 oz.			
Beef suet		1 lb. 8 oz.			
Salt	½ c.				
Milk	3 c.				
Onion, ground fine . . .		9 oz.			

Mix the meat with the crumbs and suet. Add the seasonings and milk. Weigh the mixture into balls of one pound each. Divide each one-pound portion into balls or patties — four to the pound. These may be cooked in a hot skillet on top of the stove or broiled. They are best when cooked to order and not allowed to stand.

They may be served with onions, on toast or between buns. Ground pork, which is frequently found in recipes for hamburgers, should not be used, since the quick cooking demanded by this type of steak is insufficient to cook the pork. In the above recipe the fat is supplied by the suet.

Total Weight: 13 lb. 8 oz.
Yield: 54 servings, 4 oz. each.
Per Serving: Cost_____ Selling Price_____ Calories_____

HUNGARIAN GOULASH WITH NOODLES

INGREDIENTS	AMOUNT	WEIGHT	MULTIPLE	UNIT COST	TOTAL COST
Beef rump or round, boned		10 lb.			
Suet		10 oz.			
Onion		3 lb.			
Garlic, chopped	1 clove				
Dry mustard	1 tbsp.				
Paprika	¼ c.				
Red pepper	⅛ tsp.				
Brown sugar		7 oz.			
Salt	¼ c.				
Worcestershire sauce . .	2 c.				
Vinegar	2 tbsp.				
Catsup	1 qt.				
Water	4 qt.				
Flour		10 oz.			
Noodles		3 lb. 3 oz.			
Water	3 gal.				
Salt	4 tbsp.				

Cut the meat into one-inch cubes and brown in the suet with the onion and garlic. Add the mixed mustard, paprika, pepper, sugar and salt to the Worcestershire sauce, vinegar and catsup. Add this to the browned meat and pour over the water, reserving a small amount to mix with the flour for the gravy. Let simmer in a heavy-bottomed kettle, closely covered, for two and one half or three hours, or until the meat is tender.

Strain out the meat to avoid breaking it up during the thickening process. Thicken the stock with a paste made of the flour and part of the water.

Cook the noodles in three gallons of boiling water with four tablespoons of salt until tender. Put into a colander and pour cold water over to remove the excess starch. Drain. Mix one quart of the gravy from the meat with the noodles.

Serve in separate containers. Place one half cup of noodles on the plate and cover with one half cup of the meat and gravy. This makes eight and one fourth quarts of meat and gravy.

Total Weight: Approximately 32 lb. 10 oz.

Noodles, 16 lb. 5 oz.

Meat and gravy, 16 lb. 5 oz.

Yield: 58 servings, 9 oz. each (approximately 4½ oz. noodles and 4½ oz. meat and gravy).

Per Serving: Cost____ Selling Price____ Calories____

JELLIED BEEF À LA MODE

Ingredients	Amount	Weight	Multiple	Unit Cost	Total Cost
Beef round, boned and tied		10–12 lb.			
Beef suet		4 oz.			
Veal bone		4 lb.			
Water	2 qt.				
Salt	¼ c.				
Onion, ground		4 oz.			
Tomatoes, strained . .	1 qt.				
Carrots, small whole . .		2 lb. 6 oz.			
Gelatin		3 oz.			
Cold water	1 c.				
Green pepper rings . .		4 oz.			
Celery, cut fine		4 oz.			
Parsley sprigs	½ c.				

Sear the beef in the suet in a kettle on top of the stove. Add the water and veal bone. Cover and cook below the boiling point until the meat is tender, for about three to four hours.

Add the salt and the vegetables, except the green peppers, the last hour, and cook until tender. Remove the veal bone. Soften the gelatin in the cold water and dissolve in the kettle of meat and stock. Add the green peppers. Pour into a mold and let set. If fat floats to the top while the meat is cooling it should be skimmed off.

This may be molded in a decorative mold if it is to be used on a cold buffet, or the meat may be cut in pieces and the meat and stock put in bread tins so that uniform slices of meat and jelly may be obtained when sliced.

This recipe is an adaptation of the beef à la mode served in the old "Bœuf à la Mode" restaurant in Paris.

Total Weight. Meat and jelly, 15 lb.
Yield: 60 servings, 4 oz. each.
Per Serving: Cost_____ Selling Price_____ Calories_____

MACARONI — NEAPOLITAN STYLE

INGREDIENTS	AMOUNT	WEIGHT	MULTIPLE	UNIT COST	TOTAL COST
Navy beans		1 lb. 11 oz.			
Water	6 qt.				
Salt	2 tbsp.				
Macaroni, broken . . .		13 oz.			
Water	6 qt.				
Salt	2 tbsp.				
Salad oil	2 c.				
Garlic		¾ oz.			
Parsley, chopped . . .	1 c.				
Tomatoes	4 qt.				
Dried beef		3 lb.			

Soak the beans overnight and drain. Cook in the six quarts of boiling water with the two tablespoons of salt until tender. Drain again. Cook the macaroni in the six quarts of boiling water with the two tablespoons of salt until tender. Drain. Pour cold water over to remove the excess starch. Cook the sliced garlic and the parsley in one cup of the oil. Add the strained tomatoes and continue cooking until almost as thick as conserve, and until the volume is reduced to about half. Cut the beef in small pieces and sauté in the remaining cup of oil. Mix with the drained beans, macaroni and tomato mixture. Bake forty-five minutes to one hour to develop flavor.

Total Weight: 15 lb. 12 oz.
Yield: 42 servings, 6 oz. each (approximately ¾ c.).
Per Serving: Cost____ Selling Price____ Calories____

MEAT CROQUETTES

Ingredients	Amount	Weight	Multiple	Unit Cost	Total Cost
Rice, uncooked		1 lb. 14 oz.			
Meat stock	1 gal.				
Onion, ground		10 oz.			
Meat, cooked and ground		7 lb.			
Fat		4½ oz.			
Flour		1½ oz.			
Stock	1 qt.				
Salt	¼–⅓ c.				
Eggs	6				
Milk	¾ c.				
Crumbs, sifted		1½–2 lb.			

Cook the rice in the gallon of boiling stock to which the onion has been added, until the rice is tender. Do not drain. Add the ground meat. Melt the fat, stir in the flour and add to the quart of boiling stock. Cook seven to ten minutes and mix this gravy with the rice and meat mixture. Salt to taste.

Using a number-eight icecream dipper, dish out into sixty mounds on crumb-covered trays or flat pans. Form all into cylindrical croquettes with the hands, being careful to leave no cracks or holes which will show up later in the frying. Dip in a dipping mixture of the eggs and milk. Drain carefully. Roll again in crumbs lightly so as not to crack or misshape. Keep cool. Fry as needed in deep fat 360–375 degrees F.

Total Weight: 15 lb.

Yield: 60 croquettes, 4 oz. of mixture (approximately ½ c. each).

Per Serving: Cost____ Selling Price____ Calories____

MEAT LOAF

INGREDIENTS	AMOUNT	WEIGHT	MULTIPLE	UNIT COST	TOTAL COST
Ground beef		8 lb.			
Ground pork		2 lb. 8 oz.			
Cayenne	¼ tsp.				
Black pepper	¼ tsp.				
Salt	¼ c.				
Onion, ground		6 oz.			
Bread crumbs		2 lb.			
Whole eggs	5				
Milk	3 c.				
Tomato juice	3 c.				

Mix the ground beef, ground pork, seasonings and bread crumbs until thoroughly blended. Beat the eggs and add with the milk and tomato juice to the above mixture. Mix thoroughly. Scale into well-greased loaf tins, using two pounds twelve ounces per loaf. Bake in a 350-degree (F.) oven for one and one half hours to insure thorough cooking of the pork. This loaf may be served with tomato, mushroom or pea sauce, or with chili sauce or catsup.

Total Weight: 16 lb. 8 oz.

Yield: 6 loaves, 2 lb. 12 oz. per loaf; 9 servings per loaf or 54 servings.

Per Serving: Cost____ Selling Price____ Calories____

MEAT PIE

Ingredients	Amount	Weight	Multiple	Unit Cost	Total Cost
Beef round or rump . .		10 lb.			
Water	1 gal.				
Onion, peeled		8 oz.			
Carrots, diced		1 lb. 8 oz.			
Potatoes, peeled . . .		5 lb.			
Flour		8 oz.			
Salt	¼ c.				
Biscuits	40				

Cut the meat into one-inch pieces and sauté in a kettle on top of the stove until browned. Cover with the gallon of boiling water and cook covered just below the boiling point until tender, approximately three to four hours. About one hour before serving time add the onion, diced carrots and salt. The potatoes may be added later, since they require less cooking. When done drain out the vegetables and the meat. Thicken the gravy by mixing the flour to a paste with water and pouring into the boiling stock. This will prevent the vegetables from being broken by too much stirring. Pour back over the meat and vegetables. The biscuits may be baked separately or the stew may be poured into baking pans, covered with biscuits and the biscuits baked in the oven.

Total Weight: 20 lb.
Yield: 40 servings, 8 oz. each (approximately ¾–1 c.); 40 biscuits, 1⅓ oz. each (2⅝ inches in diameter).
Per Serving: Cost____   Selling Price____   Calories____

MEAT PIE WITH DRESSING

Ingredients	Amount	Weight	Multiple	Unit Cost	Total Cost
Onion		4 oz.			
Beef fat		1 lb.			
Flour		9 oz.			
Meat stock	3 qt.				
Salt to taste					
Caramel coloring . . .					
Meat, cubed		6 lb.			
Dressing	5 qt.				

Sauté the onion until a golden brown in the beef fat. Stir in the flour and add to the boiling stock. Salt to taste and color with caramel coloring, if needed. Trim the meat and cube in three-fourths to one-inch cubes and add to the gravy. Line the sides of three baking or shallow steam-table pans (about 9″ × 15″) with dressing. Fill the center with the meat and gravy. Bake in a hot oven until brown. When serving, both the meat and the dressing should be given.

Total Weight: Meat and gravy, 13 lb. 1 oz.; dressing, 7 lb. 10 oz.

Yield: Approximately 40 servings, 8 oz. each.

Per Serving: Cost____ Selling Price____ Calories____

MINCED BEEF AND CHEESE SANDWICH

Ingredients	Amount	Weight	Multiple	Unit Cost	Total Cost
Cooked beef, ground or chopped fine		3 lb. 2 oz.			
Prepared mustard (see page 143)	$\frac{2}{3}$ c.				
Mixed-pickle relish . .	$2\frac{1}{2}$ c.				
Mayonnaise	$3\frac{3}{4}$ c.				
Cooked salad dressing .	$3\frac{3}{4}$ c.				
Bread slices	60				
Nippy cheese, ground . .		2 lb. 4 oz.			
Cream, 18%	$1\frac{1}{2}$ c.				

Grind or chop the cooked leftover beef and mix with the seasonings and dressings. Use the stiff cooked dressing without mixing with whipped cream. (This filling may be stored in the refrigerator to use as needed.)

Using a number-sixteen scoop, cover toasted bread with the mixture and over the meat spread a number-forty scoop of the cheese, which has been mixed with the cream to a soft paste. Put under the broiler and toast until brown. Brown only as needed and serve at once.

Total Weight: Meat, 7 lb. 8 oz.; cheese mixture, 3 lb.

Yield: 60 sandwiches, 2 oz. each of meat mixture; $\frac{4}{5}$ oz. each of cheese.

Per Serving: Cost____   Selling Price____   Calories____

ROAST BEEF

INGREDIENTS	AMOUNT	WEIGHT	MULTIPLE	UNIT COST	TOTAL COST
Rib roast of beef . . .		22–24 lb.			
Salt	$\frac{1}{4}-\frac{1}{3}$ c.				
Water for gravy . . .	1 gal.				
Flour		9 oz.			

To Prepare for the Oven:

Cut out the bladebone. The backbone and the short ribs should have been cut off before delivery.

To Roast:

Place rib, fat side uppermost, in an open roasting pan. Rub salt on cut surfaces. Without water, roast in a 300-degree (F.) oven about three to three and one half hours. While not essential, the use of a meat thermometer is desirable. Insert the bulb in the center of the roast. For rare roast beef the temperature should reach 142 degrees F., for medium rare, 154 degrees F., and for well done, 167 degrees F. Commercially, roasts should not be cooked beyond the rare or medium-rare stage. This gives well-done slices from the ends and rare from the center cuts.

To Make Gravy:

Remove the roast from the pan. Add the water, and when boiling and when all drippings have been scraped and stirred from the bottom and sides of the pan, add the flour mixed to a smooth paste with cold water. Bring to a boil and cook thoroughly to develop flavor.

Yield: A 22–24 lb. rib roast as purchased yields approximately:
Short ribs, 3 lb.
Backbones, 2¾ lb.
Rib ready for oven, 16–17 lb.
Rib after roasting, 14–15 lb.
Number servings, 38–41, 4 oz. each.

Per Serving: Cost____ Selling Price____ Calories____

SPANISH SPAGHETTI

INGREDIENTS	AMOUNT	WEIGHT	MULTIPLE	UNIT COST	TOTAL COST
Spaghetti		1 lb. 12 oz.			
Water	3 gal.				
Salt	¼ c.				
Meat, cooked		3 lb. 12 oz.			
Onion, ground		3 oz.			
Beef fat		12 oz.			
Flour		3 oz.			
Chili powder	4½ tsp.				
Tomatoes	2¼ qt.				
Stock	4½ c.				
Pimentos, chopped . .	¾ c.				
Celery, ½″ lengths . . .	2¼ c.				
Green peppers, chopped .	½ c.				
Nippy cheese		12 oz.			

Cook the spaghetti in the three gallons of boiling water with the one-fourth cup salt until tender. Drain into a colander and pour cold water over to remove the excess starch. Brown the ground meat and the onion in one half of the fat. Melt the remaining fat, add the well-mixed flour and chili powder and when well blended add to the boiling stock and tomatoes. Combine the remaining ingredients, except the cheese. Put in baking pans and bake slowly for at least two hours. During the last half hour of baking sprinkle with the grated or ground cheese and brown.

Total Weight: 18 lb., after baking.
Yield: 48 servings, 6 oz. each (approximately $\frac{2}{3}$–$\frac{3}{4}$ c.).
Per Serving: Cost____   Selling Price____   Calories____

SWISS STEAK

Ingredients	Amount	Weight	Multiple	Unit Cost	Total Cost
Round steak, one inch thick		20 lb.			
Flour		1 lb. 2 oz.			
Salt	$\frac{1}{2}$ c.				
Fat		1 lb.			
Water	1 gal.				
Onion, ground		12 oz.			
Flour for gravy		8 oz.			

Trim the steak and cut into pieces about three to the pound. Mix the flour and the salt and pound into the steak. Sauté in a skillet on top of the stove until brown. Put into a roasting pan. Add the ground onion, cover with the water and cook slowly for two and one half to three hours. When done drain off the stock and thicken with a paste made of the eight ounces of flour mixed to a smooth paste with cold water. If the gravy is not a good color, caramel coloring may be added. More salt may also be added to the gravy, if necessary. For a tomato sauce substitute one half gallon of tomato purée for one half gallon of the water.

Total Weight: 20 lb., before cooking.
Yield: 56–60 servings, 5$\frac{1}{3}$ oz. each, before cooking.
Per Serving: Cost____   Selling Price____   Calories____

BAKED HAM

Ingredients	Amount	Weight	Multiple	Unit Cost	Total Cost
Hams, cured, 15 lb. each	2				
Sugar, brown		1 lb. 7 oz.			
Vinegar	2⅔ c.				
Cloves, whole	2⅔ tbsp.				
Crumbs	⅔ c.				

Put the hams in a kettle, cover with water and bring to a boil. Simmer for three to four hours, or until they are tender. Remove from the stock. Peel off the skin and place in a baking pan. Stick the fat with cloves about one inch apart. Make a syrup of the vinegar and brown sugar and pour over the hams. Sprinkle them with crumbs and brown in a hot oven for about one hour.

Yield: two 15-lb. hams yield 22–24 lb. cooked ham (bone in); 56–62 servings, 4 oz. each.

Per Serving: Cost_____   Selling Price_____   Calories_____

HAM LOAF

Ingredients	Amount	Weight	Multiple	Unit Cost	Total Cost
Pork, ground		7 lb.			
Cooked ham, ground . .		3 lb. 8 oz.			
Bread crumbs		1 lb. 5 oz.			
Salt	2½ tbsp.				
Eggs, whole	7				
Milk	2 qt.				
Tomato purée	1 qt.				

Mix the ground pork and ground cooked ham together with the bread crumbs and salt. Beat the eggs and add to the milk and pour over the ground meat. Mix well. Weigh two and three fourths pounds of the meat mixture into each of six greased loaf tins. Press the meat down until smooth on top and pour the tomato purée over. Set the loaf pans in pans of hot water and bake one and one half to two hours in a 325–350-degree (F.) oven. If desired, the same amount of mixture may be molded into loaves and baked on sheet pans, though it is more difficult to produce uniform servings by this method. Serve with horse-radish sauce. Cut each loaf in nine servings.

Total Weight: 16 lb. 8 oz.
Yield: 6 loaves or 54 servings.
Per Serving: Cost____ Selling Price____ Calories____

SCALLOPED HAM, CELERY AND MUSHROOMS

Ingredients	Amount	Weight	Multiple	Unit Cost	Total Cost
Celery, ⅓-inch pieces . .	5¼ qt.				
Mushrooms, sliced . . .		1 lb. 8 oz.			
Onion, ground		2 oz.			
Fat		4 oz.			
Ham, cooked and diced .		6 lb. 12 oz.			
Milk	4½ qt.				
Fat		14 oz.			
Flour		7 oz.			
Salt	2½ tbsp.				
Egg yolks	½ c.				
Crumbs		8 oz.			
Butter		1 oz.			

Boil or steam the celery until tender. Brown the mushrooms and the onion in the four ounces of fat. Combine all with the ham. Scald the milk, melt the fourteen ounces of fat and add the flour. When well blended add to the scalded milk, stirring vigorously. Cook from seven to ten minutes. Add the beaten egg yolks to a small amount of the hot mixture and add to the remainder of the white sauce, stirring vigorously. Add the salt. Pour the white sauce over the ham mixture and mix lightly.

Put in baking dishes or steam-table pans and cover with the buttered crumbs. Bake until brown in a 350-degree (F.) oven, about forty-five minutes.

Total Weight: 22 lb. 8 oz.
Yield: 60 servings, 6 oz. each (approximately $\frac{2}{3}$–$\frac{3}{4}$ c.).
Per Serving: Cost_____   Selling Price_____   Calories_____

KITCHENETTE SQUASH WITH HAM PATTY AND DRESSING

Ingredients	Amount	Weight	Multiple	Unit Cost	Total Cost
Individual squash (1 lb. 2 oz. — 1 lb. 4 oz. each)	25–30				
Bread dressing	7½ qt.				
Ham Patties:					
Pork, ground		4 lb. 2 oz.			
Cooked ham, ground .		2 lb. 1 oz.			
Bread crumbs . . .		13 oz.			
Eggs	4				
Milk	5 c.				
Cream Gravy:					
Milk	5 qt.				
Ham fat		1 lb. 8 oz.			
Flour		12 oz.			
Salt to taste					

Select squash weighing from one pound two ounces to one pound four ounces each. Wash and cut into halves or thirds lengthwise to make uniform servings. Remove the seeds. Steam until almost tender. Put a number-eight scoop of dressing in each half squash. Mix together the pork, ham, crumbs, beaten eggs and milk. Weigh into one-pound balls and form each ball into patties six to the pound. Place a patty on top of the dressing in each squash and bake in a 350-degree (F.) oven an hour or until the patty is done. Make a cream gravy by scalding the milk and adding the blended fat and flour to it, stirring vigorously. Cook seven to ten minutes. Salt to taste. Serve over the squash, dressing and ham patty.

Yield: 60 servings (2¾ oz. dressing, 2⅔ oz. patties and 3 oz. cream gravy).
Per Serving: Cost_____   Selling Price_____   Calories_____

ROAST PORK

INGREDIENTS	AMOUNT	WEIGHT	MULTIPLE	UNIT COST	TOTAL COST
Pork loins, 10–12 lb. each	2				
Salt	3 tbsp.				
Water	6 qt.				
Onion, ground		8 oz.			
Flour		14 oz.			

To Prepare for Oven:

The loins of pork should be chimed before delivery. Cut out the tenderloin strip. Wipe off the roast. A pork loin of this size will produce an average of one pound of chimed bones and twelve to sixteen ounces of tenderloin.

To Roast:

Place in an open roasting pan fat side up. Rub on salt. Cook in a 300–325-degree (F.) oven uncovered without water for about four hours. If a meat thermometer is used, cook to an interior temperature of 185 degrees F. Pork must be thoroughly cooked. Add the onion the last hour.

To Make Gravy:

Remove the meat from the pan. Add the water and when boiling and all of the drippings have been stirred from the sides and bottom of the pan add flour mixed to a smooth paste with cold water. Bring to a boil and cook thoroughly. Strain to remove the onion. Coloring may be added if a darker gravy is desired.

Since bread dressing is usually served with pork roast, three-ounce servings of meat may be considered adequate.

Total Weight: 14–16 lb., after cooking.
Yield: 60–65 servings, 3 oz. each.
Per Serving: Cost____ Selling Price____ Calories____

BAKED THURINGER SAUSAGES WITH SAUERKRAUT

INGREDIENTS	AMOUNT	WEIGHT	MULTIPLE	UNIT COST	TOTAL COST
Sauerkraut	7½ qt.				
Ham bones	3				
Bay leaves	7				
Onion, cut fine		12 oz.			
Raw potatoes, grated . .		1 lb. 11 oz.			
Brown gravy	2¼ qt.				
Thuringer sausages (approximately 4 to 1 lb.) .		14 lb.			

Simmer the kraut one and one half to two hours with the ham bones, bay leaves and onion. Remove the ham bones and bay leaves and add the grated raw potatoes. Cook the sausages for ten minutes in boiling water. Line the bottom of seven long shallow steam-table pans (15″ × 9″) with one quart of the seasoned kraut. Pour over the kraut mixture in each pan one and one half cups of brown gravy and place eight sausages on top. Put into the oven and bake the sausages until brown. Turn and brown on the other side. This requires from three fourths to one hour's baking in a moderate oven.

Total Weight: Sausages, 14 lb.; kraut mixture, 14 lb. 11 oz.
Yield: 56 servings, 8 oz. each (4 oz. sausage and 4 oz. kraut).
Per Serving: Cost____ Selling Price____ Calories____

CURRIED LAMB — EAST INDIA STYLE

Ingredients	Amount	Weight	Multiple	Unit Cost	Total Cost
Milk	5½ qt.				
Flour		10 oz.			
Fat		1 lb. 6 oz.			
Salt	4⅔ tbsp.				
Red pepper	1/16 tsp.				
Curry powder	3½ tbsp.				
Cinnamon	¼ tsp.				
Cloves	¼ tsp.				
Nutmeg	¼ tsp.				
Allspice	¼ tsp.				
Onion, ground		1 lb. 2 oz.			
Apples, sliced		2 lb.			
Lamb, cooked and cubed		8 lb.			
Rice, uncooked		4 lb.			
Boiling water	9 qt.				
Salt	3 tbsp.				

Make a white sauce by blending one half of the fat with the ten ounces of flour and adding to the scalded milk, stirring rapidly. Cook seven to ten minutes. Melt the remaining fat and add the well-mixed seasonings. When well blended add the onion, sliced apples and lamb and cook together, covered, for one hour. Add to the white sauce. Cook the rice in the nine quarts of boiling water with the salt until tender. Drain into a colander and pour water through to remove the excess starch. To serve, reheat the rice as needed and put in individual molds or a ring mold. Pour the curried lamb around it.

This recipe furnishes an excellent outlet for small pieces of leftover roast lamb. If none is available, lamb shoulder may be purchased and cooked for use in the recipe. In this case, it will take approximately thirteen to fourteen pounds to make the eight pounds of cooked lamb called for in the recipe.

Total Weight: Lamb, 22 lb. 8 oz.

Rice, 17 lb. 12 oz., cooked weight.

Yield: Lamb, 60 servings, 6 oz. each (approximately $\frac{2}{3}$ c.).

Rice, 60 servings, $4\frac{1}{2}$–$4\frac{3}{4}$ oz. each (approximately $\frac{1}{2}$ c.).

Per Serving: Cost_____ Selling Price_____ Calories_____

LAMB OR IRISH STEW

INGREDIENTS	AMOUNT	WEIGHT	MULTIPLE	UNIT COST	TOTAL COST
Lamb, shoulder		7 lb. 8 oz.			
breast		4 lb.			
Water	4 qt.				
Salt	$4\frac{1}{2}$ tbsp.				
Onion, chopped		2 oz.			
Flour		12 oz.			
Water	$2\frac{1}{4}$ c.				
Potatoes		3 lb. 9 oz.			
Peas		1 lb. 5 oz.			
Carrots		2 lb. 4 oz.			
Onion		2 lb.			

Cover the meat with the four quarts of boiling water. Add the salt and the onion and cook just below the boiling point until tender. Drain off the stock and thicken with a paste made of the flour and two and one fourth cups of water. Cook the vegetables quickly on top of the stove and add to the stew just before serving. They may be mixed through the stew, or, where eye appeal is a consideration, as in a cafeteria, the vegetables may be put over the top of the serving pans.

Total Weight: Meat, gravy and vegetables, 26 lb.

Yield: 52 servings, 8 oz. each (approximately $\frac{3}{4}$–1 c.).

Per Serving: Cost_____ Selling Price_____ Calories_____

ROAST LAMB

Ingredients	Amount	Weight	Multiple	Unit Cost	Total Cost
Legs of lamb, 3, 7¼–7½ lb. each		21–23 lb.			
Salt	⅓ c.				
Water	1 gal.				
Flour		9 oz.			

To Roast:

Wipe the lamb legs which have been boned and tied and place in an open roasting pan, together with the lamb bones which add flavor to the gravy. Rub in salt. Cook without water three and one fourth to four hours in a 300–325-degree (F.) oven. Lamb should be cooked until medium to well done or, if a meat thermometer is used, to an interior temperature of 175–180 degrees F.

To Make Gravy:

Remove the meat and bones from the pan. Add water and when boiling and all the drippings have been scraped and stirred from the bottom and sides of the pan thicken with a smooth paste made of flour mixed with cold water. Bring to a boil and cook several minutes to develop flavor.

The average leg of lamb, weighing 7¼–7½ lb. before cooking and boning, weighs approximately 4 lb. after boning and cooking. Each leg of lamb will yield approximately 18–20 servings, 3½ oz. each, cooked weight; or 4–5 oz. each as purchased.

Yield: Three 7¼–7½-lb. legs of lamb as purchased yield approximately 4 lb. each after boning and cooking. 54–60 servings, 3½ oz. each.

Per Serving: Cost＿＿   Selling Price＿＿   Calories＿＿

ROAST VEAL

INGREDIENTS	AMOUNT	WEIGHT	MULTIPLE	UNIT COST	TOTAL COST
Veal leg, boned and tied .		16 lb.			
Salt	¼ c.				
Onion, ground		2 oz.			
Flour		9 oz.			
Water	1 gal.				

To Prepare for the Oven:

Order the veal leg boned and tied. Wipe the meat.

To Roast:

Place in a roasting pan. Rub in salt. Do not add water. Cook at 300 degrees F. for about four hours. If a meat thermometer is used, insert in center of roast and cook to 170 degrees F. Add the ground onion the last hour.

To Make Gravy:

Remove the meat from the roasting pan. Add water and when boiling and when the drippings have been scraped from the bottom and sides of the pan add the flour mixed to a paste with cold water. Bring to a boil and cook five to seven minutes and strain to remove the onion. The gravy may be colored with caramel coloring if a darker color is desired.

In ordering, allow 5 to 6 oz. veal as purchased per serving. Repeated tests show that 14–16-lb. legs of veal after boning and tying weigh approximately 11 to 12 lb. The same roasts will weigh approximately 8 to 9 lb. after cooking.

Yield: 45–50 servings, 3 oz. each (cooked weight).
Per Serving: Cost____   Selling Price____   Calories____

VEAL BIRDS

Ingredients	Amount	Weight	Multiple	Unit Cost	Total Cost
Veal, round steak . . .		15 lb.			
Salt	⅜ c.				
Bread dressing	6 qt.				
Flour		8 oz.			
Fat		1 lb. 8 oz.			
Milk	1½ qt.				
Water	1½ qt.				

The veal steak should be cut about one third inch thick. Trim and cut into pieces about three and one half to four ounces each. Pound the veal to make it tender and to shape it into rectangular pieces. (The small pieces of meat that are trimmed off may be chopped and added to the dressing.) Salt the meat and cover with dressing, using a ten-to-a-quart icecream dipper to make the servings uniform. Roll up and fasten with toothpicks. Roll in flour. Melt the fat in a skillet on top of the stove and sear the birds until brown. Put in a baking pan or steamtable pan in a single layer and pour the milk and water around them. Bake covered in a moderate 325-350-degree (F.) oven until tender, about one and one half to two hours. Remove the toothpicks and serve.

Yield: 60 servings, 6-7 oz. each.
Per Serving: Cost_____ Selling Price_____ Calories_____

VEAL HEARTS EN CASSEROLE

Ingredients	Amount	Weight	Multiple	Unit Cost	Total Cost
Veal hearts		20 lb.			
Flour		11 oz.			
Salt	½ c.				
Bacon fat		1 lb.			
Onion, ground		1 lb.			
Stock	1½ gal.				

VEAL HEARTS EN CASSEROLE (*Continued*)

Ingredients	Amount	Weight	Multiple	Unit Cost	Total Cost
Celery salt	¼ c.				
Peppercorns	2 tbsp.				
Flour		9 oz.			
Caramel coloring . . .					
Green peppers, chopped .		5 oz.			
Carrots, diced	1 c.				
Parsley, chopped . . .	¼ c.				

Wash and slice the veal hearts. Trim out the arteries and the gristle. Dredge in flour and salt and brown in the bacon fat, to which the onion has been added. Put the hearts into a roasting pan, pour the stock over them and add the spices. Cook in a slow oven until tender. Mix the nine ounces of flour to a thin paste with water. Add to the stock to thicken. If necessary, the gravy may be colored with caramel coloring. Boil or steam the carrots until tender. As needed for serving, place the veal hearts in a pan and sprinkle with the diced green peppers, the cooked carrots and the chopped parsley.

Total Weight: Cooked hearts, 12 lb.; gravy, 11 lb.
Yield: 48 servings, 4 oz. of meat and 3–4 oz. of gravy (approximately ⅓–½ c.).
Per Serving: Cost_____   Selling Price_____   Calories_____

VEAL ROSETTES

Ingredients	Amount	Weight	Multiple	Unit Cost	Total Cost
Ground veal		5 lb.			
Ground pork		1 lb.			
Bread crumbs		1 lb. 8 oz.			
Onion, grated		2 oz.			
Salt	2 tbsp.				
Milk	1 qt.				
Bacon	48 slices	1 lb. 9 oz.			

Mix the ground veal, pork, crumbs, onion and salt together. Add the milk and mix thoroughly. Weigh into one-pound balls and form each ball into flat patties, allowing five to the pound. Put a strip of bacon around the outside of the patty and fasten with a toothpick. Cook in the oven until the rosette and bacon are done. Allow one rosette per serving. They may be made up ten to the pound and two rosettes given for each serving, in which case twice the amount of bacon will be required. Serve with jelly.

Total Weight: 11 lb. 3 oz., before cooking.
Yield: 48 patties, approximately 3¾ oz. each.
Per Serving: Cost____   Selling Price____   Calories____

VEAL OR BEEF STEW

Ingredients	Amount	Weight	Multiple	Unit Cost	Total Cost
Rump or round of beef or veal		10 lb.			
Fat		6 oz.			
Boiling water	1 gal.				
Salt	5 tbsp.				
Onion		8 oz.			
Carrots		1 lb. 8 oz.			
Potatoes, diced		5 lb.			
Flour		8 oz.			

Cut the meat into one-inch pieces and sauté in the fat until well browned. Cover with the boiling water and simmer until tender. About one hour before serving time add the salt, onion and carrots cut in three-fourths-inch cubes. The potatoes may be added later since they require less cooking. When done drain off the stock and thicken with the flour mixed to a thin paste with a small amount of water. Cook seven to ten minutes. Pour back over the meat. This will prevent the vegetables from being broken by the thickening process. The stew may be garnished with new peas, if desired.

In cafeteria service, where eye appeal is essential, the vegetables should be cooked separately and put on top of the stew as it is served.

Total Weight: Approximately 20 lb.
Yield: 40 servings, 8 oz. each (approximately $\frac{3}{4}$–1 c.).
Per Serving: Cost_____   Selling Price_____   Calories_____

LIVER AND BACON

INGREDIENTS	AMOUNT	WEIGHT	MULTIPLE	UNIT COST	TOTAL COST
Liver		9 lb.			
Eggs	4				
Milk	$\frac{1}{4}$ c.				
Salt	2 tbsp.				
Crumbs		14 oz.			
Bacon, sliced 24 per lb. .		1 lb. 10 oz.			

Slice the liver thin and cut into servings weighing three and one half ounces each. Mix the eggs, milk and salt. Dip the liver in the dipping mixture, then into crumbs and place in a baking pan with about one eighth to one fourth inch of fat on the bottom. Put a slice of bacon on top of each serving and cook in a slow oven until well browned and until the liver and bacon are done. Do not overcook.

Frying liver is the most popular way of serving it. When beef liver is used the oven method of cooking is preferable. Cooking the bacon slices on top as in the above method adds fat and flavor. Young calves' liver may be pan fried, but overcooking should be avoided.

Total Weight: Bacon, 1 lb. 10 oz.; liver, 9 lb.
Yield: 40 servings, $3\frac{1}{2}$ oz. each with 1 strip of bacon.
Per Serving: Cost_____   Selling Price_____   Calories_____

CREAMED SWEETBREADS AND PEAS

Ingredients	Amount	Weight	Multiple	Unit Cost	Total Cost
Sweetbreads		7 lb. 8 oz.			
Water	6 qt.				
Vinegar.	¾ c.				
Salt	3 tbsp.				
Milk	4½ qt.				
Fat		1 lb. 2 oz.			
Flour		6¾ oz.			
Salt	2½ tbsp.				
Egg yolks	½ c.				
Paprika	1½ tsp.				
Fresh peas		3 lb. 12 oz.			

Parboil the sweetbreads in the water to which the vinegar and salt have been added, about half an hour or until tender. When cooked, drain and plunge into cold water. Remove the tough connective membrane. Make a white sauce by scalding the milk, melting the fat and adding the paprika and flour to the fat. When well blended add to the scalded milk, stirring vigorously. Cook from seven to ten minutes. Beat the egg yolks and mix with a little of the hot mixture and add to the white sauce, stirring vigorously. Reheat the sweetbreads in the sauce. Cook the peas, drain and add to the sweetbreads and white sauce. Serve in bread cases, patty shells or on toast.

Total Weight: 16 lb. 8 oz.
Yield: 44 servings, 6 oz. each (approximately ⅔ c.).
Per Serving: Cost____   Selling Price____   Calories____

BREAD DRESSING

Ingredients	Amount	Weight	Multiple	Unit Cost	Total Cost
Bread, cubed		4 lb.			
Salt	$\frac{1}{4}$ c.				
Sage	2 tbsp.				
Onion, finely chopped .		10 oz.			
Fat		1 lb. 9 oz.			
Hot water to moisten . .	2–2$\frac{1}{4}$ qt.				

Add the salt and the sage to the cubed bread. Mix well.
Fry the onion in the fat until golden brown. Add to the
cubed bread. Add hot water sufficient to moisten. Mix
lightly to keep from packing. Bake three fourths to one
hour in a moderate oven until brown. This may be used
as dressing for fish, veal, pork, or as stuffing for veal birds
or fowl.

Total Weight: 8 lb. 7 oz., after baking.
Yield: 45 servings, 3 oz. each (approximately $\frac{1}{2}$ c.).
Per Serving: Cost_____ Selling Price_____ Calories_____

STEAMED DUMPLINGS

Ingredients	Amount	Weight	Multiple	Unit Cost	Total Cost
Flour		1 lb. 14 oz.			
Baking powder, S.A.S.-phosphate type . . .	3$\frac{1}{4}$ tbsp.				
Salt	1$\frac{1}{2}$ tbsp.				
Fat		9 oz.			
Eggs	3				
Milk to make soft dough	2–2$\frac{1}{2}$ c.				

Mix and sift the dry ingredients. Work in the fat
lightly with the finger tips. Combine the beaten eggs
and milk and add to the dry ingredients. Place boiling
stew or creamed chicken in the pans from which it is to be

served and with a number-twenty-four scoop or a spoon drop dumplings in rows on top of the stew. Place in the steamer for twelve to fifteen minutes. If desired, the dumplings may be dropped on top of a kettle of stew, covered tightly and allowed to cook on top of the stove for the same length of time.

Total Weight: 3 lb. 12 oz.
Yield: 40 dumplings, 1½ oz. each (number-24 scoop).
Per Serving: Cost_____   Selling Price_____   Calories_____

METHOD FOR STEWING CHICKENS

Ingredients	Amount	Weight	Multiple	Unit Cost	Total Cost
To each:					
5-6 lb. fowl, New York dressed					
Use:					
Celery leaves		½ oz.			
Onion, ground . . .		6 oz.			
Salt	2 tbsp.				
Water	3 qt.				

Cut off the feet and head and clean and draw the fowl. If desired, cut off the legs, thighs and wings and separate the neck and back from the breast. For each five- to six-pound fowl use seasonings as outlined above and add three quarts of water. Cover and simmer about four to four and one half hours, or until tender. Remove from the fire and take the meat from the stock and cool quickly.

The meat is now ready to remove from the bones for use in slicing, cubing or chopping, as required; for chicken pies, sandwiches, salads, pressed chicken, creamed chicken and chicken à la king or any other purpose. When a number of fowl have been cooked, sort the meat as it is taken from the bones into four pans, *i.e.:*

1. White meat.
2. Dark meat.
3. Small pieces not suitable for slicing.
4. Skin and bones (for the soup kettle).

The stock in which the fowl has been cooked should be strained in order to remove the onion and celery and cooled quickly.   When cold, put into cans or jars and place in the ice box so that the fat may harden on top.   This forms a seal on the top of the stock and helps to prevent spoilage. The giblets from the chicken may be cooked separately, as they tend to darken the stock.   When practical from the standpoint of time and labor the feet may be blanched and peeled and added to the stock.   They add materially to the flavor.

In large quantity preparation, fowl should be handled with utmost care and a technique and routine developed which will render spoilage impossible.   A few pounds of meat allowed to spoil through haphazard handling represents several dollars in food cost.

Experience shows that heavy hens weighing five to six pounds yield a higher percentage of meat and are therefore more economical to use.

The chicken meat, the gravy or the stock of one day should never be mixed with that of another but used separately.   This is mentioned, since under certain weather conditions chicken stock taken from the stove to cool at night may be spoiled by the next morning.

Yield: From one 5–6-lb. hen :
    Approximately 1 lb. 2 oz. to 1 lb. 4 oz. meat ;
    2½ qt. stock ;
    6 oz. fat.

Per Serving: Cost____   Selling Price____   Calories____

CHICKEN À LA KING

Ingredients	Amount	Weight	Multiple	Unit Cost	Total Cost
Chicken fat		12 oz.			
Flour		14 oz.			
Chicken stock	1 gal.				
Milk	1 qt.				
Mushrooms, sliced . . .		1 lb.			
Onion, chopped	2 tbsp.				
Fat		8 oz.			
Egg yolks	⅔ c.				
Salt to taste					
Chicken meat, cooked and cubed		5 lb.			
Green peppers, chopped .	2 c.				
Pimentos, chopped . .	2 c.				

Melt the chicken fat, add the flour and when well blended add to the boiling stock, stirring rapidly with a wire whisk. Add the scalded milk and let cook seven to ten minutes. Sauté the mushrooms and onion in the eight ounces of fat and add. Beat the egg yolks and mix with a small amount of the hot mixture to blend and add to the above, stirring vigorously. Salt to taste. Fold in the cubed chicken, green peppers and pimentos. Serve on toast, in bread cases or patty shells.

Total Weight: 18 lb.
Yield: 48 servings, 6 oz. each (approximately ⅔–¾ c.).
Per Serving: Cost____   Selling Price____   Calories____

CHICKEN CROQUETTES

INGREDIENTS	AMOUNT	WEIGHT	MULTIPLE	UNIT COST	TOTAL COST
Rice		1 lb. 6 oz.			
Chicken stock	3 qt.				
Parsley	1 tbsp.				
Celery salt	1 tsp.				
Paprika	1 tsp.				
Onion juice	2 tbsp.				
Chicken stock	1 qt.				
Flour		6¾ oz.			
Chicken meat, cubed . .		5 lb.			
Salt to taste					
DIPPING MIXTURE:					
Eggs	6				
Milk	¾ c.				
Crumbs, sifted		2 lb. 6 oz.			

Wash the rice and cook until tender in the three quarts of chicken stock to which all the seasonings have been added.

Mix the flour to a smooth paste with part of the one quart of stock and add to the remainder, which has been brought to a boil. Stir this gravy and the cubed chicken meat carefully into the rice. Taste for salt. Let cool.

Using a number-eight scoop measure out into fifty-four molds. Shape into smooth cylindrical croquettes, being careful to avoid cracks and holes, which will be dark when fried. Roll carefully in fine crumbs and dip in egg and milk mixture. Drain and roll in crumbs. Fry as needed in deep fat at 360 degrees F.

For method of cooking and handling chickens see page 115.

Total Weight: 13 lb. 8 oz.
Yield: 54 servings, 4 oz. each (approximately ½ c.).
Per Serving: Cost_____ Selling Price_____ Calories_____

CHICKEN AND CHEESE CROQUETTES

Ingredients	Amount	Weight	Multiple	Unit Cost	Total Cost
Milk	3 qt.				
Chicken fat		9 oz.			
Onion juice	2 tbsp.				
Celery leaves, finely chopped	1 tsp.				
Parsley, finely chopped .	1 tbsp.				
Flour		1 lb. 6 oz.			
Nippy cheese		2 lb. 8 oz.			
Salt	¼ c.				
Paprika	1 tsp.				
Chicken, cubed cooked .		2 lb. 8 oz.			
Whole eggs	4				
Milk	½ c.				
Crumbs		2 lb.			

Reserve a portion of the cold milk to mix to a paste with the flour. Scald the remainder of the milk to which has been added the chicken fat, the onion juice, celery leaves and parsley to season. Add the flour paste, stirring vigorously. Cook seven to ten minutes. This should be cooked in a heavy-bottomed kettle, as it is a very thick mixture and scorches easily. Add the cheese, salt and paprika and stir until the cheese has melted. Add the cubed cooked chicken, from which all gristle has been trimmed, and mix lightly. Do not break up the chicken. Cool. Using a number-ten icecream scoop, measure out uniform servings onto crumbed sheets or trays. Mold into balls, dip into crumbs, into the dipping mixture made of the eggs and milk and again into crumbs. Fry in deep fat at 360 degrees F. until brown. Serve with jelly.

Total Weight: 12 lb. 8 oz.
Yield: 50 servings, approximately 4 oz. each (one No. 10 scoop).
Per Serving: Cost____   Selling Price____   Calories____

CHICKEN AND SPAGHETTI

Ingredients	Amount	Weight	Multiple	Unit Cost	Total Cost
Spaghetti		2 lb. 7 oz.			
Chicken stock	6 qt.				
Celery salt	1½ tsp.				
Chicken stock	2¼ qt.				
Chicken fat		1 lb. 2 oz.			
Onion, ground		7 oz.			
Flour		3 oz.			
Pimento, chopped . . .	6 tbsp.				
Green pepper, chopped .	6 tbsp.				
Parsley, chopped . . .		1 oz.			
Chicken meat, cubed . .		3 lb. 12 oz.			

Cook the spaghetti until tender in the six quarts of chicken stock and celery salt. Taste the cooked spaghetti and add salt, if necessary.

Bring the remaining chicken stock to a boil. Brown the onion in the chicken fat, add the flour and when blended add to the boiling stock and cook seven to ten minutes. Add the pimento, green pepper, parsley and chicken meat and mix with the cooked spaghetti.

Total Weight: 21 lb. 14 oz.
Yield: 50 servings, 7 oz. each (approximately ¾ c.).
Per Serving: Cost____ Selling Price____ Calories____

CREAMED CHICKEN

Ingredients	Amount	Weight	Multiple	Unit Cost	Total Cost
Onion, ground		9 oz.			
Chicken fat		2 lb. 4 oz.			
Flour		1 lb. 8 oz.			
Celery salt	1½ tsp.				
Chicken stock	4½ qt.				
Milk	3 qt.				
Egg yolks	¾ c.				
Chicken meat, cubed . .		4 lb.			

Brown the onion in the chicken fat.   Add the flour and celery salt and when blended add to the boiling stock. Heat the milk, reserving a small amount to mix with the egg yolks.   Add the yolks to the hot milk and combine with the thickened stock.   Salt to taste.   Add the chicken which has been cut in three-fourths-inch cubes.   Serve on toast, with biscuits or in patty shells.

Total Weight: 21 lb.
Yield: 56 servings, 6 oz. each (approximately ¾ c.).
Per Serving: Cost＿＿   Selling Price＿＿   Calories＿＿

INDIVIDUAL CHICKEN PIES

Ingredients	Amount	Weight	Multiple	Unit Cost	Total Cost
CRUST:					
Flour		4 lb.			
Baking powder, S.A.S.-phosphate type . .	4 tbsp.				
Salt	2⅔ tsp.				
Fat		2 lb.			
Cold water to moisten .	3½–4 c.				
FILLING:					
Chicken, cooked and cubed		4 lb.			
Chicken fat		2 lb. 4 oz.			
Onion		9 oz.			
Flour		1 lb. 8 oz.			
Celery salt	1½ tsp.				
Rich chicken stock . .	4½ qt.				
Milk	3 qt.				
Egg yolks	¾ c.				

Crust:

Mix and sift the dry ingredients.   Work in the fat with the tips of the fingers.   Add the water a little at a time, being careful to distribute the water evenly through the mixture.   Avoid getting the dough too wet.   Roll out to about one fourth inch in thickness and cut to fit shallow eight-ounce casseroles. Crescents cut out of the dough will allow the steam to escape and add to the appearance as well. These unbaked crusts may be put on trays in the refrigerator and held until needed. Place brown paper between the layers of crusts to prevent sticking together.

Filling:

Melt the fat, add the onion and cook until a golden brown. Add the flour and celery salt and when well blended add to the boiling stock, stirring rapidly with a wire whip. Cook from seven to ten minutes. Heat the milk, mix with the egg yolks and add to the thickened stock. In eight-ounce casseroles place one and one third ounces of dark and white meat (twelve casseroles per pound of chicken meat), add three fourths cup of hot gravy and cover with the crust. Brush the top of the crust with milk and bake in a hot oven until the crust is brown. It is important that the gravy be hot when it is poured over the chicken meat or the crust will be soggy when baked.

When making large numbers of individual chicken pies it facilitates preparation to place the required number of casseroles on trays and divide each pound of chicken meat between twelve casseroles. Repeat until the desired number are filled. Stack the trays and place in the refrigerator until meal time, when they may be removed from the refrigerator as needed, filled with the hot gravy, covered with crust and baked on the trays twelve at a time.

Yield: 48 pies with approximately $1\frac{1}{3}$ oz. meat, 6 oz. gravy and $2\frac{1}{2}$ oz. crust four inches in diameter.

Per Serving: Cost____   Selling Price____   Calories____

SCALLOPED CHICKEN AND RICE WITH MUSHROOMS

Ingredients	Amount	Weight	Multiple	Unit Cost	Total Cost
Rice, uncooked		1 lb. 14 oz.			
Water	2 gal.				
Salt	2⅔ tbsp.				
Chicken fat or butter . .		12 oz.			
Onion, ground		2 oz.			
Mushrooms, sliced . . .		2 lb.			
Flour		5 oz.			
Chicken stock	3 qt.				
Milk	1 qt.				
Pimento	2 c.				
Almonds, blanched and cut lengthwise . . .		6½ oz.			
Chicken, cubed		2 lb. 10 oz.			
Salt to taste					
Crumbs		6 oz.			
Butter		1 oz.			

Cook the rice in the boiling salted water until tender. Pour cold water over it to remove the excess starch.

Sauté the mushrooms and onion in the chicken fat. When golden brown add the flour, blend and, stirring rapidly, add to the milk and the chicken stock, which have been brought to a boil. Let cook seven to ten minutes.

Add the cubed chicken, pimento and almonds and mix lightly with the rice to prevent breaking. Salt to taste. Put into casseroles or steam-table pans. Cover with buttered crumbs and bake forty-five minutes to one hour in a moderate oven. This will make three shallow pans, 9″ × 15″.

Total Weight: 18 lb. 12 oz.
Yield: 50 servings, 6 oz. each (approximately ¾ c.).
Per Serving: Cost____   Selling Price____   Calories____

SCALLOPED CHICKEN WITH MUSHROOMS, SWEETBREADS AND ALMONDS

Ingredients	Amount	Weight	Multiple	Unit Cost	Total Cost
Sweetbreads		3 lb. 4 oz.			
Water	3 qt.				
Vinegar	6 tbsp.				
Salt	1½ tbsp.				
Chicken fat or butter . .		12 oz.			
Onion, ground		3 oz.			
Mushrooms, sliced . . .		1 lb. 8 oz.			
Flour		13 oz.			
Chicken stock	3 qt.				
Cream	1½ qt.				
Milk	1½ qt.				
Chicken, cooked and cubed		4 lb. 2 oz.			
Almonds, blanched and sliced		14½ oz.			
Salt to taste					
Bread crumbs		9 oz.			
Butter		1 oz.			

Parboil the sweetbreads in the acidulated salted water until tender, about one half hour. When cooked, drain, plunge into cold water and remove the tough connecting membrane. Melt the butter or chicken fat, add the onion and mushrooms and sauté until tender. Add the flour and when blended add to the hot chicken stock, milk and cream, stirring vigorously. Cook from seven to ten minutes. Add the cubed chicken, sweetbreads and almonds. Salt to taste. Put into casseroles or individual baking dishes. Cover with buttered crumbs and brown in the oven.

Total Weight: **21 lb. 14 oz.**
Yield: 50 servings, 7 oz. each (approximately ¾–1 c.).
Per Serving: Cost_____ Selling Price_____ Calories_____

CHICKEN GIBLETS, CUBAN STYLE

Ingredients	Amount	Weight	Multiple	Unit Cost	Total Cost
Rice		2 lb. 13 oz.			
Chicken stock	8 qt.				
Chicken fat		1 lb. 8 oz.			
Onion, ground		12 oz.			
Salt to taste					
Yellow vegetable coloring	3¾ tsp.				
Giblets, cooked		4 lb. 8 oz.			
Green peppers		1 lb. 2 oz.			
Red peppers		1 lb. 2 oz.			

Cook the rice in the chicken stock to which the fat and onion have been added. Salt to taste and add vegetable coloring to give a light yellow color. Trim the giblets, cutting off all gristle, and cut in large pieces. Put a layer of giblets in the bottom of three long shallow baking pans, approximately 9″ × 15″. Cover with rice and bake. When almost done cover the top with large pieces, approximately 2″ × 2″, of red and green peppers and bake until they begin to soften but have not lost their color. The contrast of the yellow rice and the red and green peppers makes a very attractive dish.

Total Weight: 24 lb. 1 oz.
Yield: 55 servings, 7 oz. each (approximately ¾–1 c.).
Per Serving: Cost___   Selling Price___   Calories___

CHICKEN GIBLETS AND NOODLES

Ingredients	Amount	Weight	Multiple	Unit Cost	Total Cost
Chicken stock	6½ qt.				
Celery salt	1½ tsp.				
Ground onion		6 oz.			
Noodles		2 lb.			
Chicken fat		12 oz.			
Flour		3 oz.			
Milk	1½ qt.				
Egg yolks	1 c.				
Giblets, cooked		3 lb. 12 oz.			
Salt to taste					

Bring the stock to a boil and add the celery salt, and onion. Break the noodles into three- to four-inch lengths, add to the boiling stock and cook until tender. Melt the chicken fat, stir in the flour and add to the scalded milk. Cook until thickened, about seven to ten minutes. Add the egg yolks, stirring vigorously. Add this mixture to the noodles. Cube the giblets, being very careful to trim out all the gristle. Add these to the noodle mixture and taste for salt. As the chicken and noodles are served the serving pans or plates may be garnished with green pepper, pimento or chopped parsley.

Total Weight: 22 lb. 4 oz.

Yield: 50 servings, 7 oz. each (approximately ¾ c.).

Per Serving: Cost_____ Selling Price_____ Calories_____

SCALLOPED EGGPLANT WITH CHICKEN GIBLETS AND MUSHROOMS

Ingredients	Amount	Weight	Multiple	Unit Cost	Total Cost
Eggplant		7 lb. 14 oz.			
Water	3 gal.				
Salt	¼ c.				
Mushrooms		3 lb.			
Onion, chopped		1 lb.			
Fat		12 oz.			
Giblets, cooked and cubed		2 lb. 5 oz.			
Green pepper, chopped .		14 oz.			
Crumbs		1 lb. 8 oz.			
Salt	1½ tbsp.				
Milk	4½ qt.				
Fat		1 lb.			
Flour		6¾ oz.			
Salt	2½ tbsp.				
Crumbs		12 oz.			
Butter		1½ oz.			

Slice the eggplant into one-inch slices. Peel and cut into one-inch cubes. Cook in boiling salted water until tender. Drain thoroughly.

Wash and slice the mushrooms and sauté with the onion in the twelve ounces of fat.

Combine the giblets with the eggplant, mushrooms and chopped pepper and one and one half pounds of crumbs. Add the salt.

Scald the milk, melt the one pound of fat and blend with the six and three fourths ounces of flour, stirring vigorously. Add to the milk and cook seven to ten minutes. Pour over the combined mushroom, giblet and eggplant mixture. Stir lightly to blend. Pour into steam-table pans or baking dishes. This will fill three long shallow pans, 9″ × 15″. Cover with the twelve ounces of crumbs mixed with one and one half ounces of butter and bake thirty minutes in a 350–375-degree (F.) oven until well browned.

Total Weight: 20 lb. 2 oz., after baking.
Yield: 46 servings, 7 oz. each (approximately ⅔–¾ c.).
Per Serving: Cost____   Selling Price____   Calories____

CODFISH BALLS

INGREDIENTS	AMOUNT	WEIGHT	MULTIPLE	UNIT COST	TOTAL COST
Codfish, dried		3 lb.			
Potatoes, raw diced . .		10 lb.			
Egg whites	3¾ c.				
Egg yolks	2½ c.				
Fat		6 oz.			
Paprika	⅔ tsp.				

Grind the codfish and steam with the potatoes until the potatoes are done. Beat the egg whites until stiff. Beat the egg yolks thoroughly. Mash the potatoes and the codfish on a mixing machine at high speed for about eight minutes or until the mixture is fluffy and all of the potato lumps are removed. Add the fat, paprika, beaten egg yolks and whites and mix just enough to combine. Using an eight-to-the-quart size icecream dipper to keep the servings uniform, drop (without dipping or crumbing) into deep fat and fry at 360 degrees F. until golden brown. Serve with parsley-cream sauce.

Total Weight: 14 lb. 4 oz.
Yield: 48 servings, 4¾ oz. each (approximately ½ c.).
Per Serving: Cost____   Selling Price____   Calories____

SCALLOPED CRABMEAT, NOODLES AND ALMONDS

INGREDIENTS	AMOUNT	WEIGHT	MULTIPLE	UNIT COST	TOTAL COST
Noodles		1 lb. 8 oz.			
Water	3 gal.				
Salt	¼ c.				
WHITE SAUCE:					
Milk	1 gal.				
Fat		1 lb. 8 oz.			
Flour		6 oz.			
Salt	2¼ tbsp.				
Egg yolks	¼ c.				
Onion juice	⅓ c.				
Almonds, sliced		13 oz.			
Crabmeat, canned . . .		4 lb.			
Pimento, chopped . . .	3 c.				
Nippy cheese, grated . .		10 oz.			

Cook the noodles in the three gallons of boiling water with the one fourth cup of salt until tender. Drain into a colander and pour cold water over until the excess starch has been removed.

Scald the milk. Melt the fat and add the flour and when well blended add to the milk, stirring vigorously, and cook seven to ten minutes. Add the egg yolks to a little of the white sauce, mixing thoroughly, and add slowly to the thickened mixture. Add the salt.

Mix the noodles, white sauce, onion, almonds, pimento and crabmeat, which has been carefully looked over to remove the stiff, bony tissue.

Place in individual casseroles or shallow baking pans with grated cheese on top. Bake in a moderate oven about forty-five minutes to an hour.

Total Weight: 21 lb. 12 oz.
Yield: 58 servings, 6 oz. each (approximately ⅔ c.).
Per Serving: Cost____   Selling Price____   Calories____

FISH SOUFFLÉ

Ingredients	Amount	Weight	Multiple	Unit Cost	Total Cost
Milk	1½ qt.				
Onion, finely ground . .	2 tbsp.				
Fat		6 oz.			
Flour		7 oz.			
Egg yolks	2¼ c.				
Fish (left over), flaked .		3 lb. 4 oz.			
Salt	2 tsp.				
Egg whites	3½ c.				

Scald the milk. Sauté the onion in the fat and add the flour. When blended add to the scalded milk, stirring vigorously. Cook from seven to ten minutes. Beat the egg yolks and add to a small amount of the white sauce and combine with the remaining sauce. Add the flaked fish and salt. Fold in the stiffly beaten egg whites. Bake in greased individual or ring molds in a pan of water in a moderate oven until the mixture has set. Serve with a crabmeat, lobster or cheese sauce. This amount will make five molds holding thirty ounces each and cutting into eight servings per mold.

Total Weight: 9 lb. 6 oz.
Yield: Ring molds, 5; 40 servings of 3–4 oz. each.
Per Serving: Cost____   Selling Price____   Calories____

SALMON LOAF

Ingredients	Amount	Weight	Multiple	Unit Cost	Total Cost
Salmon	8 lb.				
Bread crumbs		2 lb. 11 oz.			
Celery, cut fine, cooked .	1⅓ qt.				
Paprika	1 tsp.				
Salt	3 tbsp.				
Fat		8 oz.			
Milk	2⅔ qt.				
Bay leaves	5				
Onion		1⅓ oz.			
Eggs	11				

Mix the salmon (which has been looked over to remove the bones and skin), the bread crumbs, the celery, paprika, salt and melted fat. Scald the milk with the bay leaves and onion and add to the well-beaten eggs. Remove the bay leaves, pour over the other ingredients and mix. Put the mixture into well-greased loaf tins. Set the pans into a pan of water to prevent overcooking or crusting and bake until firm. This will make six loaves weighing two pounds twelve ounces each.

Total Weight: 16 lb. 8 oz. (6 loaves with 2 lb. 12 oz. in each loaf and 9 servings per loaf).

Yield: 54 servings, approximately 5 oz. each.

Per Serving: Cost_____ Selling Price_____ Calories_____

SCALLOPED SALMON

Ingredients	Amount	Weight	Multiple	Unit Cost	Total Cost
Bay leaves	⅛ c.				
Parsley sprigs	¼ c.				
Onion, ground		2 oz.			
Milk	4 qt.				
Fat		8 oz.			
Flour		6 oz.			
Salt	1½ tbsp.				
Paprika . .	½ tsp.				

SCALLOPED SALMON (*Continued*)

INGREDIENTS	AMOUNT	WEIGHT	MULTIPLE	UNIT COST	TOTAL COST
Salmon		10 lb.			
Bread, broken		1 lb. 12 oz.			
Crumbs		12 oz.			
Butter	3 tbsp.				

Add the bay leaves, parsley and onion to the milk and bring to the boiling point. Melt the fat, add the flour, blend and add to the milk, stirring rapidly. When the milk has thickened add the salt, paprika and strain out the seasonings. Look over the salmon to remove the skin and bones. Break into pieces, not too small, and mix with the broken bread. Pour the hot cream sauce over and mix well but lightly. Do not make the bread pasty by overstirring. Weigh into well-greased baking pans or steam-table pans, and cover with buttered crumbs. Bake for one half hour in a moderate oven to brown and develop the flavor.

Total Weight: 17 lb. 8 oz.
Yield: 56 servings, 5 oz. each (approximately $\frac{2}{3}$ c.).
Per Serving: Cost____ Selling Price____ Calories____

CREAMED SHRIMP

INGREDIENTS	AMOUNT	WEIGHT	MULTIPLE	UNIT COST	TOTAL COST
Green Shrimp		7 lb. 8 oz.			
Water	6 qt.				
Salt	2 tbsp.				
or					
Canned Shrimp		3 lb. 10 oz.			
Milk	$4\frac{1}{2}$ qt.				
Fat		1 lb. 2 oz.			
Flour		9 oz.			
Catsup	$4\frac{1}{2}$ c.				
Worcestershire sauce . .	9 tbsp.				
Cayenne	$\frac{1}{2}$ tsp.				
Salt	$1\frac{1}{2}$ tbsp.				

If green shrimp are used, cover with the six quarts of water to which the two tablespoons of salt have been added. Cook until tender, about twenty minutes. Drain and pour cold water over them. Remove the hard shell and clean the shrimp by carefully removing the black intestinal line around the outside. Cut in half. Melt the fat, add the flour and when well blended add to the scalded milk. Cook seven to ten minutes. When thickened add the catsup and Worcestershire sauce, cayenne and salt. Add the shrimp to the sauce. Serve on toast.

Total Weight: 15 lb.
Yield: 40 servings, 6 oz. each (approximately $\frac{2}{3}$–$\frac{3}{4}$ c.).
Per Serving: Cost_____ Selling Price_____ Calories_____

CURRIED SHRIMP AND RICE

INGREDIENTS	AMOUNT	WEIGHT	MULTIPLE	UNIT COST	TOTAL COST
Rice, uncooked		3 lb. 2 oz.			
Water	3 gal.				
Salt	4 tbsp.				
Green shrimp		8 lb.			
Onion juice	$\frac{1}{4}$ c.				
Chicken stock	3 qt.				
Milk	1 qt.				
Chicken fat		1 lb. 8 oz.			
Flour		11 oz.			
Salt	5 tbsp.				
Curry powder	4 tbsp.				

Cook the rice in the three gallons of boiling water with four tablespoons of salt until tender. Drain into a colander and pour cold water over until the excess starch has been removed.

Cook the fresh shrimp in boiling salted water for about twenty minutes or until tender. Peel the shell and remove the dark intestinal tract. Cut in half. If canned shrimp are used, no cooking is necessary, but they must be cleaned in the same way as the fresh.

Add the onion juice to the milk and chicken stock and bring to a boil.   Blend the fat, well-mixed flour and curry powder and add to the stock mixture, stirring constantly. Cook seven to ten minutes.   Add the shrimp.

Serve with mounds of the boiled rice which should be reheated in a steamer before serving.   On the cafeteria counter fill a steam-table pan one half to three fourths full of shrimp and place rice mounds on top.   Sprinkle the rice with paprika for color.

Total Weight: Curried shrimp, 12 lb. 8 oz.; boiled rice, 10 lb.
Yield: Shrimp, 40 servings, 5 oz. each (approximately $\frac{1}{2}-\frac{2}{3}$ c.);
    rice, 40 servings, 4 oz. each (approximately $\frac{1}{2}$ c.).
Per Serving: Cost____   Selling Price____   Calories____

CHEESE FONDUE

Ingredients	Amount	Weight	Multiple	Unit Cost	Total Cost
Nippy cheese		3 lb. 5 oz.			
Mustard	4 tsp.				
Salt	2 tbsp.				
Paprika	1⅓ tsp.				
Fat		4 oz.			
Bread crumbs		2 lb.			
Milk	4 qt.				
Egg yolks	2 c.				
Egg whites	3 c.				

Add the grated or chopped cheese, mustard, salt, paprika and fat to the crumbs.   Scald the milk and add to the well-beaten egg yolks and pour over the above ingredients.   Fold in the stiffly beaten egg whites and bake in a greased pan in a slow oven in a pan of hot water.

This may be baked in individual cups, allowing three fourths cup per serving.

Total Weight: 16 lb.
Yield: 57 servings, 4½ oz. each (approximately ¾ c.).
Per Serving: Cost____ Selling Price____ Calories____

CHEESE RAREBIT WITH BACON

INGREDIENTS	AMOUNT	WEIGHT	MULTIPLE	UNIT COST	TOTAL COST
Fat		1 lb. 8 oz.			
Flour		11 oz.			
Mustard	4 tsp.				
Cayenne	¼ tsp.				
Onion juice	1 tbsp.				
Chili powder	2 tsp.				
Milk	4 qt.				
Nippy cheese		3 lb.			
Salt	5 tsp.				
Egg yolks	⅓ c.				
Bacon	100 slices				
Toast slices	50				

Melt the fat and blend with the flour, mustard, cayenne, onion juice and chili powder. Add to the scalded milk and cook seven to ten minutes. Add the grated cheese, salt and beaten egg yolks. Cook the bacon on sheet pans in the oven. To keep the bacon from curling a similar shaped pan may be placed on top of the bacon during the cooking process. Serve the rarebit on toast with two slices of crisp bacon. Garnish with a dash of paprika.

Total Weight: 12 lb. 8 oz.
Yield: 50 servings, 4 oz. each (approximately ½ c.).
Per Serving: Cost____ Selling Price____ Calories____

CORN OYSTERS WITH BACON

INGREDIENTS	AMOUNT	WEIGHT	MULTIPLE	UNIT COST	TOTAL COST
Corn, cut from cob . .		5 lb.			
Eggs, whole	15				
Flour		1 lb. 2 oz.			
Baking powder	3 tbsp.				
Salt	2¼ tbsp.				
Fat, melted		3 oz.			
Bacon, sliced 24 per lb. .		3 lb. 9 oz.			

Use frozen whole kernel corn or fresh uncooked corn cut off the cob. Chop lightly in a chopping machine or bowl. Mix and sift the flour, baking powder and salt. Mix the corn and lightly beaten eggs and combine with the dry ingredients. Add the melted fat. Stir as little as possible to mix. Fry on a griddle allowing one sixth cup of mixture for each oyster, or a number-twenty-four scoop may be used. Serve with crisp bacon, allowing two slices of bacon and two oysters for each serving. Syrup may also be served, if desired.

Yield: 88 oysters or 44 servings, 2 oysters each.
Per Serving: Cost____   Selling Price____   Calories____

EGG CUTLETS

INGREDIENTS	AMOUNT	WEIGHT	MULTIPLE	UNIT COST	TOTAL COST
Flour		1 lb. 6 oz.			
Milk	3 qt.				
Fat		9 oz.			
Salt	⅓–½ c.				
Eggs, hard-cooked . . .	6 doz.				
Eggs	6				
Milk	¾ c.				
Bread crumbs		1 lb. 12 oz.			

Make a paste of part of the cold milk and the flour. Scald the remaining milk. Add the fat. Add the thin, smooth flour paste to the scalded milk and fat, stirring rapidly. Cook seven to ten minutes. This is a very thick mixture and needs to be stirred constantly or it will scorch. A heavy-bottomed kettle should therefore be used.

Peel and chop the hard-cooked eggs. Add to the thick white sauce with the salt and cool in shallow pans. When thoroughly cold, mold in the shape of a cutlet and dip in crumbs, then in a dipping mixture made of the eggs and milk beaten together. Dip in crumbs and fry in deep fat at 360 degrees F. until a golden brown. Be sure to form the cutlet into the desired shape before crumbing as cracks form if the cutlets are handled and shaped after crumbing. A number-eight icecream dipper may be used in order to obtain uniform servings.

Total Weight: 14 lb.
Yield: 56 servings, 4 oz. each (approximately ½ c.).
Per Serving: Cost_____   Selling Price_____   Calories_____

MACARONI LOAF

INGREDIENTS	AMOUNT	WEIGHT	MULTIPLE	UNIT COST	TOTAL COST
Macaroni		1 lb. 9 oz.			
Water	2 gal.				
Salt	2⅔ tbsp.				
Onion, ground		4 oz.			
Salt	3 tbsp.				
Fat		12 oz.			
Bread crumbs, white . .		7 oz.			
Nippy cheese		1 lb. 5 oz.			
Pimento, chopped . . .	1¾ c.				
Parsley	⅚ c.				
Milk	2⅓ qt.				
Eggs	14				

Cook the macaroni in the two gallons of boiling water with two and two thirds tablespoons of salt until tender. Drain into a colander and pour cold water over to remove the excess starch. Add the seasonings, fat, crumbs, cheese, pimento and chopped parsley. Scald the milk and add to the well-beaten eggs and pour over the macaroni-cheese mixture. Stir well and pour into greased loaf tins. Bake the loaves in a pan of hot water in a 350-degree (F.) oven about an hour, until the loaf is firm. Serve with a cheese or a mushroom sauce.

Total Weight: 16 lb. 8 oz.
Yield: 6 loaves, 2 lb. 12 oz. each (9 servings per loaf or 54 servings).
Per Serving: Cost____   Selling Price____   Calories____

CREAMED FRESH MUSHROOMS

Ingredients	Amount	Weight	Multiple	Unit Cost	Total Cost
Mushrooms		4 lb.			
Onion		1 lb.			
Butter		1 lb. 8 oz.			
Cream	2 qt.				
Milk	3 qt.				
Flour		9 oz.			
Salt	2⅔ tbsp.				

Wash and slice the mushrooms. Sauté the onion and mushrooms in the fat until tender and a golden brown. Add the flour and when blended pour the mixture into the scalded milk and cream, stirring vigorously. Cook seven to ten minutes. Add the salt. Serve on toast, in patty shells or bread cases.

Total Weight: 15 lb. 2 oz.
Yield: 44 servings, 5½ oz. each (approximately ⅔–¾ c.).
Per Serving: Cost____   Selling Price____   Calories____

MUSHROOMS AND EGGS À LA KING

Ingredients	Amount	Weight	Multiple	Unit Cost	Total Cost
Fat		9 oz.			
Flour		9 oz.			
Milk	4½ qt.				
Mushrooms, sliced . . .		1 lb. 8 oz.			
Onion, ground	3 tbsp.				
Fat		12 oz.			
Eggs, hard-cooked . . .	3 doz.				
Green pepper, chopped .	2¼ c.				
Pimento, chopped . . .	1½ c.				
Cayenne	¼ tsp.				
Salt	3 tbsp.				

Melt the nine ounces of fat, add the flour and when well blended add to the scalded milk, stirring rapidly. Cook seven to ten minutes. Wash and slice the mushrooms and sauté with the ground onion in the twelve ounces of fat. Add the cooked mushrooms, cubed hard-cooked eggs, green pepper and pimento to the white sauce. Add the seasonings. Serve on slices of toast, in fresh-cooked spinach rings or with individual spinach mounds.

Total Weight: 16 lb. 14 oz.
Yield: 54 servings, 5 oz. each (approximately ⅔–¾ c.).
Per Serving: Cost____ Selling Price____ Calories____

MUSHROOMS AND SPAGHETTI

Ingredients	Amount	Weight	Multiple	Unit Cost	Total Cost
Tomatoes	3 qt.				
Salt	3 tbsp.				
Red pepper	½ tsp.				
Black pepper	¾ tsp.				
Cloves, whole	7				
Mushrooms, sliced . . .		3 lb.			
Fat		4 oz.			
Spaghetti, uncooked . .		2 lb. 4 oz.			
Water	4 gal.				
Salt	5 tbsp.				
Nippy cheese, grated . .		9 oz.			

Cook the tomatoes with the three tablespoons of salt, red and black pepper and cloves and strain. Brown the sliced mushrooms in the fat. Cook the spaghetti in the four gallons of water with the five tablespoons of salt until tender. Drain into a colander and pour cold water over it until the excess starch has been removed. Add the mushrooms and strained tomatoes to the spaghetti. Put in baking dishes or steam-table pans, sprinkle the grated cheese on top and bake one hour in a moderate oven.

Total Weight: 15 lb., after baking.
Yield: 40 servings, 6 oz. each (approximately $\frac{2}{3}$–$\frac{3}{4}$ c.).
Per Serving: Cost_____   Selling Price_____   Calories_____

SCOTCH WOODCOCK

Ingredients	Amount	Weight	Multiple	Unit Cost	Total Cost
Celery, cut fine		3 lb.			
Fat		2 lb. 4 oz.			
Flour		13½ oz.			
Mustard	4 tsp.				
Chili powder	3 tsp.				
Milk	6 qt.				
Nippy cheese, ground . .		3 lb.			
Pimento olives, chopped .	3 c.				
Onion juice	2 tbsp.				
Salt	6 tsp.				

Cook the celery in boiling salted water until tender. Melt the fat, add the flour, mustard and chili powder mixed well together, and when blended add to the scalded milk. When this has thickened add the cheese, olives, celery, onion juice and salt. Serve on toast.

Total Weight: 21 lb.
Yield: 56 servings, 6 oz. each (approximately $\frac{2}{3}$–$\frac{3}{4}$ c.).
Per Serving: Cost_____   Selling Price_____   Calories_____

CHEESE SAUCE

Ingredients	Amount	Weight	Multiple	Unit Cost	Total Cost
Milk	1 gal.				
Fat		12 oz.			
Flour		6 oz.			
Mustard	2 tsp.				
Cayenne	⅛ tsp.				
Nippy cheese, ground .		1 lb. 8 oz.			
Salt	1⅔ tbsp.				

Scald the milk. Melt the fat, add the flour, mustard and cayenne, and when thoroughly blended add to the scalded milk, stirring vigorously. Cook from seven to ten minutes. Add the cheese and stir until melted and well blended. Add the salt.

Total Weight: 10 lb. 5 oz.
Yield: 55 servings, 3 oz. each (approximately ⅓ c.).
Per Serving: Cost_____   Selling Price_____   Calories_____

CRABMEAT SAUCE

Ingredients	Amount	Weight	Multiple	Unit Cost	Total Cost
Crabmeat		1 lb. 11 oz.			
Milk	4 qt.				
Butter		1 lb.			
Flour		6 oz.			
Salt	2¼ tbsp.				
Egg yolks	½ c.				

Look over the crabmeat and remove the stiff bony tissue. Scald the milk, melt the fat, add the flour and when well blended add to the scalded milk, stirring vigorously. Cook from seven to ten minutes. Beat the egg yolks, mix with a portion of the thickened milk and add to the remaining white sauce. Add the salt and the flaked crab-meat.

Total Weight: 9 lb. 6 oz.
Yield: 50 servings, 3 oz. each (approximately ⅓ c.).
Per Serving: Cost____ Selling Price____ Calories____

HORSE-RADISH SAUCE

Ingredients	Amount	Weight	Multiple	Unit Cost	Total Cost
Horse-radish	½ c.				
Vinegar	2 tbsp.				
Salt	½ tsp.				
Prepared mustard . . .	½ c.				
Cayenne	a few grains				
Cream, before whipping .	½ c.				

Drain the horse-radish. Mix together the horse-radish, vinegar, salt, prepared mustard and cayenne. Whip the cream until stiff and fold into the other ingredients. Serve with meat. This is especially good with ham loaf.

Total Weight: 12 oz.
Yield: 54 servings, ¾–1 tbsp. each.
Per Serving: Cost____ Selling Price____ Calories____

CREAMED FRESH MUSHROOM SAUCE

Ingredients	Amount	Weight	Multiple	Unit Cost	Total Cost
Fat		12 oz.			
Onion, ground		1½ oz.			
Mushrooms, sliced . . .		12 oz.			
Milk	3 qt.				
Flour		4½ oz.			
Egg yolks	3 tbsp.				
Salt	2 tbsp.				

Melt the fat, add the onion and mushrooms and cook slowly until the mushrooms are tender. Scald the milk. Add the flour to the sautéed mushroom mixture and when well blended add to the scalded milk, stirring vigorously. Cook from seven to ten minutes. Add the beaten egg yolks and the salt. Serve with meats, soufflés or other entrées.

Total Weight: 7 lb.
Yield: 56 servings, 2 oz. each (approximately ¼ c.).
Per Serving: Cost____ Selling Price____ Calories____

FRESH MUSHROOM SAUCE, WITH STOCK

Ingredients	Amount	Weight	Multiple	Unit Cost	Total Cost
Carrots, chopped . . .		3 oz.			
Onion, chopped		3 oz.			
Bay leaves	3				
Parsley, chopped . . .	3 tbsp.				
Peppercorns	1½ tsp.				
Meat stock	3 qt.				
Mushrooms		1 lb. 8 oz.			
Fat		12 oz.			
Flour		7½ oz.			
Salt	1 tbsp.				

Cook the vegetables and seasonings in the meat stock until tender, and strain. Wash and slice the mushrooms and sauté in the melted fat. Add the flour to the mushrooms and stir until the flour and fat are blended. Add the seasoned meat stock and cook seven to ten minutes. Add the salt. Serve hot with meat loaves, tenderloins or other meat dishes.

Total Weight: 6 lb.
Yield: 48 2-oz. servings (approximately ¼ c. each).
Per Serving: Cost____ Selling Price____ Calories____

MUSTARD SAUCE

Ingredients	Amount	Weight	Multiple	Unit Cost	Total Cost
Egg yolks	⅔ c.				
Sugar	2 tbsp.				
Salt	2 tsp.				
Paprika	1 tsp.				
Mustard, dry		4 oz.			
Vinegar	6 tbsp.				
Boiled salad dressing . .	1 c.				
Mayonnaise	3½ c.				

Beat the egg yolks until lemon-colored and thick. Add the well-mixed sugar, salt, paprika and mustard. Add the vinegar and salad dressings slowly and continue beating until the mixture is the consistency of mayonnaise. This has the keeping quality of mayonnaise.

Total Weight: 2 lb. 12 oz.
Per Serving: Cost____   Selling Price____   Calories____

TARTARE SAUCE

Ingredients	Amount	Weight	Multiple	Unit Cost	Total Cost
Dill pickles, chopped . .		8 oz.			
Onion, chopped	2 tbsp.				
Parsley, chopped . . .	2 tbsp.				
Mayonnaise	1 qt.				

Chop the pickles, onion and parsley fine and add to the mayonnaise. Chopped olives may be substituted for part of the pickles, if desired, although the dill pickles alone make a very good and inexpensive sauce, suitable for serving with hash or fish. Tartare sauce should be made as needed since it deteriorates on standing.

Total Weight: 2 lb. 9 oz.
Per Serving: Cost____   Selling Price____   Calories____

TOMATO SAUCE

Ingredients	Amount	Weight	Multiple	Unit Cost	Total Cost
Bay leaves	3				
Parsley, chopped . . .	3 tbsp.				
Salt	2⅔ tbsp.				
Peppercorns	3				
Meat stock	2¾ qt.				
Tomatoes, cooked . . .	2¼ qt.				
Celery salt	1⅓ tbsp.				
Carrots, chopped . . .		1 oz.			
Onion, ground	2 tbsp.				
Fat		8 oz.			
Flour		9 oz.			

Add the bay leaves, parsley, salt and peppercorns to the boiling stock and vegetables and cook until the vegetables are tender and the stock seasoned. Melt the fat, add the flour and when blended stir into the hot liquid. Cook five to seven minutes. Strain to remove the chopped vegetables. This sauce may be served with meat loaf, cheese fondue or with other meat or fish dishes.

Total Weight: 8 lb. 10 oz.
Yield: 50 servings, 2¾ oz. each (approximately ⅓ c.).
Per Serving: Cost___ Selling Price___ Calories___

CHAPTER VIII

Vegetables

Vegetable Cookery Has for Its Aim the Preparation of Vegetables in Such a Way As to Increase Eye Appeal, Palatability and Retention of Nutritives. These aims are achieved by following certain principles which the experimental food laboratories have developed. Holiday and Noble, in their book *Hows and Whys of Cooking*, have presented these principles clearly and in terms which may be understood even by those without special scientific background. The problem in quantity cookery is to apply the principles which have been worked out in such research departments.

From the Commercial Standpoint Eye Appeal or Appearance Undoubtedly Comes First. The consumer must be tempted, a fact which holds not only for self-service institutions but for service restaurants as well. The waiter who brings food to the table, and proudly displays it before serving, is acting on this principle. This eye appeal is dependent largely on the preservation of color and form. These are most commonly destroyed by overcooking and, while vegetables must be cooked until done, it must also be recognized that cooking continues to a slight degree in the *bain-marie* or the steam table. "Cook quickly and often" is a good rule, thereby reducing to a minimum the time between the preparation of the vegetable and the time it is eaten. The most scientifically prepared vegetable may be spoiled by standing. Peas, cabbage and cauliflower are especially good examples of this.

Where maintenance of the form of the vegetable is desired, it should be handled as little as possible during the preparation and serving. Where practical, vegetables should be cooked in the pan or dish in which they are to be served. Transferring from one pan to another, as well as stirring or handling on the steam or serving table, should be avoided.

Palatability or Pleasing Taste Is the Second Consideration. This depends on three main factors. First, on buying in the proper amounts. Purchasing in amounts too large to allow vegetables to be used before wilting, or otherwise deteriorating, is often a cause of poor flavor in the cooked product. Freshness, especially in such vegetables as corn, beans and peas, is of primary importance.

In the second place, after purchasing, the fresh vegetables must be stored properly. They should not be kept near stoves, hot chimneys or in sunny windows. In some instances, they must be kept in the icebox until consumed. In any case, a free circulation of air is essential and all containers avoided which preclude good ventilation.

The last factor in producing pleasing taste is proper preparation. Of all types of cookery, vegetable cookery has been one of the last to be standardized. Hit-or-miss methods still obtain, such as cooking the same vegetable at one time on top of the stove, the next time in the steam-jacketed kettle or steamer; with salt one time, without salt the next; cooking covered or uncovered, as chance dictates; and guessing on the amount of salt, butter or sauce. These are common practices and make for unstandardized results. The only method to be recommended is to develop recipes for each dish and to be sure that they are followed accurately and carefully.

The Third Aim in Vegetable Cookery Is to Retain the Valuable Nutritives. The responsibility for maintaining the maximum of nutritive essentials rests upon the food-production manager and is an obligation which he owes to the public. As a guide, it may be said that, if the vegetables are cooked so as to preserve color and form and to develop or maintain flavor, the amount of salts and vitamins retained will be better than average and the responsibility, dietetically speaking, will probably be met.

FRIED APPLES

INGREDIENTS	AMOUNT	WEIGHT	MULTIPLE	UNIT COST	TOTAL COST
Apples		15 lb.			
Bacon fat		15 oz.			
Granulated sugar . . .		15 oz.			
Salt	1 tbsp.				

Wash, quarter, core and slice the apples. Do not peel. Melt the fat in a skillet. Add the apples and fry on top of the stove until almost tender. Add the sugar and the salt and finish cooking.

Total Weight: 13 lb.
Yield: 52 servings, 4 oz. each (approximately ½ c.).
Per Serving: Cost____   Selling Price____   Calories____

BAKED BEANS

INGREDIENTS	AMOUNT	WEIGHT	MULTIPLE	UNIT COST	TOTAL COST
Beans		5 lb.			
Salt pork		2 lb. 9 oz.			
Mustard	3 tbsp.				
Sugar		14 oz.			
Molasses	½ c.				
Water	6 qt.				

Soak the beans twelve hours or more. Drain. Cube the salt pork in one-third-inch cubes, fry until brown and mix the pork and fat with the remaining ingredients. Add to the beans. Put into jars, crocks or pans with small evaporating surface and add the water. Cover and bake seven to eight hours at 250 degrees F. Uncover and brown the last hour. Add extra hot water while baking, if necessary.

Total Weight: 16 lb. 5 oz.
Yield: 58 servings, 4½ oz. each (approximately ½ c.).
Per Serving: Cost____ Selling Price____ Calories____

BAKED LIMA BEANS

INGREDIENTS	AMOUNT	WEIGHT	MULTIPLE	UNIT COST	TOTAL COST
Lima beans		3 lb.			
Water , ...	2 qt.				
Salt	2 tbsp.				
Pimentos		6 oz.			
Bacon fat		6 oz.			
Onion, ground		8 oz.			
Paprika	1 tbsp.				
Green peppers		3 oz.			
Molasses	2 tbsp.				
Corn syrup	⅓ c.				

Soak the lima beans in water to cover, overnight. Drain and cook them in the two quarts of boiling salted water until almost tender. Add the remaining ingredients and pour into baking or steam-table pans. Bake in a moderate oven until the beans are tender and well browned.

Total Weight: 10 lb. 8 oz., after baking.
Yield: 42 servings, 4 oz. each (approximately ½ c.).
Per Serving: Cost____ Selling Price____ Calories____

BEET GREENS

Ingredients	Amount	Weight	Multiple	Unit Cost	Total Cost
Young beet greens . . .		10 lb.			
Salt pork, cubed . . .		1 lb. 8 oz.			
Onion, ground		12 oz.			
Vinegar	½ c.				

Cook the beet greens uncovered about fifteen to twenty minutes in ample boiling salted water until tender. Do not steam as it destroys the color. Drain thoroughly. While the beet greens are cooking fry the salt pork, which has been diced in one-fourth-inch pieces, together with the onion until crisp and brown. Add the vinegar and serve.

Total Weight: 10 lb.
Yield: 40 servings, 4 oz. each (approximately ½ c.).
Per Serving: Cost____ Selling Price____ Calories____

BUTTERED BEETS

Ingredients	Amount	Weight	Multiple	Unit Cost	Total Cost
Beets		12 lb.			
Butter		12 oz.			
Salt	3 tbsp.				

Wash the beets and steam or boil them until tender. Remove the skin, cube or slice and reheat. Add the salt and pour the melted butter over them. Beets should never be cut before cooking since they tend to lose color and shrivel when cut. Because they darken on standing, especially on standing on a steam table, it is advisable to steam the amount necessary for a meal but to cut or slice and season only as they are needed.

Total Weight: 10 lb. 8 oz.
Yield: 42 servings, 4 oz. each (approximately ½–⅔ c.).
Per Serving: Cost____ Selling Price____ Calories____

BUTTERED CABBAGE

Ingredients	Amount	Weight	Multiple	Unit Cost	Total Cost
Cabbage		12 lb.			
Water	3 gal.				
Salt	½ c.				
Butter		1 lb. 8 oz.			

Remove the coarse outer leaves of the cabbage, wash and cut the heads in eighths. Cook ten to fifteen minutes in boiling salted water uncovered until tender. Avoid over-cooking to prevent the cabbage from discoloring and from developing a strong flavor. The cabbage should be light green or white and should present an almost crisp appearance, at the same time being tender. Drain off the water and add the butter. A steamer should never be used for cooking cabbage since its appetizing color and good flavor depend wholly on quick cooking uncovered in ample boiling water.

Total Weight: 10 lb. 8 oz.
Yield: 42 servings, 4 oz. each (approximately ½–⅔ c.).
Per Serving: Cost_____ Selling Price_____ Calories_____

CREAMED CABBAGE

Ingredients	Amount	Weight	Multiple	Unit Cost	Total Cost
Cabbage		8 lb.			
Salt	½ c.				
Water	3 gal.				
Milk	3 qt.				
Butter		12 oz.			
Flour		3 oz.			
Egg yolks	6 tbsp.				
Salt	1¾ tbsp.				

Remove the coarse outside leaves from the cabbage. Wash and cut the heads into eighths. Do not shred.

Cook in boiling salted water uncovered until tender, ten to fifteen minutes. Avoid overcooking. Cabbage should be white or light green when served. Drain. To make the white sauce melt the fat, stir in the flour and add to the scalded milk, stirring vigorously. Cook seven to ten minutes. Beat the yolks with a small amount of the white sauce and then stir into the remainder of the white sauce. Pour the sauce over the very well-drained cabbage.

In serving larger numbers over a period of time vegetables should be prepared as needed. However, in this case, the white sauce for as many servings as desired may be prepared and the cabbage cut for a like number. The cabbage may then be cooked as needed and white sauce added only as served.

Total Weight: 10 lb. 8 oz.
Yield: 42 servings, 4 oz. each (approximately ½ c.).
Per Serving: Cost_____   Selling Price_____   Calories_____

HOT SLAW

Ingredients	Amount	Weight	Multiple	Unit Cost	Total Cost
Cabbage		6 lb.			
Fat		2 oz.			
Salt	4 tsp.				
Pepper	2 tsp.				
DRESSING:					
Sour cream	1 qt.				
Vinegar	1 c.				
Water	½ c.				
Sugar		1 lb. 7 oz.			
Egg yolks	⅔ c.				

Shred the cabbage and plunge into boiling water to wilt slightly. Drain and add the fat, salt and pepper. Heat the sour cream, vinegar and water. Blend the sugar and yolks and thicken the hot liquid. As needed, combine the cabbage with the dressing and serve.

Total Weight: 10 lb. 8 oz.
Yield: 42 servings, 4 oz. each (approximately ⅓–½ c.).
Per Serving: Cost_____   Selling Price_____   Calories_____

RED CABBAGE, GERMAN STYLE

INGREDIENTS	AMOUNT	WEIGHT	MULTIPLE	UNIT COST	TOTAL COST
Red cabbage, shredded .		7 lb. 8 oz.			
Tart apples, peeled and sliced		1 lb. 13 oz.			
Allspice	1 tbsp.				
Cloves	1 tsp.				
Sugar		2 oz.			
Salt	4 tbsp.				
Bacon fat		12 oz.			
Vinegar	½ c.				
Boiling water . .	3 qt.				

Add the cabbage and the remaining ingredients to the boiling water. Cover and cook slowly about four hours until thoroughly tender and well seasoned.

Total Weight: 12 lb. 11 oz.
Yield: 58 servings, 3½ oz. each (approximately ½ c.).
Per Serving: Cost_____   Selling Price_____   Calories_____

BUTTERED CARROTS

INGREDIENTS	AMOUNT	WEIGHT	MULTIPLE	UNIT COST	TOTAL COST
Carrots		7 lb. 8 oz.			
Water	7 c.				
Salt	4½ tbsp.				
Butter		8 oz.			

Scrape the carrots. If they are young and small they may be left whole. If not, cut in slices or julienne pieces.

Place in a kettle and add the water, salt and butter. Cover and cook slowly until the carrots are tender, about thirty to forty-five minutes. The aim is to use as little water as possible to prevent the loss of mineral salts and vitamins. Serve without draining.

Total Weight: 7 lb. 14 oz.
Yield: 42 servings, 3 oz. each (approximately ⅓–½ c.).
Per Serving: Cost____ Selling Price____ Calories____

CREAMED CARROTS

INGREDIENTS	AMOUNT	WEIGHT	MULTIPLE	UNIT COST	TOTAL COST
Carrots		10 lb.			
Salt	3 tbsp.				
Water	5 qt.				
WHITE SAUCE:					
Milk.	1 gal.				
Butter		1 lb.			
Flour		4 oz.			
Egg yolks	½ c.				
Salt	2¼ tbsp.				

Wash, scrape or pare and slice the carrots. Cook in the boiling salted water until tender, about thirty to forty-five minutes. Drain. Scald the milk, melt the fat and blend with the flour. Add to the milk, stirring vigorously. Cook seven to ten minutes. Stir in the egg yolks mixed with a small amount of the thickened milk. Add the salt. Combine the white sauce with the thoroughly drained carrots.

Total Weight: 15 lb.
Yield: 60 servings, 4 oz. each (approximately ½–⅔ c.).
Per Serving: Cost____ Selling Price____ Calories____

CREAMED CELERY

Ingredients	Amount	Weight	Multiple	Unit Cost	Total Cost
Celery		6 lb. 12 oz.			
Salt	4 tbsp.				
Water	6 qt.				
White Sauce:					
Milk.	3 qt.				
Butter		12 oz.			
Flour		3 oz.			
Egg yolks	⅓ c.				
Salt	1¾ tbsp.				

Wash and clean the celery and cut in three-quarter-inch lengths. Cook in the boiling salted water until tender. Avoid overcooking to prevent discoloration. When tender, drain. Scald the milk, melt the fat and blend with the flour. Add to the hot milk, stirring rapidly. Cook seven to ten minutes. Stir in the egg yolks which have been mixed with a small amount of the thickened milk. Add the salt. Pour the white sauce over the celery and mix lightly. If the whole amount is not needed for service at once combine the white sauce and celery only as needed.

Total Weight: 11 lb. 8 oz.
Yield: 46 servings, 4 oz. each (approximately ½–⅔ c.).
Per Serving: Cost____ Selling Price____ Calories____

CORN PUDDING

Ingredients	Amount	Weight	Multiple	Unit Cost	Total Cost
Milk	3 qt.				
Eggs	12				
Corn, #10 can	1				
Sugar	3 tbsp.				
Salt	1½ tbsp.				
Bread crumbs		1 lb.			
Fat		8 oz.			
Green pepper	1 c.				
Pimento, chopped . . .	1 c.				

Scald the milk, add the well-beaten eggs and combine with the remainder of the ingredients. Pour the mixture into individual ramekins or baking pans. Place them in pans of water and bake in a moderate oven until the custard sets, approximately one and one half to one and three fourths hours. Serve hot.

Total Weight: 14 lb. 10 oz., after baking.
Yield: 52 servings, 4½ oz. each (approximately ½–⅔ c.).
Per Serving: Cost_____ Selling Price_____ Calories_____

SCALLOPED CORN

INGREDIENTS	AMOUNT	WEIGHT	MULTIPLE	UNIT COST	TOTAL COST
Milk	1¼ qt.				
Fat		1 lb. 4 oz.			
Onion, ground		2 oz.			
Salt	1 tbsp.				
Finely broken bread or crackers		1 lb. 8 oz.			
Corn, #10 can	1				
Crumbs		12 oz.			
Butter		1½ oz.			

Heat the milk, add the one pound four ounces of fat and the ground onion. Add the salt and pour over the broken bread or crackers. Add the corn and mix lightly. Pour into greased baking or steam-table pans. This will fill three shallow pans approximately 9″ × 15″. Sprinkle buttered crumbs over the top and bake in a 350-degree (F.) oven about one hour.

Total Weight: 12 lb. 8 oz., after baking.
Yield: 50 servings, 4 oz. each (approximately ½ c.).
Per Serving: Cost_____ Selling Price_____ Calories_____

HOMINY IN CREAM

Ingredients	Amount	Weight	Multiple	Unit Cost	Total Cost
Hominy, #10 cans . . .	2				
Top milk	2¾ qt.				
Salt	1¾ tbsp.				

Drain the hominy and add the top milk. Put in a heavy-bottomed kettle. Cover and simmer on the back of the stove for two hours or more until the hominy has absorbed the top milk and become creamy and tender. Add the salt.

Total Weight: 10 lb. 8 oz.
Yield: 42 servings, 4 oz. each (approximately ½ c.).
Per Serving: Cost____ Selling Price____ Calories____

FRIED EGGPLANT

Ingredients	Amount	Weight	Multiple	Unit Cost	Total Cost
Eggplant		7 lb.			
Salt	3 tbsp.				
Milk	½ c.				
Eggs, whole	4				
Crumbs, sifted		1 lb.			

Cut the eggplant into slices one third to one half inch thick and peel. Make a dipping mixture of the eggs, milk and salt. Dip the eggplant into the dipping mixture and then in the crumbs. Fry in deep fat at 360–380 degrees F. Fry only as needed as it loses its crispness quickly on standing. Eggplant is often served with powdered sugar sifted over it. Sweet crumbs wholly or in part may be used for crumbing eggplant. They tend to counteract the acidity of the eggplant and add a pleasing flavor. Eggplant is often prepared by soaking in a strong salt solution and expressing the juice. This, however, is not necessary, and in quantity work is impractical and the extra labor unjustified.

Total Weight: 7 lb. 14 oz. (after dipped, rolled in crumbs but not cooked).
Yield: 42 servings, 3 oz. each before cooking (approximately 2–3 slices).
Per Serving: Cost____ Selling Price____ Calories____

WILTED LETTUCE

Ingredients	Amount	Weight	Multiple	Unit Cost	Total Cost
Lettuce		8 lb.			
Bacon, cooked		12 oz.			
Bacon fat		8 oz.			
Flour		1 oz.			
Salt	1 tbsp.				
Sugar		10 oz.			
Vinegar	1 c.				
Water	3 c.				

Wash the lettuce leaves well and drain thoroughly. Cut coarsely. Chop the cooked bacon and add to the lettuce. Make a sauce by melting the bacon fat, stirring in the flour mixed with salt and sugar, and adding to the boiling vinegar and water. When the sauce has thickened pour hot over the lettuce leaves and bacon, tossing lightly to wilt the lettuce.

Total Weight: 11 lb. 12 oz.
Yield: 47 servings, 4 oz. each (approximately $\frac{2}{3}$ c.).
Per Serving: Cost____ Selling Price____ Calories____

MACARONI AND CHEESE

Ingredients	Amount	Weight	Multiple	Unit Cost	Total Cost
Macaroni, broken . . .		1 lb. 10 oz.			
Water	3 gal.				
Salt	¼ c.				
WHITE SAUCE:					
Milk.	3 qt.				
Butter		10 oz.			
Flour		4½ oz.			
Egg yolks	⅓ c.				
Salt	1¾ tbsp.				
Red pepper	½ tsp.				
Cheese, nippy		2 lb.			

Cook the broken macaroni in the three gallons of boiling water with the one fourth cup of salt until tender. Drain into a colander and pour cold water over it until the excess starch has been removed.

Scald the milk. Melt the fat, add the flour and blend. Add to the hot milk, stirring vigorously. Add the well-beaten yolks to part of the white sauce and combine with the remainder. Add the salt and combine with the macaroni, red pepper and the cheese which has been ground or cut fine.

Put into well-greased baking pans and bake about one hour in a medium oven until browned.

Total Weight: 13 lb. 12 oz.
Yield: 44 servings, 5 oz. each (approximately ½ c.).
Per Serving: Cost_____ Selling Price_____ Calories_____

SCALLOPED NOODLES AND VEGETABLES

Ingredients	Amount	Weight	Multiple	Unit Cost	Total Cost
Noodles		1 lb. 8 oz.			
Water	2 gal.				
Salt	2⅔ tbsp.				
WHITE SAUCE :					
Butter		6 oz.			
Flour		2 oz.			
Paprika	¾ tbsp.				
Milk	1½ qt.				
Salt	1 tbsp.				
Nippy cheese, ground . .		12 oz.			
String beans, cooked . .		12 oz.			
Carrots, cooked and cut fine		12 oz.			
Peas, cooked		12 oz.			
Tomatoes, canned . . .	1½ c.				
Onion, ground		4 oz.			

Cook the noodles in the two gallons of boiling water with two and two thirds tablespoons of salt until tender. Drain into a colander and pour water over to remove the excess starch. Make a white sauce by blending the fat, flour and paprika and stirring into the scalded milk. Cook seven to ten minutes. Add the salt and one half of the cheese to the white sauce. Stir until dissolved. Mix with the cooked vegetables and tomatoes and the cooked noodles. Pour the mixture into shallow baking pans and sprinkle the remaining cheese over the top. Bake in a moderate oven for about one hour.

Total Weight: 12 lb., after baking.
Yield: 48 servings, 4 oz. each (approximately ½ c.).
Per Serving: Cost_____   Selling Price_____   Calories_____

BUTTERED ONIONS

Ingredients	Amount	Weight	Multiple	Unit Cost	Total Cost
White onions		15 lb.			
Salt	6 tbsp.				
Water	9 qt.				
Butter		6 oz.			

Peel the onions, which should be of a uniform size. Cook uncovered in the boiling salted water for thirty to forty minutes. Avoid overcooking, which tends to make the onions yellow and bitter in flavor. When tender and white, drain and add the butter.

Total Weight: 12 lb. 8 oz.
Yield: 50 servings, 4 oz. each (approximately ½ c.).
Per Serving: Cost____ Selling Price____ Calories____

CREAMED ONIONS

Ingredients	Amount	Weight	Multiple	Unit Cost	Total Cost
Onions		15 lb.			
Salt	5½ tbsp.				
Water	9 qt.				
Milk	3 qt.				
Butter		12 oz.			
Flour		3 oz.			
Egg yolks	6 tbsp.				
Salt	1¾ tbsp.				

Peel the onions and cook uncovered in the boiling salted water about thirty to forty minutes until tender. Scald the milk, melt the fat, add the flour and when blended add to the milk, stirring vigorously. Cook seven to ten minutes. Add the egg yolks to a little of the hot liquid and pour into the remaining thickened milk. Add the salt.

Drain the onions thoroughly and pour the white sauce over them.

Total Weight: 17 lb. 14 oz.
Yield: 52 servings, 5½ oz. each (approximately ½–⅔ c.).
Per Serving: Cost____ Selling Price____ Calories____

CREAMED PEAS WITH 'DUMPLINGS

Ingredients	Amount	Weight	Multiple	Unit Cost	Total Cost
White Sauce:					
Milk	1 gal.				
Butter		12 oz.			
Flour		4 oz.			
Salt	3 tbsp.				
Egg yolks	½ c.				
Peas		5 lb.			
Salt	3 tbsp.				
Water	2 qt.				
Dumplings:					
Flour		15 oz.			
Baking powder . . .	1½ tbsp.				
Salt	¾ tbsp.				
Fat		4½ oz.			
Eggs	2				
Milk	1⅓–1½ c.				

Scald the milk. Melt the butter, add the flour and, stirring rapidly, add to the scalded milk. Cook five to seven minutes. Add a small amount of the hot liquid to the beaten egg yolks and combine with the remaining thickened liquid. Add the salt.

Cook the peas in boiling salted water, being careful not to overcook. Drain and combine with the white sauce. Pour into the pans from which the peas are to be served and drop on the dumplings, using approximately one tablespoon of dough per dumpling. See page 114 for in-

structions on the method of preparing dumplings.   Steam
ten to twelve minutes until the dumplings are light.

Total Weight: Creamed peas, approximately 12 lb.; dumplings,
1 lb. 14 oz.
Yield: 64 servings, approximately 3½ oz. each.
Per Serving: Cost____   Selling Price____   Calories____

BROWNED POTATOES

INGREDIENTS	AMOUNT	WEIGHT	MULTIPLE	UNIT COST	TOTAL COST
Potatoes, peeled . . .		18 lb.			
Beef fat		1 lb. 2 oz.			
Salt	6 tbsp.				
Paprika	3 tbsp.				

Wash and peel potatoes of even size (or cut to an even
size).   Dip in melted beef fat.   Drain off excess fat and
place in a baking pan.   Sprinkle with salt and paprika and
bake two and one half to three hours in a moderate oven.
Shake pan occasionally to baste the potatoes.

Total Weight: 11 lb. 4 oz.
Yield: 40 servings, 4½ oz. each (approximately ¾ c.).
Per Serving: Cost____   Selling Price____   Calories____

CREAMED NEW POTATOES

INGREDIENTS	AMOUNT	WEIGHT	MULTIPLE	UNIT COST	TOTAL COST
Potatoes, peeled . . .		10 lb.			
Salt	2⅔ tbsp.				
WHITE SAUCE :					
Milk	2 qt.				
Flour		2 oz.			
Butter		8 oz.			
Egg yolks	¼ c.				
Salt	1¼ tbsp.				

Cut the potatoes to an even size. Boil or steam until tender. If steamed, the two and two thirds tablespoons of salt may be sprinkled on top of the potatoes. If boiled, add the salt to the boiling water.

Scald the milk. Melt the fat, stir in the flour and when well blended add to the scalded milk, stirring vigorously. Cook from seven to ten minutes. Add the egg yolks to some of the thickened milk, mix thoroughly, and add slowly to the remainder. Add the one and one fourth tablespoons of salt. Combine the cooked potatoes and the white sauce.

Total Weight: 13 lb. 8 oz.

Yield: 54 servings, 4 oz. each (approximately $\frac{1}{3}$–$\frac{1}{2}$ c.).

Per Serving: Cost_____   Selling Price_____   Calories_____

FRENCH FRIED POTATOES

INGREDIENTS	AMOUNT	WEIGHT	MULTIPLE	UNIT COST	TOTAL COST
Potatoes, peeled . . .		15 lb.			
Salt	3 tbsp.				
Fat					

Cut the peeled potatoes into strips about $\frac{1}{2}''\times\frac{1}{2}''\times 3''$ long. Dry on a cloth. Fill the fry basket about one third full of potatoes and fry in deep fat for five to twelve minutes, at 365–370 degrees F., or until the potatoes are done but not brown. Drain and hold until needed for serving. At that time brown in deep fat at 395–400 degrees F. Drain on brown paper and sprinkle with salt. The potatoes may also be blanched by parboiling or steaming until almost tender, but the deep fat method of precooking is preferable. The weight of potatoes produced will vary with the kind of potato and the season.

Total Weight: Approximately 7 lb. 8 oz., after frying.

Yield: Approximately 40 servings, 3 oz. each (approximately 1 c.).

Per Serving: Cost_____   Selling Price_____   Calories_____

HOT OR GERMAN POTATO SALAD

Ingredients	Amount	Weight	Multiple	Unit Cost	Total Cost
Potatoes		10 lb.			
Celery, sliced	1 qt.				
Onion (Bermuda or Span-ish)		1 lb.			
Chopped parsley . . .		1 oz.			
Bacon, cut fine		1 lb.			
Salt	$\frac{1}{3}$ c.				
Black pepper	$\frac{1}{2}$ tsp.				
Vinegar	1 c.				
Water	$\frac{3}{4}$ c.				

Cook the potatoes in their jackets and peel and dice while hot. Mix the potatoes, celery, onion and parsley. Fry the bacon and add with the fat in which it has been cooked to the remaining ingredients and pour over the potato mixture. Cover and let stand thirty to forty minutes to season. Serve hot.

Total Weight: 13 lb.
Yield: 52 servings, 4 oz. each (approximately $\frac{1}{2}$–$\frac{2}{3}$ c.).
Per Serving: Cost____ Selling Price____ Calories____

MASHED POTATOES

Ingredients	Amount	Weight	Multiple	Unit Cost	Total Cost
Potatoes, peeled . . .		10 lb.			
Salt	$2\frac{2}{3}$ tbsp.				
Milk, scalded	$1\frac{3}{4}$ qt.				
Butter		8 oz.			

Steam the potatoes until thoroughly done. Beat in a mixing machine until all the lumps have been removed and the potatoes are soft and fluffy. Whip at high speed for a few minutes. Add the butter and salt. Pour in the hot milk gradually. The amount of milk will vary depending on the kind of potato. Mashed potatoes should not be allowed to stand, but should be cooked and mashed in small amounts as needed.

Total Weight: 11 lb. 8 oz.
Yield: 46 servings, 4 oz. each (approximately ½ c.).
Per Serving: Cost____   Selling Price____   Calories____

PARSLEY BUTTERED POTATOES

Ingredients	Amount	Weight	Multiple	Unit Cost	Total Cost
Potatoes, pared		15 lb.			
Butter		11 oz.			
Salt	2 tbsp.				
Parsley, chopped . . .	1⅓ c.				

Steam or boil the potatoes until tender. When done place them in the containers in which they are to be served and pour the butter, which has been melted, over them. Salt and sprinkle with parsley. Shake gently to distribute the parsley and butter evenly.

Total Weight: 13 lb. 8 oz.
Yield: 54 servings, 4 oz. each (approximately ½ c.).
Per Serving: Cost____   Selling Price____   Calories____

POTATO CHIPS

Ingredients	Amount	Weight	Multiple	Unit Cost	Total Cost
Potatoes, peeled . . .		10 lb.			
Fat					
Salt					

Select large uniform potatoes eight to twelve ounces each. Peel and cut lengthwise into thin slices with a mechanical cutter. Twenty-four slices when laid together should measure one inch. Soak in cold water and rinse thoroughly to remove the starch. Drain thoroughly and dry on towels. Fry in deep fat at 360 degrees F. until light brown and crisp. Turn frequently. Drain on brown paper. Sprinkle with salt. The amount of starch varies according to the variety of potato and time of year. This will cause a variation in the amount of potato chips obtained.

Total Weight: 2 lb. 12 oz. to 3 lb. 12 oz.
Yield: 44 to 60 servings of one ounce each.
Per Serving: Cost_____ Selling Price_____ Calories_____

SCALLOPED POTATOES (WITH COOKED POTATOES)

INGREDIENTS	AMOUNT	WEIGHT	MULTIPLE	UNIT COST	TOTAL COST
Potatoes, steamed and sliced		10 lb, 8 oz.			
Milk	3 qt.				
Butter		12 oz.			
Flour		4½ oz.			
Egg yolks	6 tbsp.				
Salt	⅓ c.				
Onion, grated		4 oz.			
Crumbs		8 oz.			
Butter		2 oz.			

Scald the milk. Melt the twelve ounces of fat, stir in the flour and when well blended add to the scalded milk, stirring vigorously. Cook from seven to ten minutes. Add the egg yolks to a small amount of the hot thickened milk and add slowly to the remaining milk, stirring constantly. Add the grated onion and salt. Grease four scalloping or steam-table pans, 9″ × 9″. Cover with a layer of potatoes and then with white sauce. Add another layer of potato and white sauce. Melt the two ounces of butter, add the crumbs and stir until well coated with butter and sprinkle over the potato mixture. Bake about forty minutes in a moderate oven until brown.

Total Weight: 18 lb. 12 oz.
Yield: 60 servings, 5 oz. each (approximately ⅔ c.).
Per Serving: Cost—— Selling Price—— Calories——

SCALLOPED POTATOES (WITH UNCOOKED POTATOES)

Ingredients	Amount	Weight	Multiple	Unit Cost	Total Cost
Potatoes, peeled . . .		14 lb.			
White Sauce:					
Milk.	2 qt.				
Butter		8 oz.			
Flour		3 oz.			
Egg yolks	¼ c.				
Salt	⅓ c.				
Onion juice	1 c.				
Crumbs		1 lb.			
Butter for crumbs . . .		4 oz.			

Slice the potatoes on a slicing machine about one sixteenth inch in thickness. Put them into the steamer and cook for ten minutes. Divide between baking dishes or three steam-table pans, 9″ × 15″. Scald the milk and melt the eight ounces of fat. Add the flour and when well blended add to the scalded milk, stirring vigorously. Cook from seven to ten minutes. Add the egg yolks to part of the white sauce, mix thoroughly and add slowly to the thickened milk. Pour the white sauce over the potatoes. Melt the four ounces of butter and stir in the crumbs until well mixed. Sprinkle over the pans. Bake in a moderate oven until the potatoes are tender and the crumbs a golden brown.

Total Weight: 16 lb. 4 oz.
Yield: 52 servings, 5 oz. each.
Per Serving: Cost—— Selling Price—— Calories——

STUFFED BAKED POTATOES

Ingredients	Amount	Weight	Multiple	Unit Cost	Total Cost
Potatoes		24 lb.			
Milk	1 qt.				
Salt	½ c.				
Paprika	1 tsp.				
Butter		4 oz.			
Chopped pimento . . .	½ c.				
Chopped parsley . . .	1 c.				
Egg whites	1½ c.				

Select smooth potatoes weighing one pound each. Wash and bake. When done, cut in half lengthwise. Scoop out the inside, mash or put through a ricer and add the milk, seasonings, fat, chopped pimento and parsley. Fold in the beaten egg whites. Fill the potato shells lightly with the seasoned mixture and brown in a hot oven.

Yield: 48 servings (approximately 5⅔ oz. each), after baking.
Per Serving: Cost____   Selling Price____   Calories____

RICE CROQUETTES

Ingredients	Amount	Weight	Multiple	Unit Cost	Total Cost
Rice		2 lb. 6 oz.			
Milk	3 qt.				
Water	1½ qt.				
Eggs	20				
Salt	2 tbsp.				
Fat		4 oz.			

Cook the rice uncovered in the milk and water until tender, stirring occasionally to prevent sticking. Remove from the fire. Do not drain. Add the well-beaten eggs, salt and fat. With a number-eight dipper drop the mixture into hot fat (360 degrees F.) and fry until brown. Serve with jelly or syrup.

Total Weight: 11 lb.
Yield: 44 servings, 4 oz. each (approximately ½ c.).
Per Serving: Cost____   Selling Price____   Calories____

SPANISH RICE

Ingredients	Amount	Weight	Multiple	Unit Cost	Total Cost
Rice, uncooked		1 lb. 14 oz.			
Water	9 qt.				
Salt	3 tbsp.				
Cooked tomatoes . . .	3 qt.				
Green peppers, chopped .	2¼ c.				
Cooked chopped bacon .		10 oz.			
Salt	1½ tbsp.				
Chili powder	1 tbsp.				
Onion, ground		2 oz.			
Bacon fat	1 c.				

Cook the rice in the boiling salted water until tender. Drain into a colander and run cold water over to separate the rice grains and remove the excess starch. Add the tomatoes, green pepper, bacon, salt, chili powder, onion and fat. Mix carefully to avoid breaking up the rice. Put in baking pans and bake for one hour at 350 degrees F., until the flavors are blended. This will make two shallow pans, approximately 9″ × 15″.

Total Weight: 13 lb., after baking.
Yield: 52 servings, 4 oz. each (approximately ½ c.).
Per Serving: Cost___ Selling Price___ Calories___

BUTTERED RUTABAGAS

Ingredients	Amount	Weight	Multiple	Unit Cost	Total Cost
Rutabagas, diced . . .		10 lb.			
Water	5 qt.				
Salt	3 tbsp.				
Sugar	3–5 tbsp.				
Butter		6 oz.			

Cook the rutabagas in the boiling salted water or in the steamer about twenty-five to thirty minutes until tender. Drain and add the sugar and butter. Because the color of rutabagas is fairly stable, they may be cooked in a steamer with no appreciable loss of color.

Total Weight: 10 lb.
Yield: 46 servings, 3½ oz. each (approximately ½ c.).
Per Serving: Cost____ Selling Price____ Calories____

MASHED RUTABAGAS

Ingredients	Amount	Weight	Multiple	Unit Cost	Total Cost
Peeled rutabagas . . .		15 lb.			
Butter or bacon fat . .		1 lb. 8 oz.			
Salt	⅔ c.				
Sugar		4–6 oz.			

Steam the rutabagas until tender and mash. Season with the fat, salt and sugar.

Total Weight: 15 lb. 14 oz.
Yield: 60 servings, 4 oz. each (approximately ½ c.).
Per Serving: Cost____ Selling Price____ Calories____

SPINACH SOUFFLÉ, CHEESE SAUCE

Ingredients	Amount	Weight	Multiple	Unit Cost	Total Cost
Soufflé :					
Milk	2 c.				
Cheese, nippy . . .		1 lb. 8 oz.			
Salt	¼ tsp.				
Egg yolks	¾ c.				
Spinach, cooked and chopped		5 lb. 12 oz.			
Bread crumbs . . .		5 oz.			
Egg whites	2¼ c.				
Sauce :					
Milk	2¾ qt.				
Fat		6 oz.			
Flour		3 oz.			
Salt	1¾ tbsp.				
Egg yolks	1 c.				
Nippy cheese, ground .		1 lb. 8 oz.			

Scald the milk and pour over the cheese and salt. When well blended add the beaten egg yolks, the chopped spinach and the crumbs. Fold in the stiffly beaten egg whites. Using a number-eight icecream scoop, put into greased individual casseroles garnished with a small piece of pimento in the bottom of each casserole. Steam for twenty to thirty minutes or until firm.

Make a white sauce by blending the fat and flour and adding to the hot milk, stirring vigorously. Add the salt and the beaten egg yolks to a small amount of the white sauce and stirring rapidly add to the remaining white sauce. When thickened add the ground cheese to the sauce and beat until thoroughly blended.

Pour the sauce into steam-table or serving dishes and place the unmolded soufflés in rows in the pans.

Total Weight: Spinach mixture, 10 lb. 1 oz.; sauce, 7 lb. 3 oz.
Yield: Soufflé — 46 servings, 3½ oz. each; cheese sauce — 46 servings, 2½ oz. each.
Per Serving: Cost____ Selling Price____ Calories____

GLAZED SWEET POTATOES

Ingredients	Amount	Weight	Multiple	Unit Cost	Total Cost
Cooked and peeled sweet potatoes		12 lb.			
Light-brown sugar . . .		2 lb. 4 oz.			
Fat		3 oz.			
Water	¼ c.				
Salt	4 tsp.				

Slice the potatoes in one-inch pieces. Place in pans. Make a syrup of the sugar, fat, water and salt. Pour over the potatoes. Bake for one and one half hours, basting occasionally.

Total Weight: 11¼ lb.
Yield: 40 servings, 4½ oz. each.
Per Serving: Cost____ Selling Price____ Calories____

SCALLOPED SWEET POTATOES AND APPLES

INGREDIENTS	AMOUNT	WEIGHT	MULTIPLE	UNIT COST	TOTAL COST
Apples, peeled and cored .		7 lb. 8 oz.			
Sweet potatoes, cooked and peeled		7 lb. 8 oz.			
Fat		1 lb.			
Light-brown sugar . . .		2 lb. 8 oz.			
Water	1½ c.				
Salt	1½ tbsp.				

Slice the apples. Steam or cook until almost tender. Put a layer of sliced sweet potatoes in a baking pan, cover with apples, add another layer of sweet potatoes and then a layer of apples. This should make three shallow pans, approximately 9″ × 9″.

Make a syrup of the fat, sugar, water and salt. Pour over the apples and potatoes. Bake for one to one and one half hours in a slow oven.

Total Weight: 18 lb. 9 oz.
Yield: 54 servings, approximately 5½ oz. each.
Per Serving: Cost____ Selling Price____ Calories____

BAKED STUFFED TOMATOES

INGREDIENTS	AMOUNT	WEIGHT	MULTIPLE	UNIT COST	TOTAL COST
Tomatoes, 6-7 oz. each .	48				
Green peppers, chopped .	2 c.				
Corn		2 lb.			
Coarse bread crumbs . .		1 lb. 12 oz.			
Onion juice	½ c.				
Salt	1⅓ tbsp.				
Fat		1 lb.			
Black pepper	½ tsp.				
Sugar	2 tbsp.				
Chili powder	¼ tsp.				

Select six- to seven-ounce tomatoes. Wash and cut a large cone-shaped piece out of the center of each. Mix the remaining ingredients and one half of the fat. Fill the tomatoes with approximately one fourth cup each of this mixture. Dot with the remaining fat and bake in a 350 degree F. oven for about forty-five minutes.

Yield: 48 servings.
Per Serving: Cost____   Selling Price____   Calories____

GRILLED TOMATOES

INGREDIENTS	AMOUNT	WEIGHT	MULTIPLE	UNIT COST	TOTAL COST
Tomatoes	40–50	15 lb.			
Eggs	18				
Salt	6 tbsp.				
Crumbs		3 lb.			
Bacon fat		2 lb. 8 oz.			

Select tomatoes uniform in size weighing about three to the pound. Wash and cut out the stem end. Do not peel. Slice into about three slices each, one third to one half inch thick. Beat the eggs, add the salt and dip the tomatoes into the egg mixture, and then into the crumbs. Sauté in bacon fat. These may be served as a vegetable, on toast with cheese sauce and bacon, as a garnish with meat dishes or on a mixed grill.

Total Weight: 14 lb. 10 oz.
Yield: 58 servings, 4 oz. each (2–3 slices per serving).
Per Serving: Cost____   Selling Price____   Calories____

SCALLOPED TOMATOES

Ingredients	Amount	Weight	Multiple	Unit Cost	Total Cost
Onion, ground		2 oz.			
Sugar		8 oz.			
Salt	¼ c.				
Fat		4 oz.			
Tomatoes, #10 cans . .	2				
Bread, cubed		1 lb. 5 oz.			
Crumbs		10 oz.			
Butter (for crumbs) . .		2 oz.			

Add the onion, sugar, salt and the fat to the tomatoes and heat. Pour over the cubed bread, which has been put into the bottom of greased baking pans. Cover with buttered crumbs and bake in the oven until brown and until the flavor has been developed.

Total Weight: 14 lb. 8 oz., after baking.
Yield: 58 servings, 4 oz. each (approximately ½—⅔ c.).
Per Serving: Cost____ Selling Price____ Calories____

STEWED TOMATOES

Ingredients	Amount	Weight	Multiple	Unit Cost	Total Cost
Fat		4 oz.			
Onion, ground		1 oz.			
Sugar		8 oz.			
Salt	3 tbsp.				
Tomatoes, #10 cans . .	2				
Bread, cubed		14 oz.			

Melt the fat. Add the onion and cook until golden brown. Add the sugar, salt and cooked onion to the tomatoes and bring to a boil. The cubed bread should be added just before serving.

Total Weight: 13 lb.
Yield: 52 servings, 4 oz. each (approximately ½ c.).
Per Serving: Cost____ Selling Price____ Calories____

MOCK HOLLANDAISE SAUCE

INGREDIENTS	AMOUNT	WEIGHT	MULTIPLE	UNIT COST	TOTAL COST
Butter, melted		8 oz.			
Flour		4 oz.			
Milk	2 qt.				
Egg yolks	⅔ c.				
Lemon juice	¼ c.				
Vinegar	½ c.				
Butter		4 oz.			
Sugar	2 tbsp.				
Salt	2 tsp.				

Blend the butter and flour and add to the scalded milk. Stir until the mixture comes to a boil. Add the egg yolks, beaten light and diluted with a little of the hot mixture. Then drop by drop add four tablespoons of lemon juice and one half cup of vinegar. Add the four ounces of butter, sugar and salt. Beat until the mixture is smooth.

Total Weight: 5 lb. 2 oz.
Yield: 50 servings, approximately 3 tbsp. each.
Per Serving: Cost____ Selling Price____ Calories____

THIN WHITE SAUCE

INGREDIENTS	AMOUNT	WEIGHT	MULTIPLE	UNIT COST	TOTAL COST
Milk, scalded	1 gal.				
Butter		1 lb.			
Flour		4 oz.			
Salt	2¼ tbsp.				
Egg yolks	½ c.				

Melt the fat, stir in the flour and add to the scalded milk, stirring vigorously. Cook seven to ten minutes. Add the egg yolks to a small amount of the white sauce and, beating with a wire whisk, add to the remaining white sauce slowly, stirring rapidly. Add the salt. This white sauce is suitable for use on vegetables such as peas or carrots, or wherever a thin sauce is desired. The above recipe is given on the basis of one gallon to make easy the division or multiplication, according to the amount desired.

Total Weight: 8 lb. 6 oz.
Per Serving: Cost_____   Selling Price_____   Calories_____

MEDIUM WHITE SAUCE

INGREDIENTS	AMOUNT	WEIGHT	MULTIPLE	UNIT COST	TOTAL COST
Milk, scalded	1 gal.				
Butter		1 lb.			
Flour		6 oz.			
Salt	2¼ tbsp.				
Egg yolks	½ c.				

Melt the fat, stir in the flour and add to the scalded milk, stirring vigorously. Cook seven to ten minutes. Add the egg yolks to a small amount of the white sauce and, beating with a wire whisk, add to the remaining white sauce slowly, stirring rapidly. Add the salt. This sauce is suitable for scalloping or for creamed dishes. The above recipe is given on the basis of one gallon to make easy the division or multiplication, according to the amount of sauce desired.

Total Weight: 8 lb. 8 oz.
Per Serving: Cost_____   Selling Price_____   Calories_____

THICK WHITE SAUCE FOR CROQUETTES

Ingredients	Amount	Weight	Multiple	Unit Cost	Total Cost
Milk, scalded	1 gal.				
Flour		1 lb. 13 oz.			
Fat		12 oz.			
Salt	2¼ tbsp.				

Mix the flour to a smooth thin paste with a small amount of cold milk. Scald the remainder of the milk and add the fat and the flour paste, stirring vigorously. Cook from seven to ten minutes. Add the salt.

Total Weight: 10 lb.
Per Serving: Cost_____ Selling Price_____ Calories_____

CHAPTER IX

Salads, Salad Dressings and Sandwiches

Salads Function in Two Ways on the Menu. On the one hand, they may serve as the main dish at luncheon, in which case they should be so planned in size and composition as to fulfill that function. On the other hand, they may be planned as an accompaniment to lunch or dinner.

Most Salads Are an Accompaniment to a Meal. Therefore, the first principle in planning them should be to have them simple, natural and attractive. They furnish a part of the needed roughage and some of the vitamins, and if served first, as is sometimes done in simple course dinners, may act as an appetizer as well. The aim will best be achieved if all ingredients are fresh, crisp and cold, giving a maximum of eye appeal.

Ornate, "dressed up," "fixey" salads may have their place, but they are excellent examples of bad art and often in the attempt to achieve a pattern, crisp freshness is sacrificed.

Seasonal Fruits and Vegetables Have Greatest Appeal. While it is true that fresh fruits and vegetables are less difficult to obtain at all times of the year than of old, it still is true that when the particular fruit or vegetable is definitely in its season it makes its greatest appeal to the public and the menu should be planned with this in mind.

Standardized Operations Make Salad Preparation Efficient. In institutions where a number of one kind of salad is to be produced standardization of processes is essential to efficient production. Bowl salad making is a good example. By spreading out the bowls and performing all of one process at a time, it takes little longer to make sixty or more salads than to assemble and make up a dozen, when each is completed individually.

Pre-preparation of Ingredients Improves Quality and Efficiency and Reduces Waste. As lettuce comes into the institution it should be looked over, the coarse outside leaves removed and the resulting heads packed in cans with close-fitting covers and stored in the cooler. From this amount a day's supply may be soaked in cold water, drained and stored in covered cans. As needed these heads may be removed from the icebox, and the leaves loosened and made ready for use in the dishing up of the salads.

Tomatoes, a standard salad ingredient, should be sorted as fast as fully ripened, then scalded, chilled and put on trays in the cooler ready to peel quickly and easily as needed. They may be further sorted for size, reserving the larger ones for stuffing.

Celery, too, should be cleaned, washed and sorted into that used for vegetable cooking and the finer, whiter stalks to be used for salads. Celery should be cut evenly and completely through to prevent strings which make salads look rough and poorly executed.

Water cress, parsley, radishes and almost all vegetables used in salad work should be washed, drained and then stored in refrigerator pans or covered jars until needed.

Cabbage should be shredded or chopped, crisped in ice water and drained thoroughly before using. To keep crisp, mix with salad dressing only as used.

Fruits that do not turn dark may be cut ahead. Uniformity in cutting, whether the pieces be large or small, makes for attractiveness and takes away a ragged, unkempt appearance that cutting fruit in uneven sizes gives to the finished salad.

Cut celery, fruits diced ready for use, washed garnishes, lettuce ready for salad making and scalded tomatoes all facilitate the actual work of making up the final salad.

The Efficient Salad Department Will Schedule the Making of Salad Dressings in Slack Periods. An adequate supply should be on hand at all times, since dressings keep well and nothing is gained by frequent making.

All Garnishes Should be Planned and Executed before the Work of Dishing Is Undertaken. Bits of parsley, water cress, cut cherries, olives, shredded nuts, carrot strips, celery curls, hard-boiled eggs, all should be assembled ready at hand to expedite the final dishing up. Thus is insured maximum crispness, coldness and freshness and a successful salad. A garnish tray on which all garnishes are kept in small containers is useful.

Made-Up Salads Should Not Stand. Since salads to be satisfactory should be crisp and fresh, they should be made up only as needed. This makes essential the careful pre-preparation outlined above, as well as the standardization of processes. This will make possible, even in serving large banquets, the maximum of crisp perfection.

APPLE, CELERY AND DATE SALAD

Ingredients	Amount	Weight	Multiple	Unit Cost	Total Cost
Apples, diced		3 lb. 12 oz.			
Dates, chopped		13 oz.			
Celery, cut fine	1½ qt.				
Mayonnaise	3 c.				

Pare and dice the apples into half-inch cubes and mix with the chopped dates. Cut the celery fine and add to the apples and dates. Mix with the salad dressing and serve in lettuce cups. To prevent the apples turning dark they may be covered with salt water or water containing

a little vinegar while they are being pared and diced.
Garnish with chopped nuts or walnut halves.

Total Weight: 7 lb. 8 oz.
Yield: 40 servings, 3 oz. each (approximately ½ c.).
Per Serving: Cost____   Selling Price____   Calories____

BOWL SALAD

INGREDIENTS	AMOUNT	WEIGHT	MULTIPLE	UNIT COST	TOTAL COST
Head lettuce, torn . . .		6 lb.			
Celery, diced		1 lb. —			
		1 lb. 8 oz.			
Cucumber, sliced . . .		1 lb. —			
		1 lb. 8 oz.			
Carrots		6 oz.			
Radishes		6 oz.			
Tomatoes, peeled . . .		6 lb.			
Green-pepper rings . .	48				
Water-cress sprigs . . .	48				
Eggs, hard-cooked . . .	5–6				

Spread out forty-eight salad bowls on trays. The insides
of the bowls may be rubbed with garlic. Scale into or fill
each with lettuce torn in medium-sized pieces. Sprinkle
one teaspoon of diced celery over. Arrange two slices of
cucumber and three slices each of carrot and radish over
the top of the lettuce. Use three to four wedges of
tomato and garnish with green-pepper rings, a slice of
hard-cooked egg and a sprig of water cress.

To facilitate the making of these salads all ingredients
should be washed, sliced or diced previously so that the
dishing up process is expedited. If the salads are not
to be used at once, a dampened cloth spread over the top
of the salads helps to keep them fresh. Serve with French
or Roquefort-cheese dressing.

Yield: 48 salads, approximately 5–7 oz. each (approximately
1½ cup each).
Per Serving: Cost____   Selling Price____   Calories____

CABBAGE, ALMOND, MARSHMALLOW AND PINEAPPLE SALAD

Ingredients	Amount	Weight	Multiple	Unit Cost	Total Cost
Cabbage		4 lb. 8 oz.			
Marshmallows		12 oz.			
Pineapple, diced . . .		2 lb. 9 oz.			
Almonds		11 oz.			
Cream, whipped . . .	¾ qt.				
Boiled dressing	¾ qt.				

Shred the cabbage fine and let stand in ice water to crisp a half hour or more. Drain thoroughly. Cut the marshmallows in quarters and dice the pineapple. Cut the almonds lengthwise. To serve, mix all of the ingredients, except the almonds, with the whipped cream and dressing. Serve on lettuce and garnish with the sliced almonds. Do not allow to stand after mixing or the cabbage loses its crispness.

Total Weight: 10 lb. 8 oz.
Yield: 56 servings, 3 oz. each (approximately ½–⅔ c.).
Per Serving: Cost——— Selling Price——— Calories———

CABBAGE RELISH

Ingredients	Amount	Weight	Multiple	Unit Cost	Total Cost
Cabbage		5 lb.			
Green peppers		1 lb. 4 oz.			
Vinegar	1¼ c.				
Sugar		2 lb. 6 oz.			
Salt	3⅓ tbsp.				

Chop the cabbage and the peppers (from which the seeds have been removed) until fine. Add the vinegar, sugar and salt. Let stand one half hour to develop the flavor.

Total Weight: 9 lb.
Yield: 48 servings, 3 oz. each (approximately ⅓–½ c.).
Per Serving: Cost____ Selling Price____ Calories____

SOUR CREAM SLAW

Ingredients	Amount	Weight	Multiple	Unit Cost	Total Cost
Cabbage, shredded . .		4 lb. 8 oz.			
Vinegar	1½ c.				
Sugar		11 oz.			
Heavy sour cream . . .	1½ qt.				
Salt	4½ tsp.				

Crisp the cabbage by allowing it to stand a half hour or more in ice water.

Whip the cream and add the sugar, salt and vinegar. Drain and combine the cabbage and dressing as needed for serving. Garnish with grated raw carrots.

Total Weight: 8 lb. 10 oz.
Yield: 46 servings, 3 oz. each (approximately ½–⅔ c.).
Per Serving: Cost____ Selling Price____ Calories____

YANKEE SLAW

Ingredients	Amount	Weight	Multiple	Unit Cost	Total Cost
Cabbage		5 lb. 8 oz.			
Carrots		1 lb. 8 oz.			
Green peppers, chopped .	1½ c.				
Mayonnaise	1 qt.				
Salt	2 tbsp.				
Sugar	2 tbsp.				

Shred the cabbage and soak in ice water a half hour or longer to crisp. Chop the carrots and the green peppers fine. Mix all together lightly with the mayonnaise, salt and sugar. Serve in lettuce cups. All cabbage salads should be mixed with the dressing only as needed in order to keep them crisp. Garnish with grated carrot.

Total Weight: 9 lb. 6 oz.
Yield: 50 servings, 3 oz. each (approximately $\frac{1}{2}$–$\frac{2}{3}$ c.).
Per Serving: Cost_____ Selling Price_____ Calories_____

CARROT AND RAISIN SALAD

INGREDIENTS	AMOUNT	WEIGHT	MULTIPLE	UNIT COST	TOTAL COST
Raw carrots		4 lb.			
Raisins		4 lb.			
Mayonnaise	1 qt.				

Wash and pare or scrape the carrots. Chop fine. Plump the raisins in the steamer and cool. Add the raisins and salad dressing and mix lightly. Serve in a lettuce cup.

Total Weight: 9 lb. 12 oz.
Yield: 52 servings, 3 oz. each (approximately $\frac{1}{2}$ c.).
Per Serving: Cost_____ Selling Price_____ Calories_____

CHICKEN SALAD

INGREDIENTS	AMOUNT	WEIGHT	MULTIPLE	UNIT COST	TOTAL COST
Chicken, cubed		5 lb. 4 oz.			
Celery, cut fine	4 qt.				
Mayonnaise	1$\frac{1}{2}$ qt.				
Salt	4 tsp.				
Onion juice	2 tsp.				
Lemon juice	4 tsp.				

Mix the chicken which has been cut into one-third- to one-half-inch cubes and the finely cut celery with the mayonnaise, salt, onion juice and lemon juice. Serve on lettuce leaves and garnish with lemon, hard-cooked eggs or capers. Because chicken salad is high in food cost, it commands a corresponding selling cost and must be carefully made in order to satisfy the customer. No particle of gristle should be found in it, nor the small scrappy pieces of meat which come from the bones. Light and dark meat may be used, but it is not desirable, as customers expect and usually demand all white meat.

Total Weight: 12 lb. 8 oz.
Yield: 50 servings, 4 oz. each (approximately $\frac{1}{2}$–$\frac{2}{3}$ c.).
Per Serving: Cost_____ Selling Price_____ Calories_____

GERMAN CUCUMBERS

Ingredients	Amount	Weight	Multiple	Unit Cost	Total Cost
Cucumbers		10 lb.			
Water	1 gal.				
Salt	$\frac{1}{4}$ c.				
Vinegar	3 c.				
Water	3 c.				
Salt	$\frac{1}{4}$ c.				
Sugar		1 lb.			
Onion, grated		6 oz.			
Parsley, chopped . . .	$\frac{1}{4}$ c.				

Peel the cucumbers and slice thin. Soak in the gallon of water with one fourth cup of salt for thirty minutes. Drain and cover with a sauce made of the vinegar, water, salt, sugar, chopped parsley and onion. Let stand at least an hour to season.

Total Weight: 10 lb. 8 oz.
Yield: 56 servings, 3 oz. each (approximately $\frac{1}{3}$–$\frac{1}{2}$ c.).
Per Serving: Cost_____ Selling Price_____ Calories_____

DEVILED EGGS

Ingredients	Amount	Weight	Multiple	Unit Cost	Total Cost
Eggs	4 doz.				
Salt	4 tsp.				
Vinegar	$\frac{2}{3}$ c.				
Mayonnaise	1 c.				
Mustard	1 tbsp.				
Paprika	2 tsp.				

In order to have the eggs firm but tender cook below the boiling point for about thirty minutes. Peel and cut in halves lengthwise. Remove the yolks. Put the yolks through a sieve and mix with the mayonnaise and seasonings. Refill the whites of the eggs with this mixture. For deviled-egg salad, place two halves on a lettuce leaf and garnish with a pickle cut in half or with pimento strips.

Yield: 48 servings (two halves each).
Per Serving: Cost_____ Selling Price_____ Calories_____

CIDER FRUIT SALAD

Ingredients	Amount	Weight	Multiple	Unit Cost	Total Cost
Gelatin	$\frac{1}{2}$ c.				
Cold water	1 c.				
Cider (or ginger ale) . .	2 qt.				
Sugar		8 oz.			
Salt	1 tsp.				
Lemon juice	2 c.				
Grapes, halved and seeded	3 c.				
Celery, diced fine . . .	3 c.				
Apples, julienne shape .		11 oz.			
Pineapple, cubed . . .	2 c.				
Candied ginger, cut fine .		3 oz.			

Soften the gelatin in the cold water and dissolve over hot water. Stirring rapidly, pour the gelatin into the cider or ginger ale and add the sugar and salt. Stir until they are dissolved. When the gelatin begins to set, add the lemon juice and the remaining ingredients. This may be molded in individual molds or allowed to set in long shallow pans and may be cut in squares. For uniformity, the fruit may be divided among the molds and the gelatin mixture poured over when it starts to set.

Total Weight: 10 lb.
Yield: 40 servings, 4 oz. each (approximately $\frac{1}{2}$ c.).
Per Serving: Cost___ Selling Price___ Calories___

FRUIT SALAD

Ingredients	Amount	Weight	Multiple	Unit Cost	Total Cost
Oranges, diced	2 qt.				
Bananas, diced	1 qt.				
Pineapple, diced . . .	2 qt.				
Grapes, seeded	2 qt.				
Cooked salad dressing .	2 c.				
Cream, whipped . . .	2 c.				
For any of the above fruits, substitute in season:					
Cherries					
Fresh apricot halves . .					
Melon balls					
Fresh plum halves . . .					
Peaches					
Pears					

Fruit salad is one of the most popular salads with men, as well as women. It should, however, be kept seasonal and, while the recipe above is on the basis of fruit commonly used, these ingredients should be varied frequently, keeping in mind harmonizing colors, textures and flavors. All fruit should be drained and mixed with the dressing and whipped cream only as needed. Garnish with melon balls, mint sprigs, berries, cherries or other appropriate fruit in season.

Total Weight: 9 lb. 6 oz.
Yield: 50 servings, approximately 3 oz. each ($\frac{1}{3}$–$\frac{1}{2}$ c.).
Per Serving: Cost_____ Selling Price_____ Calories_____

FROZEN FRUIT SALAD

INGREDIENTS	AMOUNT	WEIGHT	MULTIPLE	UNIT COST	TOTAL COST
Gelatin	6 tbsp.				
Cold water	1½ c.				
Cream, before whipping .	1½ qt.				
Sugar		1 lb. 7 oz.			
Cooked dressing . . .	3 c.				
Lemon juice	¾ c.				
Bananas, diced, ½″ cubes		1 lb. 9 oz.			
Oranges, diced, ⅓″ cubes .		10 oz.			
Peaches, diced, ⅓″ cubes .		1 lb.			
Nuts, chopped		6 oz.			
Cherries or grapes, halved	1½ c.				

Soften the gelatin in the cold water and melt over hot water. Add to the cream which has been whipped, stirring with a wire whip until blended. Fold in the sugar, the cooked dressing, lemon juice and the drained, diced fruit. Pour into molds and let stand until set. This may be frozen in a loaf and sliced as desired. Serve in lettuce cups, and serve with either mayonnaise or a cooked dressing mixed with whipped cream. If desired, this may be garnished with a cheese carrot, made by grinding yellow cheese, adding paprika and pimento for color, shaping like a tiny carrot and inserting a small parsley sprig for the top.

Total Weight: 11 lb. 4 oz.
Yield: 54 servings, 3⅓ oz. each (approximately ½ c.).
Per Serving: Cost_____ Selling Price_____ Calories_____

PEAS, CHEESE AND PICKLE SALAD

Ingredients	Amount	Weight	Multiple	Unit Cost	Total Cost
Peas, green	2 qt.				
Sweet pickles, diced . .	1½ qt.				
American cheese . . .		3 lb.			
Boiled dressing	1¼ c.				
Mayonnaise	1¼ c.				

Cook the fresh green peas in boiling salted water. Drain and cool. Cut the pickles and the American cheese into one-fourth-inch cubes. Mix all together lightly with the dressings. Serve in lettuce cups and garnish with a pimento strip.

Total Weight: 9 lb. 6 oz.
Yield: 50 servings, 3 oz. each (approximately ½ c.).
Per Serving: Cost____   Selling Price____   Calories____

PERFECTION SALAD

Ingredients	Amount	Weight	Multiple	Unit Cost	Total Cost
Gelatin	½ c.				
Cold water	2 c.				
Boiling water	2 qt.				
Sugar		15 oz.			
Salt	4 tsp.				
Mild vinegar	2 c.				
Lemon juice	¾ c.				
Shredded cabbage . . .		12 oz.			
Celery, diced	2 qt.				
Pimentos, chopped . .	1 c.				

Soften the gelatin in the cold water. Add to the boiling water to which the sugar and the salt have been added and stir until all are dissolved. When the gelatin mixture has cooled and has started to set add the mild vinegar, lemon juice and vegetables. Pour into molds or into a shallow pan to cool and set. Unmold or cut in squares and serve in lettuce cups.

Total Weight: 10 lb.
Yield: 40 servings, 4 oz. each (approximately ½ c.).
Per Serving: Cost____ Selling Price____ Calories____

POTATO SALAD

Ingredients	Amount	Weight	Multiple	Unit Cost	Total Cost
Potatoes, cooked . . .		8 lb. 4 oz.			
French dressing	½ c.				
Celery, cut fine	1½ qt.				
Hard-cooked eggs . . .	9				
Green onion, cut fine . .	⅜ c.				
Salt	3 tbsp.				
Mayonnaise	3 c.				
Prepared mustard . . .	⅜ c.				
Chopped parsley , . .	3 tbsp.				

Dice the potatoes in half-inch cubes and marinate in the French dressing for about ten minutes. Cut the celery uniformly and the eggs into half-inch cubes and add with the remaining ingredients to the potatoes. Serve in lettuce cups.

Total Weight: 13 lb.
Yield: 52 servings, 4 oz. each (approximately ½ c.).
Per Serving: Cost____ Selling Price____ Calories____

RICHARDS TREAT SPECIAL SALAD

Ingredients	Amount	Weight	Multiple	Unit Cost	Total Cost
Cold ham	3 c.				
Cold tongue	3 c.				
Cold pork or veal . . .	3 c.				
Celery, cut fine	3¾ qt.				
Salt	1 tbsp.				
Mayonnaise	4½ c.				
Hard-cooked eggs . . .	7				
Peas, fresh, cooked . .	1½ qt.				

Trim and cube the meat in one-third-inch pieces. Combine all of the ingredients, reserving two cups of peas and the hard-cooked eggs. Serve on lettuce and garnish with a slice of hard-cooked egg and the fresh green peas.

Total Weight: 10 lb. 8 oz.
Yield: 48 servings, 3½ oz. each (approximately ½ c.).
Per Serving: Cost——   Selling Price——   Calories——

SALMON SALAD

INGREDIENTS	AMOUNT	WEIGHT	MULTIPLE	UNIT COST	TOTAL COST
Salmon		4 lb.			
Celery diced	3 qt.				
Vinegar	2 tbsp.				
Sweet pickles, diced . .	½ c.				
Salt	2 tsp.				
Mayonnaise	3 c.				

Look over the salmon and remove all of the bones and the skin. Break it up and mix with the diced celery, the vinegar, pickles and salt. Fold in the mayonnaise. Serve in lettuce cups. Garnish with a slice of hard-cooked egg, a parsley sprig, chopped chives or a slice of lemon.

Total Weight: 7 lb. 8 oz.
Yield: 40 servings, 3 oz. each (approximately ½ c.).
Per Serving: Cost——   Selling Price——   Calories——

FRESH SHRIMP COCKTAIL

INGREDIENTS	AMOUNT	WEIGHT	MULTIPLE	UNIT COST	TOTAL COST
Green shrimp		10 lb.			
Finely cut celery . . .	6 c.				
SAUCE:					
Lemon juice	¾ c.				
Catsup	1 qt.				
Onion juice	1 c.				
Tobasco sauce . . .	½ tsp.				
Salt	1¼ tbsp.				
Horse-radish	¾ c.				

Cook the green shrimp twenty minutes in boiling salted water. Clean by removing the shell and the black line around the outside edge. Chill. For each cocktail, mix two tablespoons of the fine-cut celery with four or five shrimp, whole or cut as preferred, and put in a cocktail glass. Garnish with lemon. Place a whole shrimp over the edge of the glass and serve on a plate with a small cup containing about two tablespoons of the cocktail sauce. The sauce is made by combining all of the ingredients and chilling. If preferred, the sauce may be poured over the cocktail.

Green shrimp of average size will run twenty-four to thirty to the pound.

Yield: 50 servings, each approximately 5 shrimp, 2 tbsp. of celery and 2 tbsp. of sauce.

Per Serving: Cost_____ Selling Price_____ Calories_____

SHRIMP SALAD

INGREDIENTS	AMOUNT	WEIGHT	MULTIPLE	UNIT COST	TOTAL COST
Shrimp, cleaned . . .		4 lb. 4 oz.			
Mayonnaise	1½ qt.				
Celery, cut fine	4½ qt.				
Salt	1 tbsp.				
Hard-cooked eggs, diced .	18				
Lemon juice	3 tbsp.				
GARNISH:					
Green pepper, cut fine .	1½ c.				

Cut the shrimp, which has been cleaned by removing the dark line around the outside edge, in halves or quarters. Marinate in mayonnaise and add the celery, salt, lemon juice and hard-cooked eggs. Place each serving on a lettuce cup and garnish with chopped green peppers.

Total Weight: 13 lb. 2 oz.
Yield: 60 servings, 3½ oz. each (approximately ½ c.).
Per Serving: Cost_____ Selling Price_____ Calories_____

TOMATO ASPIC

Ingredients	Amount	Weight	Multiple	Unit Cost	Total Cost
Tomato juice	6 qt.				
Cloves, whole	4 tsp.				
Bay leaves	20				
Chopped onion		4 oz.			
Salt to taste					
Cayenne	$\frac{1}{4}$ tsp.				
Gelatin	$\frac{7}{8}$ c.				
Cold water	2 c.				

Cook the tomato juice with the seasonings and add to the gelatin which has been softened in the cold water. Stir until the gelatin is dissolved. Strain and cool until it begins to set. There is a tendency for any solids present in the tomato juice to settle, so the mixture should be stirred occasionally as it is setting. Mold in Mary Ann molds, individual molds or large ring molds. Serve in lettuce cups garnished with mayonnaise and green-pepper rings.

Total Weight: 12 lb. 8 oz.
Yield: 50 servings, 4 oz. each (approximately $\frac{1}{2}$ c.).
Per Serving: Cost ____   Selling Price ____   Calories ____

TOMATO ASPIC COTTAGE-CHEESE SANDWICH

Ingredients	Amount	Weight	Multiple	Unit Cost	Total Cost
Tomato juice	$4\frac{1}{2}$ qt.				
Cloves, whole	3 tsp.				
Bay leaves	15				
Chopped onion		3 oz.			
Cayenne	$\frac{1}{4}$ tsp.				
Gelatin	$\frac{2}{3}$ c.				
Cold water	$1\frac{1}{2}$ c.				
Salt to taste					
Green pepper	$\frac{3}{4}$ c.				
Cottage cheese		3 lb.			
Nut meats	$\frac{3}{4}$ c.				

Cook the tomato juice with the seasonings and add to the gelatin, which has been softened in the cold water. Stir until the gelatin is dissolved. Strain and cool until it begins to set. Pour one half into two pans, 9″ × 15″, and let set until firm. Spread with the mixed cottage cheese, nut meats and green peppers. Pour the remaining half of the aspic over the cottage-cheese layer and let the top layer set. Cut in squares and serve on lettuce.

Total Weight: 12 lb.
Yield: 48 servings, 4 oz. each.
Per Serving: Cost____   Selling Price____   Calories____

STUFFED TOMATO WITH APPLES AND CELERY

Ingredients	Amount	Weight	Multiple	Unit Cost	Total Cost
Tomatoes, 5 oz. each . .	50				
Apples, cubed	1½ qt.				
Celery, diced fine . . .	1½ qt.				
Mayonnaise	1½ c.				
Green pepper to garnish .	50 rings				

Scald, cool and peel the tomatoes. Cut out the center. Cut the apples into one-fourth- to one-third-inch cubes and cut the celery fine. Mix with the mayonnaise and fill the tomatoes, using a number-sixteen scoop. These may be garnished with green-pepper rings.

Yield: 50 servings.
Per Serving: Cost____   Selling Price____   Calories____

TUNA FISH SALAD

Ingredients	Amount	Weight	Multiple	Unit Cost	Total Cost
Tuna fish, 13 oz. cans .	3				
Celery, diced	4½ qt.				
Chopped olives	¾ c.				
Mayonnaise	3 c.				
Salt	1½ tsp.				

Break up the tuna fish slightly. Clean and cut the celery in one-fourth-inch pieces. Add to the tuna fish and mix lightly. Add the chopped olives and mayonnaise. Each serving may be garnished with one or more of the following: hard-cooked egg, tomato slices, an eighth of lemon or a tablespoon of mayonnaise.

Total Weight: 8 lb. 7 oz.
Yield: 45 servings, 3 oz. each (approximately ½–⅔ c.).
Per Serving: Cost____   Selling Price____   Calories____

TUNA FISH AND APPLE SALAD

Ingredients	Amount	Weight	Multiple	Unit Cost	Total Cost
Tuna fish, 13 oz. cans .	3				
Apples, cubed		4 lb. 8 oz.			
Celery	4½ c.				
Salt	1½ tsp.				
Lemon juice	¾ c.				
Mayonnaise	3 c.				
Green pepper, chopped .	1½ c.				

Break the tuna fish into large flakes and add the apples cut in half-inch cubes, the finely cut celery, salt and lemon juice. Fold in the mayonnaise and serve in lettuce cups. Garnish the salads with the green peppers.

Total Weight: 9 lb. 12 oz.
Yield: 52 servings, 3 oz. each (approximately ½–⅔ c.).
Per Serving: Cost____   Selling Price____   Calories____

MIXED VEGETABLE SALAD

Ingredients	Amount	Weight	Multiple	Unit Cost	Total Cost
Carrots, cooked	1 qt.				
String beans, cooked . .	1 qt.				
Kidney beans, canned .	1 qt.				
Peas, fresh, cooked . .	1 qt.				
Cucumber or celery, diced	1 qt.				
Cabbage, shredded . .	1 qt.				
Mayonnaise	3 c.				
Salt to taste					

Dice the carrots and cut the string beans in three-quarter-inch lengths. Drain the kidney beans and mix with the peas and cucumber or celery. Chill thoroughly. Keep the cabbage crisp in cold water and when needed mix with the vegetables and the mayonnaise lightly. Add salt to taste.

Total Weight: 9 lb.
Yield: 48 servings, 3 oz. each (approximately ½ c.).
Per Serving: Cost____   Selling Price____   Calories____

MOUNDED VEGETABLE SALAD

Ingredients	Amount	Weight	Multiple	Unit Cost	Total Cost
Cauliflower, medium-sized	3 heads				
Peas	1½ qt.				
Beans, drained	1½ qt.				
Beets, diced in ¼″ cubes .	1½ qt.				
Salt to taste					
French dressing	3 c.				

Cook the cauliflower in boiling salted water until tender but not soft and mushy. Do not overcook. Cook the other vegetables separately. Marinate each in French dressing for about an hour. Place a floweret of cauliflower in the center of a lettuce leaf. Using a number-thirty scoop surround the cauliflower with mounds of the marinated beans, peas and beets. Mayonnaise may be served with this, if desired, and other vegetables substituted in like amounts, as the seasons change.

Yield: 45 servings, 1 floweret cauliflower and a No. 30 scoop of peas, beans and beets.

Per Serving: Cost____ Selling Price____ Calories____

COOKED DRESSING

Ingredients	Amount	Weight	Multiple	Unit Cost	Total Cost
Flour		1 lb. 1 oz.			
Water	5 c.				
Vinegar	6 c.				
Sugar		1 lb. 14 oz.			
Paprika	2 tsp.				
Mustard	¼ c.				
Salt	⅓ c.				
Egg yolks	2½ c.				
Egg whites	1½ c.				
Thin sour cream . . .	3½ qt.				
Fat		10 oz.			

Mix the flour to a smooth paste with part of the water and add to the vinegar and remaining water, which have been brought to a boil. Add the well-mixed sugar, paprika, mustard and salt and continue cooking from seven to ten minutes. Beat the egg yolks, whites and thin sour cream together and add to the thickened mixture. Add the fat last. Beat well and cool. This dressing may be stored in the icebox and mixed with whipped cream as needed. Use equal parts of dressing and whipped cream.

Total Weight: 16 lb. 12 oz.
Per Serving: Cost____ Selling Price____ Calories____

FRENCH DRESSING

Ingredients	Amount	Weight	Multiple	Unit Cost	Total Cost
Salt		14 oz.			
Mustard	$\frac{1}{2}$ c.				
Paprika	1 c.				
Sugar, granulated . . .		4 oz.			
Black pepper	$\frac{3}{4}$ c.				
Red pepper	1 tsp.				
Vinegar, tarragon . . .	1 qt.				
Vinegar, cider	2 qt.				
Onion juice	$\frac{3}{4}$ qt.				
Oil, olive	1 gal.				
Garlic		3 oz.			

Mix the dry ingredients and add enough vinegar to make a smooth paste. Add to this the remainder of the vinegar, onion juice and oil and beat thoroughly. Slice the cloves of garlic and add to the dressing and allow to stand until seasoned. Strain out the garlic before using.

Total Weight: 31 lb. 8 oz.
Per Serving: Cost____ Selling Price____ Calories____

MAYONNAISE

Ingredients	Amount	Weight	Multiple	Unit Cost	Total Cost
Salt		9 oz.			
Sugar		10 oz.			
Mustard		$5\frac{1}{2}$ oz.			
White pepper	$4\frac{1}{2}$ tbsp.				
Onion juice	5 tbsp.				
Water	7 c.				
Egg yolks		3 lb. 13 oz.			
Oil		27 lb.			
Vinegar	$3\frac{3}{4}$ c.				

Mix the dry ingredients and add the onion juice and two cups of the water to make a smooth paste. Place the egg yolks in a mixing machine and beat on high speed two minutes or until thick. Add the above and continue beating. Start adding the oil on high speed slowly and then more rapidly as the mixture thickens. When one half of the oil has been added alternate the oil and vinegar and the remaining water until all is added. At some time in the mixing process and again at the end the sides and bottom of the bowl should be scraped down with a spatula. The dressing should be poured into crocks or jars, covered and stored in a cooler until used. It will thicken further upon standing and chilling.

Total Weight: 36 lb. 12 oz.

Per Serving: Cost_____ Selling Price_____ Calories_____

TOASTED CHEESE SANDWICHES WITH BACON

Ingredients	Amount	Weight	Multiple	Unit Cost	Total Cost
Butter, creamed . . .		1 lb.			
Bread slices	90				
Nippy cheese, ground .		3 lb. 12 oz.			
Bacon slices, 24 per pound	45 slices				

For each sandwich take two slices of bread. Trim the crust and butter one slice. Spread the other slice with one ounce of the cheese. Put the two slices together and toast the sandwich on one side under a broiler or a drawer-type toaster. Remove from the broiler and spread one third ounce of the cheese on the untoasted side of the sandwich. Cut a slice of bacon in half and lay the two pieces on top of the cheese. Return to the broiler. The bacon will broil as the cheese and bread toast. To serve, cut an inch-wide strip diagonally through the center and place this on the two remaining triangular-shaped pieces. Garnish with two slices of dill pickle, a sprig of parsley and a dash of paprika.

Yield: 45 sandwiches, $\frac{1}{4}$ c. grated cheese or $1\frac{1}{3}$ oz. for each sandwich and one strip of bacon.

Per Serving: Cost_____ Selling Price_____ Calories_____

DATE AND NUT SANDWICHES

Ingredients	Amount	Weight	Multiple	Unit Cost	Total Cost
Dates, chopped		3 lb.			
Nuts, chopped		12 oz.			
Orange juice	2 c.				
Bread slices	100				
Butter, creamed . . .		1 lb.			

Chop the dates and nuts and mix with the orange juice. Spread one side of the sandwich with butter and the other side with one and one half ounces of the date and nut mixture. These sandwiches may be cut in triangles and garnished with a parsley sprig, nut-meat halves and a half slice of orange.

Total Weight: 4 lb. 11 oz. filling.
Yield: 50 sandwiches, 1½ oz. filling (approximately ⅙ c.).
Per Serving: Cost_____   Selling Price_____   Calories_____

EGG–SALAD SANDWICHES

Ingredients	Amount	Weight	Multiple	Unit Cost	Total Cost
Eggs, hard-cooked . . .	2 doz.				50
Crumbs, sifted		5 oz.			
Salt	2 tsp.				
Mayonnaise	3 c.				29
Lemon juice	1½ tbsp.				.06
Bread slices	100				44
Butter, creamed . . .		1 lb.			.48

Hard cook the eggs.   Peel off the shells, cool and chop. Mix with the remaining ingredients.   Butter one slice of bread and spread one and one half ounces of filling on the other.   Cut in half or in fingers.   Garnish with a pickle.

Total Weight: 4 lb. 11 oz. filling.
Yield: 50 sandwiches, 1½ oz. filling (approximately ⅙ c.).
Per Serving: Cost_____   Selling Price_____   Calories_____

FRUIT SANDWICHES

Ingredients	Amount	Weight	Multiple	Unit Cost	Total Cost
Raisins		2 lb.			
Figs, layer		1 lb.			
Sugar		1 lb. 7 oz.			
Flour	2 tbsp.				
Cold water	½ c.				
Orange juice	1 c.				
Lemon juice	⅞ c.				
Grated lemon rind . . .	⅝ c.				
Chopped nuts		8 oz.			
Bread slices	120				
Butter, creamed . . .		1 lb. 4 oz.			

Chop the raisins and figs and combine with the flour and sugar. Add the orange juice, lemon juice, grated lemon rind and water. Cook in a double boiler or covered in a steamer until thick. Add the nut meats after the filling has cooked. Use one sixth cup for each sandwich.

Total Weight: 5 lb. 10 oz. filling.
Yield: Filling for 60 sandwiches, approximately 1½ oz. per sandwich (approximately ⅙ c.).
Per Serving: Cost____ Selling Price____ Calories____

MINCED HAM SANDWICHES

Ingredients	Amount	Weight	Multiple	Unit Cost	Total Cost
Ham, chopped fine . .		1 lb. 9 oz.			
Prepared mustard (see page 143)	5 tbsp.				
Mixed-pickle relish . .	1¼ c.				
Mayonnaise	1⅞ c.				
Cooked dressing . . .	1⅞ c.				
Bread slices	100				
Butter, creamed . . .		1 lb.			

Grind or chop the ham and mix with the seasonings and the dressings. Use the cooked dressing (see page 197) undiluted by cream. This filling can be stored in the refrigerator. Butter one slice of bread and spread the other with one and one half ounces of filling.

Total Weight: 4 lb. 11 oz.
Yield: 50 sandwiches, 1½ oz. filling (approximately ⅙ c.).
Per Serving: Cost＿＿＿　Selling Price＿＿＿　Calories＿＿＿

TOASTED MUSHROOM SANDWICHES

INGREDIENTS	AMOUNT	WEIGHT	MULTIPLE	UNIT COST	TOTAL COST
Mushrooms, fresh . . .		3 lb.			
Onion, ground		12 oz.			
Butter		12 oz.			
Flour		2 oz.			
Salt	1½ tsp.				
Milk	1½ c.				
Bread slices	100				
Butter, creamed . . .		1 lb.			

Wash and chop the mushrooms fine. Sauté with the onion in butter until a golden brown. Add the flour and salt to the mushrooms and when well blended add the milk. Cook five to seven minutes. For each sandwich butter one slice of bread and spread one ounce of the mushroom filling on the other slice. Put together and toast on both sides. Cut and garnish with one ripe and one green olive and a sprig of parsley.

Total Weight: 3 lb. 2 oz. filling.
Yield: 50 sandwiches, 1 oz. filling or approximately ⅛ c.
Per Serving: Cost＿＿＿　Selling Price＿＿＿　Calories＿＿＿

OLIVE AND EGG SANDWICHES

Ingredients	Amount	Weight	Multiple	Unit Cost	Total Cost
Eggs	2 doz.				
Olives, pimento-stuffed .	3 c.				
Mayonnaise	2 c.				
Salt	2 tsp.				
Bread slices	100				
Butter, creamed . . .		1 lb.			

Hard cook and peel the eggs and chop fine. Mix with the chopped olives, mayonnaise and salt. Butter one slice of the bread and spread one and one half ounces of the filling on the other slice. Cut diagonally and garnish with water cress.

Total Weight: 4 lb. 11 oz. filling.
Yield: 50 sandwiches, 1½ oz. filling (approximately ⅙ c.).
Per Serving: Cost____   Selling Price____   Calories____

TOASTED ORANGE SANDWICHES

Ingredients	Amount	Weight	Multiple	Unit Cost	Total Cost
Oranges, whole		3 lb. 4 oz.			
Sugar		1 lb. 7 oz.			
Bread slices	100				
Butter, creamed . . .		2 lb.			

Wash and cut the oranges in quarters and remove the seeds. Grind or chop the oranges (including peeling) very fine. Mix with the sugar. Butter both slices of bread and spread one side with one and one half ounces of the sandwich filling. Place the other slice on top and toast. Cut in half diagonally and garnish with parsley and candied ginger. If the bread is fresh, one slice only may be buttered, spread with the filling, rolled and toasted.

Total Weight: 4 lb. 11 oz.
Yield: 50 sandwiches, 1½ oz. filling (approximately ⅙ c. for each sandwich).
Per Serving: Cost＿＿＿ Selling Price＿＿＿ Calories＿＿＿

TOMBECHE SANDWICHES

Ingredients	Amount	Weight	Multiple	Unit Cost	Total Cost
Tomatoes, strained . .	3 c.				
Dried beef		12 oz.			
Nippy cheese, chopped .		12 oz.			
Bread slices	90				
Butter, creamed . . .		1 lb.			

Strain the tomatoes to remove the seeds. Grind the dried beef very fine and mix with tomatoes and bring to a boil. When the beef is tender, add the cheese and stir until it is melted. Let cool. Butter one slice of bread and spread the other slice with one ounce of the filling. Place the other slice on top. Cut in half diagonally and garnish with water cress and pickles.

Total Weight: 2 lb. 13 oz.
Yield: 45 sandwiches, 1 oz. filling (approximately ⅙ c.).
Per Serving: Cost＿＿＿ Selling Price＿＿＿ Calories＿＿＿

CHAPTER X

Quick Breads

Hot Breads Make Restaurants Popular. As one travels over the country eating at famous institutions, he is impressed with the part hot breads play in their popularity. There is, for instance, in New York State a famous restaurant whose cinnamon rolls are known from coast to coast. In Arkansas, a restaurant is famous for hot biscuits. In Massachusetts there is one notable for hot pecan rolls, and through the South hot breads are often passed through the dining-room as an accepted part of the service. These specific cases are cited to prove the point that good hot breads help to build a reputation. There is one characteristic common to all of these popular breads. That is the fact that they are served hot.

Hot Breads Should Be Served Hot. This obvious fact is so completely overlooked by the majority of institutions that it deserves especial emphasis here. In fact, it is the exceptional restaurant which even attempts to serve hot breads hot; that is, to bake at one time only those breads which will be consumed before they get cold. When demand is fairly steady, a schedule may be worked out for baking hot breads so that they will come out during regular intervals. The amount baked should be increased as the peak of business approaches, being decreased again as business tapers off. It has now come to be an accepted fact that vegetables must be prepared in small amounts to be of first quality; they must reach the guest fresh-cooked, bright in color and whole in shape. With refrigeration of doughs as generally accepted as it is, hot rolls and hot quick breads are as simple to accomplish as properly cooked vegetables.

Of course, there will always be some leftover cold "hot breads." Many of these can be reheated satisfactorily, if the reheating is carefully done. Probably the best method is to sprinkle the breads and reheat for ten to fifteen minutes, or approximately one half to two thirds the time of the original baking. Lowe makes the statement that: "The staling process is reversible; i.e., the stale bread when heated again to high temperature acquires the characteristics of fresh bread. This process can be repeated several times, or until the bread has lost too large a proportion of the moisture." *

Our experience has been that breads may be reheated satisfactorily provided they are reheated in lots which will be consumed immediately, but they quickly become hard and stale on cooling. That is, breads will reheat once satisfactorily. Beyond that their quality is impaired. The important thing is to reheat the breads thoroughly. Too often rolls are simply "run into the oven" and not allowed to reach the temperature which will bring them back to a satisfactorily fresh condition. The high temperature must reach to the center of the bread.

In this connection, however, the fact must be recognized that a discriminating person can almost without fail recognize the reheated bread no matter how carefully it has been done. For this reason, when possible, these leftovers should be used in other ways, such as in dressings, for crumbing, and in recipes such as sweet crumb muffins or the popular Brown Betty. The production manager who orders her hot breads according to what her records show were consumed previously will have few leftovers, and these her ingenuity will devise ways to use.

* Lowe, Belle, *Experimental Cookery*, p. 437; John Wiley and Sons.

Muffin Standards *

A Good Muffin Is Golden Brown, Crusty, Shows No Tunnels and Is Light in Weight. It should not overrun the pan or be peaked.

Overmixing is frequently the cause of poor-quality muffins. For this reason machine mixing is inadvisable in making muffins since, even on slowest speed, the machine is so fast that overmixing is almost certain. The best results in quantities are probably obtained through the use of a round-bottomed mixing bowl and hand mixing.

In quantity work, all muffins should be dished at once with as little handling as possible and baked as needed. They may be held in the refrigerator from one day to the next without appreciable loss of lift provided an S.A.S.-phosphate-type baking powder has been used.

An S.A.S.-phosphate type baking powder has been indicated in the recipes given here. If a tartrate or calcium-phosphate baking powder is used, the baking powder must be increased by one third.

Steaming, as a result of standing in the pans after coming from the oven, is a cause of loss of crustiness. Remove at once or tilt in tins to allow circulation of air.

Muffins are very popular and a great variety may be made through further variation of the following recipes.

* For further information see *Hows and Whys of Cooking*, Halliday and Noble, The University of Chicago Press.

BACON MUFFINS

Ingredients	Amount	Weight	Multiple	Unit Cost	Total Cost
Bread flour		2 lb. 13 oz.			
Baking powder, S.A.S.-phosphate type . . .	5 tbsp.				
Salt	2½ tsp.				
Sugar		7 oz.			
Milk	4½ c.				
Bacon fat		8 oz.			
Eggs	5				
Bacon, cooked and cut .		8 oz.			

Mix and sift the dry ingredients together. Beat the eggs, add the milk, bacon fat and bacon pieces. Add all at once to the dry ingredients. Stir only until the dry ingredients are moistened. Do not attempt to make a smooth batter. Using a number-sixteen icecream scoop, dish all the muffins at once with as little handling as possible into well-greased tins. Bake twenty to twenty-five minutes in a 400–425-degree (F.) oven.

Total Weight: 7 lb. 4 oz.
Yield: 48 muffins, approximately 2½ oz. each, before baking.
Per Serving: Cost_____ Selling Price_____ Calories_____

BLUEBERRY MUFFINS (CAKE METHOD)

Ingredients	Amount	Weight	Multiple	Unit Cost	Total Cost
Fat		12 oz.			
Sugar		10 oz.			
Eggs	5				
Milk	1 qt.				
Pastry flour		2 lb. 8 oz.			
Baking powder, S.A.S.-phosphate type . . .	5 tbsp.				
Salt	1 tbsp.				
Blueberries		13 oz.			
Sugar		5 oz.			

Cream the fat and the sugar. Add the well-beaten eggs and alternate the mixed and sifted dry ingredients with the milk. Pick over and wash the berries. Drain thoroughly. Mix with the five ounces of sugar. Fold into the dough. Using a number-sixteen scoop, dish all muffins at once with as little handling as possible into well-greased tins. Bake as needed in a 400–425-degree (F.) oven for twenty to twenty-five minutes.

Total Weight: 7 lb. 12 oz.
Yield: 5 dozen muffins, approximately 2 oz. each.
Per Serving: Cost____ Selling Price____ Calories____

DARK BRAN MUFFINS

INGREDIENTS	AMOUNT	WEIGHT	MULTIPLE	UNIT COST	TOTAL COST
Bread flour		2 lb.			
Bran		14 oz.			
Baking powder, S.A.S.-phosphate type . . .	4 tbsp.				
Salt	2 tbsp.				
Sugar		8 oz.			
Raisins		1 lb.			
Eggs	4				
Molasses	3 c.				
Sour milk	1½ qt.				
Soda	2 tbsp.				
Melted Fat		6 oz.			

Scale the dry ingredients and mix well. Measure the liquid ingredients, add soda and melted fat and beat thoroughly. Pour the liquid over the dry ingredients, mixing just enough to dampen. Do not stir. Using a number sixteen-to-the-quart-sized scoop, dish all muffins at once. Bake twenty-five to thirty minutes in a 400–425-degree (F.) oven until done.

Total Weight: 9 lb. 15 oz.
Yield: 6 dozen muffins, approximately 2⅕ oz. each.
Per Serving: Cost____ Selling Price____ Calories____

CORN MEAL MUFFINS OR CORN BREAD

Ingredients	Amount	Weight	Multiple	Unit Cost	Total Cost
Flour		1 lb. 7 oz.			
Corn meal		1 lb. 11 oz.			
Sugar		7 oz.			
Salt	1 tbsp.				
Baking powder, S.A.S.-phosphate type . . .	6 tbsp.				
Milk	1½ qt.				
Eggs	5				
Fat		10 oz.			

Mix and sift all dry ingredients together. Beat the eggs, add the milk and melted fat and add all at once to the dry ingredients. Stir only until dry ingredients are moistened. Do not attempt to make the batter smooth. Using an icecream scoop, number-sixteen size, dish all the muffins at once with as little handling as possible into well-greased tins. Bake as needed in a 400–425-degree (F.) oven for about twenty to twenty-five minutes. For corn bread, weigh between fifteen to sixteen ounces of dough into well-greased cake tins, 8″ × 8″. This will make eight pans cutting 3 × 3 or seventy-two pieces.

Total Weight: 8 lb.
Yield: 48 muffins, approximately 2½ oz. each, before baking.
Per Serving: Cost____ Selling Price____ Calories____

CRANBERRY MUFFINS (CAKE METHOD)

Ingredients	Amount	Weight	Multiple	Unit Cost	Total Cost
Fat		12 oz.			
Sugar		10 oz.			
Eggs	5				
Milk	1 qt.				
Flour, pastry		2 lb. 8 oz.			
Baking powder, S.A.S.-phosphate type . . .	5 tbsp.				
Salt	1 tbsp.				
Cranberries		13 oz.			
Sugar		8 oz.			

Cream the fat and sugar, add the well-beaten eggs and alternate the mixed and sifted dry ingredients with the milk. Pick over and wash the cranberries. Drain thoroughly to dry and mix with the eight ounces of sugar. Fold into the dough. Using a number-sixteen scoop, dish all muffins at once with as little handling as possible into well-greased muffin tins. Bake as needed in a 380-degree (F.) oven twenty to twenty-five minutes.

Total Weight: Approximately 8 lb. dough.
Yield: 60 muffins, approximately 2 oz. each.
Per Serving: Cost—— Selling Price—— Calories——

SWEET CRUMB MUFFINS

Ingredients	Amount	Weight	Multiple	Unit Cost	Total Cost
Bread flour		1 lb. 6 oz.			
Sugar		10 oz.			
Sweet crumbs		1 lb. 4 oz.			
Baking powder, S.A.S.-phosphate type . . .	6 tbsp.				
Salt	1¼ tbsp.				
Eggs	4				
Milk	3½ c.				
Fat		8 oz.			

Mix and sift all dry ingredients together. Beat the eggs, add the milk and melted fat and add all at once to the dry ingredients. Stir only until dry ingredients are moistened. Do not attempt to make the batter smooth. Using an icecream scoop, number-sixteen size, dish all the muffins at once with as little handling as possible into well-greased tins. Bake as needed in a 400–425-degree (F.) oven for about twenty to twenty-five minutes.

Total Weight: 6 lb. 2 oz.
Yield: 48 muffins, approximately 2 oz. each.
Per Serving: Cost—— Selling Price—— Calories——

DATE MUFFINS

Ingredients	Amount	Weight	Multiple	Unit Cost	Total Cost
Bread flour		2 lb. 13 oz.			
Baking powder, S.A.S.-phosphate type . . .	5 tbsp.				
Salt	2½ tsp.				
Sugar		7 oz.			
Dates, chopped		1 lb.			
Eggs	5				
Milk	4½ c.				
Fat		8 oz.			

Mix and sift all dry ingredients together and add the dates. Beat the eggs, add the milk and melted fat and add all at once to the dry ingredients. Stir only until dry ingredients are moistened. Do not attempt to make the batter smooth. Using an icecream scoop, number-sixteen size, dish all the muffins at once with as little handling as possible into well-greased tins. Bake as needed in a 400–425-degree (F.) oven for about twenty to twenty-five minutes.

Total Weight: 8 lb.
Yield: 48 muffins, approximately 2½ oz. each.
Per Serving: Cost_____ Selling Price_____ Calories_____

GRAHAM MUFFINS

Ingredients	Amount	Weight	Multiple	Unit Cost	Total Cost
Bread flour		1 lb.			
Graham flour		1 lb. 12 oz.			
Sugar		14 oz.			
Baking powder, S.A.S.-phosphate type . . .	5 tbsp.				
Salt	1 tbsp.				
Eggs	5				
Milk	5½ c.				
Fat		10 oz.			

Mix and sift all dry ingredients together. Beat the eggs, add the milk and melted fat and add all at once to the dry ingredients. Stir only until dry ingredients are moistened. Do not attempt to make the batter smooth. Using an icecream scoop, number-sixteen size, dish all muffins at once with as little handling as possible into well-greased tins. Bake as needed in a 400–425-degree (F.) oven for about twenty to twenty-five minutes.

Total Weight: 7 lb. 12 oz.
Yield: 48 muffins, approximately 2½ oz. each.
Per Serving: Cost____ Selling Price____ Calories____

PLAIN MUFFINS

Ingredients	Amount	Weight	Multiple	Unit Cost	Total Cost
Sugar		8 oz.			
Flour, bread		3 lb. 4 oz.			
Baking powder, S.A.S.-phosphate type . . .	5⅓ tbsp.				
Salt	2⅔ tsp.				
Eggs	5				
Milk	5 c.				
Fat		11 oz.			

Mix and sift the dry ingredients. Beat the eggs, add the milk and the melted fat. Add all at once to the dry ingredients. Do not attempt to make a smooth batter. Mix lightly, just enough to moisten. Using an icecream scoop, number-sixteen size, dish all of the muffins at once with as little handling as possible into well-greased muffin tins. Bake as needed in a hot, 400–425-degree (F.) oven, for twenty to twenty-five minutes.

Total Weight: 7 lb. 13 oz.
Yield: 48 muffins, approximately 2½ oz. each, before baking.
Per Serving: Cost____ Selling Price____ Calories____

POTATO FLOUR MUFFINS

Ingredients	Amount	Weight	Multiple	Unit Cost	Total Cost
Eggs, whole	14				
Salt	1 tsp.				
Sugar	¼ c.				
Potato flour		13 oz.			
Baking powder	2 tbsp.				
Iced water	½ c.				

Beat the whites of the eggs very stiff and dry. Add the salt and the sugar to the well-beaten yolks and fold into the whites. Sift the flour and baking powder thoroughly and fold into the egg mixture. Add the iced water last. Bake in a 325–350-degree (F.) oven in ungreased muffin pans for fifteen to twenty minutes. This dough must be baked at once after dishing.

Total Weight: 2 lb. 14 oz.
Yield: 36 muffins, approximately 1⅓ oz. each, before baking.
Per Serving: Cost____ Selling Price____ Calories____

BAKING POWDER BISCUITS

Ingredients	Amount	Weight	Multiple	Unit Cost	Total Cost
Bread flour		4 lb. 8 oz.			
Baking powder, S.A.S.-phosphate type . . .	½ c.				
Salt	4 tsp.				
Shortening		1 lb. 6 oz.			
Milk	6–7 c.				

Mix and sift the flour, salt and baking powder thoroughly. Add the fat; break it into small pieces and then rub it in lightly with the finger tips.

Add the milk gradually, using an open wire mixing spoon or a large-tined fork so as not to pack the dough. Add enough milk to form a soft dough.

Take out about one fourth of the dough at one time onto a lightly floured board, roll around lightly so as to coat with flour and knead very lightly by rotating the balls of dough and pressing down lightly with the palm of the hand. About twelve or sixteen rotations are sufficient for each portion of the dough.

Roll out lightly to one-third-inch thickness and cut with a 2⅝-inch biscuit cutter which has been dipped in flour. Place on pans and keep in the refrigerator until needed.

Take out of the refrigerator and bake twelve to fifteen minutes in a hot oven at 425 degrees F.

If a tartrate or calcium-phosphate baking powder is used, one third more baking powder will be required.

When making biscuits in this quantity, in order that the correct number may be obtained, weigh the first four biscuits. These should weigh six ounces to obtain the yield given in this recipe.

Total Weight: Approximately 9 lb. 4 oz.

Yield: 100 biscuits, approximately 1½ oz. each, 2⅝ inches in diameter.

Per Serving: Cost_____ Selling Price_____ Calories_____

CHEESE BISCUITS

INGREDIENTS	AMOUNT	WEIGHT	MULTIPLE	UNIT COST	TOTAL COST
Flour		2 lb. 4 oz.			
Baking powder, S.A.S.-phosphate type . . .	6 tbsp.				
Salt	4 tsp.				
Sugar	½ c.				
Shortening		5 oz.			
Nippy cheese, grated . .		15 oz.			
Milk	3–4 c.				

Mix and sift the dry ingredients. Break up the shortening and rub in lightly with the tips of the fingers. Add the grated cheese and mix lightly. Add the milk gradually, mixing to a soft dough with a wire spoon. Take one half the dough on the floured board and knead very lightly for a few seconds. Roll one third of an inch in thickness and cut with a floured cutter two and five eighths inches in diameter. Place on pans and keep in the refrigerator until needed. Take out and bake in a hot oven at 425 degrees F. If a tartrate or calcium-phosphate baking powder is used, one third more baking powder will be required.

Total Weight: Approximately 5 lb. 10 oz.
Yield: 60 biscuits, 1½ oz. each.
Per Serving: Cost____ Selling Price____ Calories____

BROWN BREAD

INGREDIENTS	AMOUNT	WEIGHT	MULTIPLE	UNIT COST	TOTAL COST
Graham crumbs . . .		12 oz.			
Rye crumbs		4 oz.			
Cold water	3¼ qt.				
Molasses, dark	3 c.				
Salt	2 tbsp.				
Corn meal		2 lb.			
Graham flour		2 lb. 4 oz.			
Soda	4 tbsp.				
Raisins		1 lb. 11 oz.			

Soak the crumbs in the cold water overnight. The next morning, mix the other ingredients and add to the soaked crumbs. Pour into well-greased brown-bread cans, allowing one pound of dough per can. Cover and steam three hours. These loaves will cut in eight to ten slices.

Total Weight: 16 lb.
Yield: 16 one-pound loaves.
Per Serving: Cost____ Selling Price____ Calories____

GINGERBREAD

Ingredients	Amount	Weight	Multiple	Unit Cost	Total Cost
Sugar		11 oz.			
Fat		10 oz.			
Eggs	6				
Molasses, medium dark	3 c.				
Soda	2 tbsp.				
Cinnamon	4 tsp.				
Ginger	2 tbsp.				
Flour, pastry		2 lb. 4 oz.			
Salt	1 tsp.				
Hot water	3 c.				

Cream the fat and sugar thoroughly. Add the well-beaten eggs and molasses and continue to beat. Mix the dry ingredients and add alternately with the water, mixing as little as possible to prevent the formation of tunnels. This is a very soft dough and must be baked slowly for thirty minutes in a 325–350-degree (F.) oven. This may be baked in small loaf tins, sheet cake pans or muffin tins.

Total Weight: 7 lb. 14 oz. of dough.

Yield: 7 pans, 8″ × 8″ (9 servings per pan or 63 servings), using 1 lb. 2 oz. dough per pan.

Per Serving: Cost_____ Selling Price_____ Calories_____

CHERRY NUT BREAD

Ingredients	Amount	Weight	Multiple	Unit Cost	Total Cost
Flour		4 lb. 8 oz.			
Baking powder, S.A.S.-phosphate type	½ c.				
Salt	⅔ tsp.				
Sugar		2 lb. 8 oz.			
Raisins		7 oz.			
Candied cherries, chopped		12 oz.			
Orange peel, chopped		10 oz.			
Nuts, chopped		5 oz.			
Milk	5⅓ c.				
Eggs	8				
Fat		3 oz.			

Mix the dry ingredients with the fruit. Add the milk and melted fat to the beaten eggs. Combine by adding the liquid to the dry ingredients. Mix as little as possible. Put into twelve well-greased loaf tins, approximately $7\frac{3}{4}''$ × $4\frac{3}{8}''$ × $2\frac{3}{8}''$, and garnish with whole red cherries. Let stand fifteen to twenty minutes before baking in a 325–350-degree (F.) oven about forty minutes. These loaves will cut fifteen to sixteen slices or twenty to twenty-four thin slices for sandwiches.

Total Weight: 13 lb. 2 oz.
Yield: 12 loaves, 1 lb. $1\frac{1}{2}$ oz. per loaf.
Per Serving: Cost_____ Selling Price_____ Calories_____

DARK NUT BREAD

Ingredients	Amount	Weight	Multiple	Unit Cost	Total Cost
Graham flour		2 lb. 4 oz.			
White flour		2 lb. 4 oz.			
Baking powder, S.A.S.-phosphate type . . .	$\frac{1}{2}$ c.				
Salt	1 tbsp.				
Light-brown sugar . . .		2 lb. 8 oz.			
Nuts		1 lb.			
Raisins		1 lb. 6 oz.			
Milk	$1\frac{1}{3}$ qt.				
Eggs	8				
Shortening		3 oz.			

Sift the white flour, baking powder and salt together and mix with the remaining dry ingredients. Add all of the liquids at once and stir only until all of the flour is moistened, but do not attempt to make a smooth batter. Pour into well-greased loaf pans and garnish the top with nuts and raisins. Let stand one half hour. Bake in a moderate 350-degree (F.) oven for about forty minutes. These loaves will cut in fifteen to sixteen slices or twenty to twenty-four thin slices for sandwiches.

Total Weight: 13 lb.
Yield: 12 loaves, approximately 1 lb. 1 oz. per loaf.
Per Serving: Cost____   Selling Price____   Calories____

LIGHT NUT BREAD

Ingredients	Amount	Weight	Multiple	Unit Cost	Total Cost
Flour, bread		4 lb. 8 oz.			
Baking powder, S.A.S.-phosphate type . . .	½ c.				
Nuts, chopped		1 lb. 4 oz.			
Salt	1 tbsp.				
Sugar		2 lb. 8 oz.			
Milk	1⅓ qt.				
Eggs	8				
Shortening		3 oz.			

Mix the dry ingredients, including the nuts. Add the milk and the melted fat to the well-beaten eggs. Combine by adding the liquid to the dry ingredients, stirring only until they are moistened, not to a smooth batter. Pour the mixture into greased loaf pans, approximately 7¾″ × 4⅜″ × 2⅜″, garnish the tops with nuts and let stand one half hour. Bake in a moderate 350-degree (F.) oven for about forty minutes. These loaves will cut in fifteen to sixteen slices or twenty to twenty-four thin slices for sandwiches.

Total Weight: 12 lb. 4 oz.
Yield: 12 loaves, approximately 1 lb. each.
Per Serving: Cost____   Selling Price____   Calories____

CHAPTER XI

General Instructions for Making Yeast-Raised Doughs

A Standard for Yeast-Raised Doughs Must Be Defined. The aim in making raised doughs is to control the temperature and the proportion and handling of the ingredients in such a way as to produce a light, elastic dough which will give a bread or roll of even texture, tender, moist crumb, appetizing appearance and good keeping quality. A good loaf of bread, if made according to the following instructions, presents a bold, well-rounded appearance with a golden-brown crust and a fine texture. It should be tender, slightly sweet and of excellent keeping quality. A good roll should be tender, light, crusty and golden brown. It should be soft, moist and capable of being reheated to bring back the original softness.

The Temperature of Ingredients Is the First Consideration. When assembling ingredients, the temperature of the milk should be determined by the temperature of the room and of the flour. In summer, when the room and flour may be around 90 degrees F., the milk should not be above 60 degrees F. In winter, when the room and the flour may be 65–70 degrees F., the milk should be warmed to about 100–110 degrees F. By this warming or cooling process the dough, as it leaves the machine, will be approximately 80 degrees F., which has been established as the best finished dough temperature. Under modern conditions where the milk is delivered pasteurized in sealed cans, scalding the milk as was formerly done is of doubtful value.

Doughs May Be Quickly Mixed on a Power-Mixing Machine. Add the sugar, salt, yeast and milk to the bowl of the mixing machine and when the salt and sugar are dissolved and the yeast softened, add the flour. Let mix and add the fat. When the dough "balls up" and comes clean from the sides of the mixer, put in greased containers, cover and let rise in a warm place (80 degrees F.) free from drafts. Use a proof box if one is available. Avoid overmixing the dough, particularly a rich dough for rolls, as it makes the gluten become too elastic and makes tough rolls. Bread doughs require a more vigorous mixing for proper development of the gluten.

The Usual Practice Is To Allow the Dough To Rise or " Come Up " Twice. When the dough has doubled in bulk (this will take about one and one half hours or longer, depending upon conditions) punch it down firmly to its original bulk. Let rise again for about half an hour longer and put on the board or table.

The fermentation chart given here is printed by permission of the Products Control Department of General Mills, Inc. It is intended as a guide when for any reason it is necessary to change the fermentation time of yeast doughs. It may be used when working conditions and equipment are standard but may need to be varied under other circumstances. It applies to that part of the fermentation period up to the time the dough comes to the table to be worked up into loaves or rolls.

GUIDE TO FERMENTATION TIME OF YEAST-RAISED DOUGH *

Amount of Yeast	Gallons of Water	Period of Fermentation	1st Rising	2nd Rising	Temperature
4 oz.	1	$2\frac{1}{2}$ hr.	$1\frac{1}{2}$ hr.	1 hr.	80
8 oz.	1	$1\frac{1}{2}$ hr.	1 hr.	$\frac{1}{2}$ hr.	80
12 oz.	1	1 hr.	$\frac{3}{4}$ hr.	$\frac{1}{4}$ hr.	80
16 oz.	1	$\frac{1}{2}$ hr.	$\frac{1}{2}$ hr.	—	80

* Courtesy, Products Control Department, General Mills, Incorporated.

It Is Now Time to Form the Dough into Loaves or Rolls.
Avoid sifting too much flour or brushing excess grease on
the table when forming dough into loaves or rolls.   This
unfermented flour or excess grease if mixed with the
dough will cause streaks in the finished loaf.   If the dough
has been properly mixed, proofed and handled, the gluten
developed by this process will make a smooth elastic
dough which will not adhere to either hands or board and
hence only a little flour or fat should be needed in order
to handle the dough easily.

Scale the dough into the weight desired for loaves and
roll up into balls.   Cover the balls on the table with cloths
slightly dampened and let stand for about fifteen minutes
or until doughs are fairly well relaxed.   There are various
methods of shaping the dough into loaves, but an easy
way to obtain a uniform loaf is to roll each ball lightly with
a rolling pin to a rectangle the length of the pan to be
used.   Roll up the rectangle into an even roll and place
in greased baking pans.   Do not have an excess of grease.
Let rise until double in bulk (about forty-five minutes or
longer).

The Time of Baking Depends on the Size of the Loaf.
Bake according to the size of the loaf, about thirty-five
to forty-five minutes in a 375–400-degree (F.) oven.
Remove the bread from the pans at once as it comes out
of the oven to prevent sweating.   Cool on trays covered
with cloths or on wire racks.   At this time some prefer to
brush the top of the loaves with fat to make them shiny.

For baking one-pound loaves of bread the American
Association of Cereal Chemists recommends pans $7\frac{1}{2}''$ ×
$4\frac{1}{2}''$ at the top, $7'' \times 3\frac{1}{2}''$ at the bottom and $3\frac{1}{2}''$ in height.

**Many Communities Have a Law Requiring a Label
Giving the Weight of the Loaf.**   These labels may be put in
the pan and they will adhere to the loaf in baking.   This
is usually necessary only when the loaf is to be sold to

take off the premises. In this case, an additional amount of dough must be used to allow for loss of weight in baking, and the label must give the baked weight.

WHITE BREAD

Ingredients	Amount	Weight	Multiple	Unit Cost	Total Cost
Sugar		15 oz.			
Salt	½ c.				
Yeast		4 oz.			
Milk	4 qt.				
Flour		12 lb. 8 oz.			
Fat, melted		1 lb.			

Depending upon the temperature of the room, heat or cool milk (see page 220).

Place sugar, salt, yeast and milk in mixing bowl of mixing machine. Mix on low speed, using the dough hook, until the yeast is soft and the sugar and salt dissolved. Add the flour and continue mixing. Add the fat and continue mixing. When the dough "balls up" and comes clean from the bowl in about six to eight minutes, take off the machine. (The dough will have developed a temperature to about 80 degrees F.)

Put the dough into lightly greased containers, cover and set out of drafts or in a proof box kept at 80 degrees F. Let double in bulk, one hour to one and one half hours.

Punch down to original bulk. Let rise about one half hour and put on table to work up.

Scale into one-pound one-and-one-half-ounce units and ball the dough. Cover and let rise fifteen minutes on the board or table. Form into loaves and place in lightly greased pans.

Let rise in pan until the dough doubles, about forty to forty-five minutes.

Bake in a 375–400-degree (F.) oven thirty-five minutes for a pound loaf, longer if the loaf is larger. Remove from the pans at once on coming from the oven to prevent sweating. Cool on racks or cloth-covered trays.

This dough can be made into buns and pan rolls as well.

Total Weight: 22 lb. 10 oz. dough.
Yield: Approximately 20 loaves, 1 lb. each, after baking; or 30 dozen pan rolls.
Per Serving: Cost____   Selling Price____   Calories____

PAN ROLLS

Ingredients	Amount	Weight	Multiple	Unit Cost	Total Cost
White-bread dough . .		7 lb. 8 oz.			

Scale the dough into twelve-ounce units. Ball as for bread dough and allow to rise on table for fifteen minutes. Roll into a long cylindrical shape and cut into twelve equal parts. Roll each piece between the thumb and the palm of the hand to make a fine, smooth ball. Place on greased pie pans, one dozen to the pan, and let proof until they double in bulk. Bake in a 400-degree (F.) oven about fifteen minutes until they are a golden brown.

Total Weight: 7 lb. 8 oz.
Yield: 10 dozen pan rolls, 1 oz. each.
Per Serving: Cost____   Selling Price____   Calories____

PICNIC BUNS

Ingredients	Amount	Weight	Multiple	Unit Cost	Total Cost
White-bread dough . .		6 lb.			

Scale the dough into sixteen-ounce units and ball as for bread. Let rise on a board fifteen minutes. Roll each unit into a long cylindrical roll and cut into ten equal pieces. Roll between the thumb and the palm of the hand to make a smooth ball. Place on pans. Let proof fifteen to twenty minutes in a moist proof box. At the end of this time flatten the buns with the palm of the hand and allow to finish proofing. Bake in a 400-degree (F.) oven until brown.

Total Weight: 6 lb.
Yield: 5 dozen picnic buns, 3½ inches in diameter.
Per Serving: Cost____   Selling Price____   Calories____

GRAHAM BREAD OR ROLLS

Ingredients	Amount	Weight	Multiple	Unit Cost	Total Cost
Sugar		15 oz.			
Salt	½ c.				
Yeast		4 oz.			
Milk	4 qt.				
Molasses	1 c.				
Flour, white		6 lb. 12 oz.			
Flour, graham		5 lb. 4 oz.			
Fat, melted		1 lb.			

Depending upon the temperature of the room, heat or cool milk (see page 220).

Place sugar, salt, yeast, milk and molasses in mixing bowl of mixing machine. Mix on low speed, using the dough hook, until the yeast is soft and the sugar and salt dissolved. Add the flour and continue mixing. Add the fat and continue mixing. When the dough "balls up" and comes clean from the bowl, take off the machine. This should take about ten minutes. (The dough will have developed a temperature to about 80 degrees F.)

Put the dough into lightly greased containers, cover and set out of drafts or in a proof box kept at 80 degrees F. Let double in bulk, one hour to one and one half hours.

Punch down to original bulk. Let rise about one half hour and put on table to work up.

Scale into one-pound one-and-one-half-ounce units and ball the dough. Cover and let rise fifteen minutes on the board or table. Form into loaves and place in lightly greased pans.

Let rise in pan until the dough doubles, about forty to forty-five minutes.

Bake in a 375–400-degree (F.) oven thirty-five minutes for a pound loaf, longer if the loaf is larger. Remove from the pans at once on coming from the oven to prevent sweating. Cool on racks or cloth-covered trays.

This dough may be made into bread loaves, pan rolls or buns. It makes a good Parkerhouse roll as well and hence brings a wide variety into the hot-bread service. Finger rolls with poppy-seed garnish or sesame seeds are a popular variation.

Total Weight: 23 lb.
Yield: Approximately 21 loaves, 1 lb. each after baking; or 30 dozen pan rolls, 1 oz. each.
Per Serving: Cost_____   Selling Price_____   Calories_____

RYE BREAD

Ingredients	Amount	Weight	Multiple	Unit Cost	Total Cost
Sugar		15 oz.			
Salt	½ c.				
Yeast		6 oz.			
Milk	4 qt.				
Rye flour		5 lb.			
White flour		8 lb.			
Caraway seed	5 tbsp.				
Fat		1 lb.			

Depending upon the temperature of the room, heat or cool milk (see page 220).

Place sugar, salt, yeast and milk in mixing bowl of mixing machine. Mix on low speed, using the dough hook, until the yeast is soft and the sugar and salt dissolved. Add the flour and caraway seed and continue mixing. Add the fat and continue mixing. When the dough "balls up" and comes clean from the bowl, in about six to eight minutes, take off the machine. (The dough will have developed a temperature to about 80 degrees F.)

Put the dough into lightly greased containers, cover and set out of drafts or in a proof box kept at 80 degrees F. Let double in bulk — one hour to one and one half hours.

Punch down to original bulk. Let rise about one half hour and put on table to work up.

Scale into one-pound one-and-one-half-ounce units and ball the dough. Cover and let rise fifteen minutes on the board or table. Form into loaves and place in lightly greased pans.

Let rise in pan until the dough doubles, about forty to forty-five minutes.

Bake in a 375-400-degree (F.) oven thirty-five minutes for a pound loaf, longer if the loaf is larger. Remove from the pans at once on coming from the oven to prevent sweating. Cool on racks or cloth-covered trays.

This dough can be made into bread loaves, pan rolls or rye buns. Rye buns are especially good for ham or wiener sandwiches.

Total Weight: 23 lb.
Yield: Approximately 21 one-lb. loaves after baking.
Per Serving: Cost____ Selling Price____ Calories____

BASIC SWEET-ROLL DOUGH

Ingredients	Amount	Weight	Multiple	Unit Cost	Total Cost
Milk	4 qt.				
Sugar		3 lb.			
Salt	½ c.				
Yolks of eggs		1 lb.			
Yeast		1 lb.			
Bread flour		16 lb.			
Fat		3 lb.			

Depending on the temperature of the room, heat or cool the milk (see page 220).

Place sugar, salt, yolks, yeast and milk in the bowl of the mixing machine and mix on low speed until the ingredients are dissolved. Add the flour and continue mixing. Add the fat and mix to a smooth dough for about six to eight minutes. This dough is too soft to come clean from the sides of the bowl as bread dough will do. Overmixing should be avoided.

Proof 1½–1¾ hours in a lightly greased container at 80 degrees F. Punch down to original bulk.

Let rise about one half hour to double.

Scale into desired units to make up into cinnamon, orange or pecan rolls, coffee cakes or rich Parkerhouse or cloverleaf rolls. Directions for making up each are given as separate recipes on the following pages.

Total Weight: 32 lb.
Per Serving: Cost____   Selling Price____   Calories____

CLOVERLEAF ROLLS

Ingredients	Amount	Weight	Multiple	Unit Cost	Total Cost
Basic sweet dough (see above)		7 lb. 8 oz.			

Weigh the dough into twelve-ounce units. Roll each into a long cylindrical piece and cut crosswise into twelve equal parts. Divide each of these parts into three pieces. With the palm of the hand and thumb, roll these pieces into smooth balls. Place in well-greased muffin tins, putting three balls in each section. Proof until double in bulk. Bake fifteen to twenty minutes in a 400-degree (F.) oven.

Total Weight: 7 lb. 8 oz.
Yield: 10 doz. cloverleaf rolls, each roll 1 ounce; or three ⅓-ounce balls.
Per Serving: Cost_____ Selling Price_____ Calories_____

DINNERETTE ROLLS

INGREDIENTS	AMOUNT	WEIGHT	MULTIPLE	UNIT COST	TOTAL COST
Basic sweet dough (see page 228)		8 lb. 12 oz.			

Weigh the dough into fourteen-ounce units. Roll each into a rectangular strip about 8″ × 12″. Brush with melted fat and, beginning with the short side of the rectangle, make into a roll similar to that from which a cinnamon roll is cut. Cut crosswise of the roll into twelve equal parts. Place in lightly greased muffin tins. Proof until double in bulk. Bake fifteen to twenty minutes in a 400-degree (F.) oven.

Total Weight: 8 lb. 12 oz.
Yield: 10 dozen rolls, approximately 1⅙ oz. each.
Per Serving: Cost_____ Selling Price_____ Calories_____

PARKERHOUSE ROLLS

INGREDIENTS	AMOUNT	WEIGHT	MULTIPLE	UNIT COST	TOTAL COST
Basic sweet dough (see page 228)		7 lb. 8 oz.			

Weigh the dough into twelve-ounce units. Roll each into a long cylindrical piece and cut into twelve equal parts. With the palm of the hand and thumb roll these pieces into smooth balls and place in pans to rise. When they have become light brush the table top with melted fat, place the rolls in a double row on the greased table top and with a rolling pin or stick roll the balls flat. Fold over on the greased side to form a pocket book and press down. Replace in pans, putting fifteen rolls in a 10″ × 10″ pan. Proof until double in bulk. Bake fifteen to twenty minutes in a 400-degree (F.) oven.

Total Weight: 7 lb. 8 oz.
Yield: 10 dozen Parkerhouse rolls, 1 oz. each.
Per Serving: Cost_____   Selling Price_____   Calories_____

CINNAMON ROLLS

INGREDIENTS	AMOUNT	WEIGHT	MULTIPLE	UNIT COST	TOTAL COST
For each dozen rolls:					
Basic sweet dough (see page 228)		1 lb. 4 oz.			
Glazing mixture (see page 231)		4 oz.			
Sugar mixture (see page 231)	⅓ c.				
Raisins	⅓ c.				

Roll the one-pound four-ounce unit of dough into a rectangular strip about 9″ × 14″. Spread the rectangle with one ounce of the glazing mixture, one third cup of the sugar mixture and one third cup of raisins. Roll up and cut across into twelve equal parts.

Spread the remaining three ounces of the glazing mixture on the bottom of a 10″ × 10″ square pan. Place the dozen rolls in the pan and proof until light. Bake twenty-five to thirty minutes in a 375-degree (F.) oven. Turn upside down on a tray immediately upon taking from the oven so that the caramelized syrup will run down over the rolls and not harden in the pan.

This recipe has been given for a unit of one dozen only, to permit an easy figuring of any number of dozen rolls desired.

Yield: One dozen cinnamon rolls (1⅔ oz. dough each).
Per Serving: Cost_____ Selling Price_____ Calories_____

GLAZING MIXTURE FOR SWEET ROLLS

Ingredients	Amount	Weight	Multiple	Unit Cost	Total Cost
Granulated sugar . . .		6 lb.			
Fat		6 lb.			
Glucose	3 c.				
Honey, strained . . .	3 c.				

Cream the fat and sugar until thoroughly blended. Add the glucose and honey and mix well. Keep in the refrigerator and use as needed for cinnamon or pecan rolls.

Total Weight: 16 lb. 6 oz.
Per Serving: Cost_____ Selling Price_____ Calories_____

CINNAMON SUGAR MIXTURE FOR SWEET ROLLS

Ingredients	Amount	Weight	Multiple	Unit Cost	Total Cost
Sugar		6 lb.			
Cinnamon		4 oz.			

Weigh the ingredients, mix well and store in a covered can for use as needed.

Yield: 6 lb. 4 oz.
Per Serving: Cost_____ Selling Price_____ Calories_____

PECAN ROLLS

Ingredients	Amount	Weight	Multiple	Unit Cost	Total Cost
For each dozen rolls:					
Basic sweet dough (see page 228)		1 lb.			
Glazing mixture (see page 231)		4 oz.			
Sugar mixture (see page 231)	3 tbsp.				-
Pecans		2 oz.			

Roll the one-pound unit of sweet dough into a rectangular strip about 9″ × 14″. Spread this rectangle with one ounce of the glazing mixture and three tablespoons of the sugar mixture. Roll up as for cinnamon rolls and cut across into twelve equal parts.

Grease muffin tins or individual roll tins. Divide three ounces of the glazing mixture and two ounces of pecans evenly over the bottoms of a dozen individual pans. Place the rolls in the pans. Proof until light. Bake twenty-five to thirty minutes at 375 degrees F. Invert on a tray immediately on taking from the oven or the glaze will harden in the bottom of the pan.

This recipe has been given for a unit of one dozen only, to facilitate figuring for any number of dozen rolls required.

Yield: One dozen pecan rolls, approximately 1¾ oz. each.
Per Serving: Cost_____ Selling Price_____ Calories_____

COFFEE-CAKE TOPPING

Ingredients	Amount	Weight	Multiple	Unit Cost	Total Cost
Granulated sugar . . .		5 lb. 10 oz.			
Crumbs, light		3 lb. 10 oz.			
Cinnamon		3 oz.			

Mix the granulated sugar, light crumbs and cinnamon together. Keep on hand to use as a topping for coffee cakes.

Total Weight: 9 lb. 7 oz.
Yield: Topping for 50 coffee cakes, 8″ in diameter; 3 oz. topping per cake.
Per Serving: Cost____   Selling Price____   Calories____

DUTCH APPLE COFFEE CAKE

Ingredients	Amount	Weight	Multiple	Unit Cost	Total Cost
For each coffee cake:					
Basic sweet dough (see page 228)		11 oz.			
Apples, one-eighth-inch slices		5 oz.			
Fat		1½ oz.			
Coffee-cake topping (see page 232) . . .		3 oz.			

For each coffee cake desired, weigh eleven ounces of sweet dough. Roll or pat into shape to fit into an eight-inch square cake pan. Pare and cut the apples in one-eighth-inch slices and place in even rows on top of the cake with the edges overlapping. Put one and one half ounces of fat over the apples and dough. Spread the coffee-cake topping evenly over the apples and fat. Place in the proof box until double in bulk. Bake in a 375-degree (F.) oven from twenty-five to thirty minutes.

This recipe is given for one coffee cake to permit easy figuring for any number desired.

Yield: One cake, 8″ × 8″.
Per Serving: Cost____   Selling Price____   Calories____

GERMAN COFFEE CAKE

Ingredients	Amount	Weight	Multiple	Unit Cost	Total Cost
For each coffee cake:					
Basic sweet dough (see page 228)		11 oz.			
Fat		1½ oz.			
Coffee-cake topping (see page 232) . . .		3 oz.			

For each coffee cake required, weigh eleven ounces of sweet dough. Roll or pat into shape to fit an eight-inch round cake pan. Brush the top with melted fat. Pour one and one half ounces of fat over the top of the dough. Sprinkle three ounces of coffee-cake topping over the fat evenly. Place in a proof box until double in bulk. Bake in a 375-degree (F.) oven twenty-five to thirty minutes.

This recipe is given for a single coffee cake to facilitate figuring for as many as are required.

Yield: 1 cake, 8 inches in diameter.

Per Serving: Cost_____ Selling Price_____ Calories_____

SWEDISH COFFEE CAKE

Ingredients	Amount	Weight	Multiple	Unit Cost	Total Cost
For each coffee cake:					
Basic sweet dough (see page 228)		14 oz.			
Fat		½ oz.			
Almonds, sliced . . .	2 tbsp.				
Sugar		1 oz.			
Ground cardamon seed	½ tsp.				

For each coffee cake required, weigh fourteen ounces of basic sweet dough. Roll into an oblong strip the width and length of a loaf tin. Cut the dough into three equal lengthwise strips to within an inch of the end. Braid loosely and put into a lightly greased pound loaf pan. Pour one half ounce of fat over the braided loaf. Mix the almonds, cardamon seed and sugar and sprinkle the loaf with this mixture. Proof until double in bulk. Bake about thirty to thirty-five minutes at 375–400 degrees F.

This recipe is given for a single loaf to permit easy figuring of any number.

Yield: 1 coffee cake.
Per Serving: Cost____   Selling Price____   Calories____

CANDIED ORANGE PEEL FOR ORANGE ROLLS

INGREDIENTS	AMOUNT	WEIGHT	MULTIPLE	UNIT COST	TOTAL COST
Orange peel, cooked, scraped and ground .		9 lb. 6 oz.			
Sugar		16 lb.			
Water	2 qt.				

Save the peel from which orange juice has been extracted. Cook this fresh peel until tender. Drain and scrape out all of the white membrane and chop or grind the remaining yellow peel.

Combine the sugar and water and cook to 220 degrees F. Add the ground peel and after the syrup comes to a boil again, cook for ten minutes. Drain, leaving a little of the syrup around the peel to keep it moist. Cool and store to use as needed for filling and for making topping for orange rolls.

Save the syrup which has been drained off to use for making orange topping as well as for further candying of peel. When using the syrup a second time, add four pounds more sugar to every quart of syrup and cook to 220 degrees F., proceeding as before.

Total Weight: 16 lb. candied peel.
Per Serving: Cost____   Selling Price____   Calories____

ORANGE TOPPING FOR ORANGE ROLLS

Ingredients	Amount	Weight	Multiple	Unit Cost	Total Cost
Ground candied orange peel (see page 235) . .		3 lb. 12 oz.			
Orange syrup from candying peel (see page 235)	1½ qt.				
Strained honey	3 c.				

Add the ground candied orange peel to the orange syrup and honey and mix well. This may be kept on hand to use for brushing the tops of orange rolls.

Total Weight: 10 lb. 8 oz.
Per Serving: Cost_____ Selling Price_____ Calories_____

ORANGE ROLLS

Ingredients	Amount	Weight	Multiple	Unit Cost	Total Cost
For each dozen rolls:					
Basic sweet dough (see page 228)		14 oz.			
Chopped candied orange peel (see page 235) .		4 oz.			
Orange topping (see above)	¼ c.				

Weigh the dough into fourteen-ounce units and roll into a rectangular strip about 8″ × 12″. Brush with melted fat. Sprinkle with four ounces of chopped candied orange peel. Beginning with the short side of the dough, make into a roll. Cut crosswise of the roll into twelve equal parts. Place in greased muffin tins. Put one teaspoon of orange topping on each roll. Proof until light. Bake twenty to twenty-five minutes in a hot oven (375–400 degrees F.). Remove from the pans at once to prevent the topping from hardening and sticking to the sides of the pans.

This recipe is given for a unit of one dozen only, to permit easy figuring for any number of dozen rolls desired.

Yield: 1 dozen rolls, approximately $1\frac{1}{6}$ oz. each.
Per Serving: Cost____   Selling Price____   Calories____

CHAPTER XII

Desserts

APPLE FRITTERS

Ingredients	Amount	Weight	Multiple	Unit Cost	Total Cost
Sugar		6 oz.			
Flour		2 lb. 2 oz.			
Salt	1½ tsp.				
Baking powder	4½ tbsp.				
Soda	1½ tsp.				
Eggs	9				
Sour cream (20–25%) . .	3 c.				
Sweet milk	1½ c.				
Diced apples, ½-inch cubes		1 lb.			

Mix and sift the dry ingredients. Beat the eggs and add the sour cream and milk. Pour over the dry ingredients, mixing only to wet them. Do not beat. Fold in the diced fruit. Using a number-thirty or number-twenty-four scoop, depending on the size of fritter desired, drop the batter into deep fat, 360 degrees F., and cook about five minutes. Serve two fritters to an order. Maple or sugar syrup may be served with these. Variety may be obtained by substituting other fruits or vegetables for the apples — such as oranges, pineapple, hominy or corn.

Total Weight: 7 lb.

Yield: 42 servings, 2 fritters per serving, No. 24 scoop (1⅓ oz. batter); 52 servings, 2 fritters per serving, No. 30 scoop (1 1/12 oz. batter).

Per Serving: Cost____ Selling Price____ Calories____

DESERTS

BAKED APPLES

Ingredients	Amount	Weight	Multiple	Unit Cost	Total Cost
Apples (88 size)	50				
Sugar		3 lb. 12 oz. to 5 lb. 10 oz.			
Water	4 qt.				

Wash and core the apples and pare down one third of the way from the top.   Place the apples in a baking pan and steam from ten minutes to one half hour until partly done. This will vary according to the season and variety of apple used.   Make a syrup of the sugar and water and pour over the apples.   The amount of sugar varies, depending on the acidity of the apples.   Bake in a 400-degree F. oven thirty to forty-five minutes, basting frequently to produce a glaze or shine.   Cover the apples if they begin to brown before getting thoroughly done.

Yield: 50 servings, approximately 11 oz. each.
Per Serving: Cost_____ Selling Price_____ Calories_____

JELLIED APRICOTS

Ingredients	Amount	Weight	Multiple	Unit Cost	Total Cost
Gelatin	½ c.				
Cold water	2 c.				
Sugar		1 lb. 14 oz.			
Boiling water	1½ qt.				
Apricot juice	1½ qt.				
Lemon juice	⅔ c.				
Apricot halves, canned .	96				
Cream, before whipping .	1½ qt.				

Soften the gelatin in cold water.   Dissolve the sugar in the boiling water and pour over the gelatin.   Stir until it is dissolved. Add the unheated apricot juice and allow the mixture to cool. When it begins to set add the lemon juice. Arrange two apricot halves, rounded side out, in individual molds. Pour the gelatin mixture into these molds and allow to set. Unmold and garnish with whipped cream around the mold and on top, using a pastry tube for the cream and allowing one fourth cup, whipped, per serving.

Total Weight: Approximately 13 lb. 8 oz.
Yield: 48 servings, 4½ oz. each.
Per Serving: Cost_____ Selling Price_____ Calories_____

CARAMEL BAVARIAN

Ingredients	Amount	Weight	Multiple	Unit Cost	Total Cost
Gelatin	½ c.				
Cold water	1½ c.				
Sugar		15 oz.			
Hot water	1½ qt.				
Milk scalded	2 qt.				
Egg yolks	1⅓ c.				
Sugar		2 lb. 6 oz.			
Egg whites	2 c.				

Add the cold water to the gelatin. Caramelize the fifteen ounces of sugar. Add the hot water and cook until all of the caramelized sugar has dissolved. Add the gelatin and let cool.

Scald the milk, add the egg yolks and the two pounds six ounces of sugar beaten together and cook as for soft custard. When both mixtures have cooled, combine. When this has set to a jellylike consistency pour into the stiffly beaten egg whites and beat on a mixing machine until blended. Pour into shallow pans to set. Cut into squares and serve with whipped cream. The color of the pudding will be determined by the degree to which the sugar is caramelized.

Total Weight: 10 lb. 8 oz.
Yield: 48 servings, $3\frac{1}{2}$ oz. each (approximately $\frac{1}{2}$ c.).
Per Serving: Cost____ Selling Price____ Calories____

ORANGE BAVARIAN

Ingredients	Amount	Weight	Multiple	Unit Cost	Total Cost
Gelatin	$\frac{1}{4}$ c.				
Orange juice	$\frac{1}{3}$ c.				
Cream, before whipping .	2 qt.				
Sugar		15 oz.			
Lemon juice	$\frac{1}{4}$ c.				
Diced oranges	1 qt.				
Salt	$\frac{1}{2}$ tsp.				
Orange sections	40				

Soften the gelatin in the orange juice and dissolve over hot water. Whip the cream and continue beating while adding the sugar, salt, lemon juice and the dissolved gelatin. Fold in the oranges. Pour into individual molds to set. To serve, garnish each serving with whipped cream and a section of orange.

Total Weight: 7 lb. 8 oz.
Yield: 40 servings, 3 oz. each (approximately $\frac{1}{2}$ c.).
Per Serving: Cost____ Selling Price____ Calories____

RICE BAVARIAN WITH MAPLE SYRUP

Ingredients	Amount	Weight	Multiple	Unit Cost	Total Cost
Rice		2 lb. 2 oz.			
Boiling water	9 qt.				
Salt	3 tbsp.				
Gelatin	$4\frac{1}{2}$ tbsp.				
Cold water	$\frac{3}{4}$ c.				
Whipping cream, before whipping	$2\frac{1}{4}$ qt.				
Maple syrup	$3\frac{1}{2}$ qt.				

Cook the rice in the boiling salted water until tender. Pour into a colander and let cold water run over to separate the rice grains. Drain thoroughly. Soften the gelatin in the three fourths cup of cold water, dissolve over hot water and mix with the cream, which has been whipped. Fold in the cold rice and mold in cups which have been rinsed in cold water. This pudding is served with a maple syrup, the sweet syrup contrasting with the blandness of the rice.

Total Weight: 11 lb. 13 oz.
Yield: 54 servings, 3½ oz. rice each (approximately ½ c.) and 2 oz. of maple syrup.
Per Serving: Cost____   Selling Price____   Calories____

CHOCOLATE BLANCMANGE

INGREDIENTS	AMOUNT	WEIGHT	MULTIPLE	UNIT COST	TOTAL COST
Cornstarch		8 oz.			
Sugar		1 lb. 14 oz.			
Cocoa		1 lb.			
Salt	1½ tsp.				
Milk	1½ gal.				
Vanilla	3 tbsp.				

Mix the cornstarch, sugar, cocoa and salt together thoroughly. Add three to three and one half cups of cold milk to make a smooth paste. Scald the remainder of the milk and pour in the cornstarch and cocoa mixture, stirring rapidly with a wire whip. Cook seven to ten minutes. Remove from the fire and add the vanilla. Pour into sherbet glasses or individual molds. Serve with cream. Nuts may be added, if desired.

Total Weight: 14 lb. 10 oz.
Yield: 52 servings, 4½ oz. each (approximately ½ c.).
Per Serving: Cost____   Selling Price____   Calories____

DATE NUT BLANCMANGE

Ingredients	Amount	Weight	Multiple	Unit Cost	Total Cost
Cornstarch		6¾ oz.			
Brown sugar		2 lb. 3 oz.			
Salt	1½ tsp.				
Boiling water	2 qt.				
Egg whites	1½ c.				
Vanilla	1 tbsp.				
Nut meats, chopped . .		6 oz.			
Dates		10 oz.			

Mix the cornstarch, sugar and salt and add to the boiling water, stirring rapidly with a wire whip. Cook seven to ten minutes. Beat the egg whites stiff. When the cornstarch mixture is clear add to the egg whites and beat on a mixing machine, about five minutes on high speed until smooth and creamy. This will increase volume and improve the consistency. Remove from the machine and add the dates, nut meats and vanilla by hand. Wet ramekins or molds, pour in the pudding mixture and let set until cold. Unmold and serve with a chilled custard sauce.

Total Weight: 7 lb. 5 oz.
Yield: 50 servings, 2⅓ oz. each (approximately ½ c.).
Per Serving: Cost____ Selling Price____ Calories____

MAPLE NUT MOLD

Ingredients	Amount	Weight	Multiple	Unit Cost	Total Cost
Brown sugar		2 lb. 3 oz.			
Cornstarch		6¾ oz.			
Water	2 qt.				
Egg whites	1½ c.				
Nut meats, chopped . .		8 oz.			
Mapleline	1½ tsp.				
Salt	1½ tsp.				

Mix the cornstarch, sugar and salt and add to the boiling water, stirring rapidly with a wire whip. Cook seven to ten minutes. Beat the egg whites stiff and when the cornstarch mixture is clear add to the egg whites and beat on a power machine at high speed until smooth and a creamy white, about five minutes. Remove from the machine and add the mapeline and nut meats by hand. Wet ramekins or molds, pour in the pudding mixture and let set until cool. Unmold and serve with a chilled custard sauce.

Total Weight: 6 lb. 14 oz.
Yield: 48 servings, approximately $2\frac{1}{3}$ oz. each or $\frac{1}{2}$ cup.
Per Serving: Cost____   Selling Price____   Calories____

RAISIN BREAD PUDDING

INGREDIENTS	AMOUNT	WEIGHT	MULTIPLE	UNIT COST	TOTAL COST
Eggs	15				
Sugar		1 lb. 7 oz.			
Salt	$2\frac{1}{4}$ tsp.				
Vanilla	$1\frac{1}{2}$ tbsp.				
Fat		8 oz.			
Scalded milk	3 qt.				
Cubed bread		15 oz.			
Raisins		1 lb. 7 oz.			
Nutmeg	1 tsp.				

Add the beaten eggs, sugar, salt, vanilla and melted fat to the scalded milk. Pour this over the bread and raisins, which have been distributed over three shallow baking pans. Sprinkle the nutmeg over the top and bake in a pan of water in a moderate oven (350 degrees F.) until the custard sets, about forty-five to fifty minutes. Serve with vanilla sauce or whipped cream.

Total Weight: 11 lb. 4 oz., after baking.
Yield: 45 servings, 4 oz. each (approximately $\frac{1}{2}$ c.).
Per Serving: Cost____   Selling Price____   Calories____

APPLE BROWN BETTY

Ingredients	Amount	Weight	Multiple	Unit Cost	Total Cost
Apples, peeled		4 lb. 4 oz.			
Crumbs, sweet		1 lb. 12 oz.			
Brown sugar		1 lb. 4 oz.			
Nutmeg	$\frac{3}{4}$ tsp.				
Cinnamon	$\frac{1}{2}$ tbsp.				
Allspice	$\frac{1}{2}$ tbsp.				
Water	$2\frac{2}{3}$ c.				
Lemon juice	$1\frac{1}{3}$ tbsp.				
Grated rind	2 tbsp.				
Fat		13 oz.			

Steam the apples until tender and chop until fine. Line three greased baking pans (9″ × 9″) with crumbs, cover with apples, then with a mixture of the sugar and spices. Add one half of the water, lemon juice and grated rind. Repeat the above and cover the top with crumbs. Dot with fat. The puddings should be two to three inches in thickness. Bake forty-five minutes to one hour in a moderate oven, 375 degrees F., until brown. Serve hot with a hot lemon sauce.

Total Weight: 8 lb. 12 oz., after baking.
Yield: 40 servings, $3\frac{1}{2}$ oz. each (approximately $\frac{1}{2}$ c.).
Per Serving: Cost____   Selling Price____   Calories____

CHOCOLATE SOUFFLÉ

Ingredients	Amount	Weight	Multiple	Unit Cost	Total Cost
Sugar		1 lb. 14 oz.			
Flour		7 oz.			
Cocoa		8 oz.			
Water	$1\frac{3}{4}$ qt.				
Egg yolks	$1\frac{1}{3}$ c.				
Vanilla	2 tbsp.				
Egg whites	4 c.				

Mix the flour, sugar and cocoa and, stirring rapidly, add to the boiling water. When thickened, add the egg yolks and the vanilla. Fold this custard mixture into the stiffly beaten egg whites. Pour into baking dishes or into individual molds and set in a pan of hot water to bake. Bake in a 350-degree (F.) oven until the soufflé sets. Serve hot or cold with whipped cream.

Total Weight: 7 lb. 13 oz., after baking.
Yield: 40 servings, approximately 3 oz. each.
Per Serving: Cost____ Selling Price____ Calories____

MARY'S CHOCOLATE PUDDING

INGREDIENTS	AMOUNT	WEIGHT	MULTIPLE	UNIT COST	TOTAL COST
Chocolate		1 lb. 2 oz.			
Sugar		1 lb. 7 oz.			
Eggs, yolks	3 c.				
whites	4½ c.				
Vanilla	6 tbsp.				

Put the chocolate into a bowl and melt over hot water. Beat the sugar and the egg yolks to a creamy consistency and add to the chocolate gradually and continue cooking, stirring constantly until the mixture is thick. Beat the egg whites until stiff, remove from the machine and fold in the chocolate mixture and vanilla by hand. Stir only until the mixture is smooth and an even color. This pudding should be smooth and velvety — not coarse or foamy. Pour into sherbet glasses and put in the refrigerator to cool and set. Serve with whipped cream.

Total Weight: 6 lb. 4 oz.
Yield: 50 servings, 2 oz. each (approximately ⅓–½ c.).
Per Serving: Cost____ Selling Price____ Calories____

COTTAGE PUDDING

Ingredients	Amount	Weight	Multiple	Unit Cost	Total Cost
Shortening		6 oz.			
Sugar		1 lb. 14 oz.			
Eggs	5				
Milk	3½ c.				
Flour, pastry		2 lb. 9 oz.			
Baking powder, S.A.S.-phosphate type . . .	4½ tbsp.				
Salt	2 tsp.				
Vanilla	2 tbsp.				

Cream the sugar and the shortening. Add the well-beaten eggs and alternate the liquid and the dry ingredients. Add the vanilla. Weigh the batter into eight-inch square cake pans, using one pound of batter per pan. Bake in a 375-degree (F.) oven. Cut the pudding 3 × 3 and serve hot with lemon, vanilla, fruit or chocolate sauce.

Total Weight: 7 lb.
Yield: 7 8-inch cake pans, 1 lb. batter per pan; 9 servings per pan (63 servings).
Per Serving: Cost_____ Selling Price_____ Calories_____

CREAM PUFFS

Ingredients	Amount	Weight	Multiple	Unit Cost	Total Cost
Boiling water	1 qt.				
Fat		1 lb.			
Flour		1 lb. 2 oz.			
Salt	⅛ tsp.				
Eggs, whole	18				

Melt the fat in the boiling water and add the flour and salt all at once, stirring rapidly. Cook until the mixture forms a ball and leaves the sides of the pan. Put this mixture in the bowl of the mixing machine and, adding the eggs one at a time, continue the beating at high speed until all of the eggs are added and the dough is well mixed and smooth. Drop with a number-sixteen scoop onto a well-greased sheet and bake about forty minutes in a hot oven, about 375–400 degrees F. Do not attempt to bake the shells until perfectly dry inside. They should be slightly moist. When cool, the shells may be filled with whipped cream and served with chocolate sauce, or they may be filled with chocolate cream filling and served with whipped cream or powdered sugar over the top.

Total Weight: 5 lb. 10 oz.
Yield: 45 cream puffs, 2 oz. each.
Per Serving: Cost____ Selling Price____ Calories____

BAKED CUSTARDS

INGREDIENTS	AMOUNT	WEIGHT	MULTIPLE	UNIT COST	TOTAL COST
Eggs, whole	18				
Sugar		1 lb. 1 oz.			
Salt	1½ tsp.				
Milk	4½ qt.				
Vanilla	1½ tbsp.				
Nutmeg	¾ tsp.				

Beat the eggs, sugar and salt. Add the scalded milk and the vanilla and pour into custard cups. Sprinkle the tops with nutmeg. Set in a pan of water and bake thirty to forty minutes in a moderate, 325–350-degree (F.) oven, until the custard is firm. When a case knife inserted into the custard comes out clean, the custard is done.

Total Weight: 12 lb.
Yield: 48 servings, 4 oz. each (approximately ½ c.).
Per Serving: Cost____ Selling Price____ Calories____

GRAPENUT CUSTARD PUDDING

Ingredients	Amount	Weight	Multiple	Unit Cost	Total Cost
Eggs	8				
Sugar		5 oz.			
Salt	⅙ tsp.				
Milk	3½ qt.				
Grapenuts		8 oz.			
Bread crumbs		5 oz.			
Raisins		13 oz.			

Beat the eggs with the sugar and salt and add to the scalded milk. Pour over the grapenuts, crumbs and raisins. Put into baking pans. Set in a pan of water and bake in a moderate oven (350 degrees F.) about fifty minutes or until the custard sets. Serve hot with a lemon sauce.

Total Weight: 9 lb. 10 oz.
Yield: 44 servings, 3½ oz. each.
Per Serving: Cost_____   Selling Price_____   Calories_____

PRUNE CREAM CUSTARD

Ingredients	Amount	Weight	Multiple	Unit Cost	Total Cost
Milk	3 qt.				
Cornstarch		6 oz.			
Sugar		11 oz.			
Egg yolks	¾ c.				
Salt	3 tsp.				
Vanilla	1½ tbsp.				
Prunes, after cooking . .		3 lb.			
MERINGUE :					
Egg whites		9 oz.			
Glucose	1⅛ c.				
Granulated sugar . .		4½ oz.			
Powdered sugar . . .		3⅜ oz.			
Cream of tartar . . .	⅓ tsp.				

Mix and sift the cornstarch and the sugar and add to the scalded milk, stirring rapidly with a wire whip. Cook for seven to ten minutes. When the cornstarch has thickened add the egg yolks mixed with a small amount of the thickened milk and the salt. Cook for a few minutes. Add the vanilla. Pour this custard mixture over the prunes, which have been seeded and cut in halves and placed in the bottom of shallow pudding pans.

Pour the egg whites, glucose, granulated and powdered sugar with the cream of tartar into a mixing machine and mix on high speed five to eight minutes. Spread the meringue over the mixture in swirls and brown in a moderate oven. Serve either hot or cold.

Total Weight: 11 lb. 8 oz. (2 long shallow pans, 9″ × 15″).
Yield: 46 servings, 4 oz. each (approximately ½ c.).
Per Serving: Cost_____ Selling Price_____ Calories_____

DATE TORTE

INGREDIENTS	AMOUNT	WEIGHT	MULTIPLE	UNIT COST	TOTAL COST
Sugar		2 lb. 3 oz.			
Flour		2 oz.			
Baking powder	2 tbsp.				
Nuts, chopped		1 lb. 4 oz.			
Dates, chopped		3 lb. 10 oz.			
Egg whites	3 c.				
Salt	1 tsp.				

Sift the sugar, flour and baking powder together and add to the nuts and dates. Fold into the slightly beaten egg whites to which salt has been added. Divide between two greased shallow pans 9″ × 15″. Set in pans of hot water and bake in a 350-degree (F.) oven thirty to forty minutes until done.

Total Weight: 8 lb.
Yield: 48 servings, approximately 2⅔ oz. each.
Per Serving: Cost_____ Selling Price_____ Calories_____

FRUIT COCKTAIL

Ingredients	Amount	Weight	Multiple	Unit Cost	Total Cost
Oranges, ¾″ cubes . . .	2¼ qt.				
Bananas, ¾″ cubes . . .	3¾ qt.				
Pineapples, diced . . .	3 c.				
Sugar		11 oz.			
Water or fruit juice . .	4½ c.				
Lemon juice	¾ c.				
Cherries, Maraschino or glacé		1 lb. 3 oz.			

With a sharp knife cut the fruit carefully into three-quarter-inch cubes. Orange seeds and tough connective tissue should be removed. Make a syrup of the sugar and water or fruit juice and cool. Add the lemon juice and pour over the diced fruit. Serve in sherbet glasses with a cherry and a sprig of mint for garnish. Other fruits may be substituted in season.

Total Weight: 13 lb. 8 oz.
Yield: 48 servings, 4¼ oz. each (approximately ½ c.).
Per Serving: Cost___ Selling Price___ Calories___

FRUIT GELATIN

Ingredients	Amount	Weight	Multiple	Unit Cost	Total Cost
Gelatin	½ c.				
Cold water	2 c.				
Boiling water	3 c.				
Sugar		1 lb. 14 oz.			
Orange juice	1½ qt.				
Pineapple juice	3 c.				
Lemon juice	⅔ c.				
Diced canned pineapple .	2 c.				
Diced oranges	1 qt.				
Diced bananas	2 c.				
Halved cherries	2 c.				

Soften the gelatin in the cold water and dissolve in the boiling water. Add the sugar. Cool and add the fruit juice. When the gelatin mixture has started to set, add the diced fruit. This may be molded in individual molds or allowed to set in shallow pans. If individual molds are used the diced fruit may be divided equally between the molds, and the gelatin, after it has begun to set, poured over.

Uncooked pineapple cannot be used in fruit gelatin, since it contains an enzyme which acts on the protein of the gelatin preventing its setting.

In season, substitute fresh fruits as they appear in the market for one or all of those named above.

Total Weight: 13 lb.
Yield: 52 servings, 4 oz. each (approximately ½ c.).
Per Serving: Cost_____   Selling Price_____   Calories_____

FRUIT WHIP

INGREDIENTS	AMOUNT	WEIGHT	MULTIPLE	UNIT COST	TOTAL COST
Fruit pulp		2 lb. 4 oz.			
Sugar		1 lb. 14 oz.			
Egg whites	½ c.				
Lemon juice	¼ c.				

Put the fruit pulp, sugar and unbeaten egg whites into the bowl of a mixing machine and beat on high speed until stiff, about ten to fifteen minutes. Add the lemon juice. In making large amounts, the desired volume and texture cannot be produced without using a power mixer. Vegetable coloring may be added, if necessary, for appetizing color, but it must be done carefully and not used to excess.

Total Weight: 4 lb. 4 oz.
Yield: 50 servings, approximately 1⅓ oz. each.
Per Serving: Cost_____   Selling Price_____   Calories_____

GINGER MUFFINS, BUTTERSCOTCH SAUCE

Ingredients	Amount	Weight	Multiple	Unit Cost	Total Cost
Gingerbread dough (see page 217)		7 lb. 14 oz.			
Butterscotch Sauce:					
Brown sugar		2 lb. 10 oz.			
Flour	3 tbsp.				
Light corn syrup . .	1 qt.				
Coffee cream	1 qt.				
Salt	1 tsp.				
Vanilla	2 tsp.				

Make the gingerbread dough and with a number-sixteen-size icecream scoop dish into muffin tins. Bake in a 350-degree F. oven about twenty-five to thirty minutes until done.

Mix the brown sugar and flour together and add to the corn syrup and coffee cream. Cook to 220 degrees F. Remove from the fire and add the salt and vanilla.

Serve the muffins hot with butterscotch sauce and whipped cream.

Total Weight: 7 lb. 8 oz. sauce.
Yield: 48 servings (approximately 2½ oz. of ginger muffin and approximately 2½ oz. butterscotch sauce each).
Per Serving: Cost____ Selling Price____ Calories____

MERINGUES

Ingredients	Amount	Weight	Multiple	Unit Cost	Total Cost
Egg whites	3 c.				
Sugar		3 lb. 12 oz.			
White vinegar	¼ c.				
Vanilla	¼ c.				

Beat the egg whites and when light add one half of the sugar gradually and continue beating until very stiff. Add the vinegar, vanilla and the remainder of the sugar gradually and continue beating until stiff and dry. If a mixing machine is available, beat in all about twelve minutes. If the beating is done by hand a longer time will be necessary.

Drop the meringue by spoonfuls or put through a pastry bag onto greased paper on a baking sheet. Bake in a very slow oven (250 degrees F.) for about an hour. For a medium-sized meringue use two ounces of mixture. These may be served with icecream, whipped cream, fresh berries or a combination of these.

Total Weight: 5 lb. 4 oz.
Yield: 42 servings, 2 oz. each.
Per Serving: Cost_____ Selling Price_____ Calories_____

FRESH PEACH COBBLER

Ingredients	Amount	Weight	Multiple	Unit Cost	Total Cost
Pie dough (see pages 303, 304)		4 lb. 8 oz.			
Peach Filling:					
Peaches, peeled and sliced		8 lb.			
Sugar		4 lb. 12 oz.			
Cornstarch		3 oz.			
Nutmeg	2 tsp.				
Salt	2 tsp.				
Fat, melted		10 oz.			
Lemon juice	6 tbsp.				

Line the bottom and sides of two shallow 9″ × 15″ pans with the pie dough. To the peaches add the dry ingredients, the melted fat and lemon juice. Fill the crusts. Lattice the remaining dough over the top. Bake in a moderate oven, 350–375 degrees F., until crust and peaches

are done, approximately forty-five minutes to one hour.
Serve hot with whipped cream.

Total Weight: Approximately 16 lb. 14 oz., after baking.
Yield: 60 4½-oz. servings.
Per Serving: Cost——   Selling Price——   Calories——

PINEAPPLE DELIGHT

Ingredients	Amount	Weight	Multiple	Unit Cost	Total Cost
Water	3 qt.				
Sugar		2 lb. 13 oz.			
Cornstarch		7½ oz.			
Lemon juice	½ c.				
Pineapple, grated . . .	2¼ qt.				
Salt	½ tsp.				

Mix the sugar and the cornstarch and add to the boiling
water, stirring constantly. Cook from seven to ten minutes. When clear remove from the fire and add the pineapple, lemon juice and salt. Serve cold with whipped
cream.

Total Weight: 13 lb. 2 oz.
Yield: 50 servings, approximately 4 oz. each.
Per Serving: Cost——   Selling Price——   Calories——

BAKED PRUNE WHIP

Ingredients	Amount	Weight	Multiple	Unit Cost	Total Cost
Prunes, cooked and seeded		3 lb. 6 oz.			
Sugar		2 lb. 13 oz.			
Egg whites	¾ c.				
Lemon juice	6 tbsp.				
Chopped nuts		12 oz.			

Put the prunes into a mixing machine with the sugar and egg whites. Beat until light. This will take approximately ten to fifteen minutes at high speed. Remove from the machine and fold in the lemon juice and one half of the nuts by hand. Put into baking dishes and bake in a 300–350-degree (F.) oven in a pan of water until the egg is cooked, about thirty minutes. Avoid overbaking, which reduces the volume and makes the pudding tough. Serve in sherbet glasses. Garnish with whipped cream and the remaining nuts.

Total Weight: 6 lb. 4 oz., baked.
Yield: 50 servings, approximately 2 oz. each.
Per Serving: Cost____ Selling Price____ Calories____

NORWEGIAN PRUNE PUDDING

INGREDIENTS	AMOUNT	WEIGHT	MULTIPLE	UNIT COST	TOTAL COST
Prunes, after cooking . .		6 lb.			
Cinnamon	1½ tbsp.				
Sugar		2 lb. 2 oz.			
Salt	¾ tsp.				
Cornstarch		10 oz.			
Prune juice or prune juice and water	3 qt.				
Lemon juice	¾ c.				

Seed and chop the cooked prunes. Mix the cinnamon, sugar, salt and cornstarch together and add to the boiling prune juice, stirring rapidly with a wire whip. Cook from seven to ten minutes. Remove from the fire and add the lemon juice and prunes.

Total Weight: 14 lb. 4 oz.
Yield: 48 servings, 4¾ oz. each (approximately ½ c.).
Per Serving: Cost____ Selling Price____ Calories____

OLD-FASHIONED BAKED RICE PUDDING

Ingredients	Amount	Weight	Multiple	Unit Cost	Total Cost
Rice		1 lb. 4 oz.			
Milk	7½ qt.				
Raisins		14 oz.			
Salt	⅔ tsp.				
Sugar		15 oz.			

Wash the rice and add to the scalded milk and bake in a slow oven. As a brown skin forms on the milk, fold under and lift the rice from the bottom gently. This must be done several times during the baking. Avoid stirring, which crushes the rice. When the rice is almost tender add the sugar, raisins and salt and continue cooking until the rice is done.

Total Weight: 14 lb. 1 oz., after baking.
Yield: 50 servings, 4½ oz. each (approximately ½ c.).
Per Serving: Cost____   Selling Price____   Calories____

SCHAUM TORTE

Ingredients	Amount	Weight	Multiple	Unit Cost	Total Cost
Torte:					
Egg whites	3 c.				
Sugar		3 lb. 12 oz.			
White vinegar . . .	¼ c.				
Vanilla	¼ c.				
Filling:					
Cream, before whipping	2 qt.				
Gelatin	1⅓ tbsp.				
Water	⅓ c.				
Strong coffee	¼ c.				
Candied cherries . .		4 oz.			

Beat the egg whites and when light add one half of the sugar gradually and continue beating until very stiff.

Add the vinegar, vanilla and the remainder of the sugar gradually and continue beating until stiff and dry. If a mixing machine is available, beat in all about twelve minutes. If the beating is done by hand a longer time will be necessary.

For the torte, put into paper-lined eight-inch square cake pans, allowing ten ounces of mixture per pan. Bake in a very slow, 250-degree (F.), oven for sixty minutes.

To make the filling, whip the cream. Soften the gelatin in the cold water and dissolve over hot. Add to the whipped cream with the coffee. Put this cream mixture between layers of the torte and on top. Garnish with candied cherries.

Total Weight: 5 lb. 4 oz. torte; 4 lb. 8 oz. filling.
Yield: 48 servings, approximately 3¼ oz. each.
Per Serving: Cost_____ Selling Price_____ Calories_____

SNOW PUDDING

INGREDIENTS	AMOUNT	WEIGHT	MULTIPLE	UNIT COST	TOTAL COST
Gelatin		2 oz.			
Cold water	1⅓ c.				
Boiling water	5⅓ c.				
Sugar		1 lb. 14 oz.			
Lemon juice	1⅓ c.				
Egg whites	1¾ c.				
Grated rind of lemon . .	1 tbsp.				

Soak the gelatin in the cold water. Add the sugar to the boiling water and pour over the softened gelatin, stirring until the gelatin is dissolved. Cool and add the lemon juice. When the gelatin has set to a soft jellylike consistency beat the egg whites stiff and add the gelatin mixture. Continue beating until of an even texture. For best results this should be done on a high-speed kitchen machine. Pour into shallow pans which have been rinsed in cold water and let the mixture set. Cut into squares and serve with a chilled custard sauce.

Total Weight: 6 lb. 4 oz.
Yield: 50 servings, 2 oz. each.
Per Serving: Cost_____   Selling Price_____   Calories_____

SOUR CREAM PUDDING

INGREDIENTS	AMOUNT	WEIGHT	MULTIPLE	UNIT COST	TOTAL COST
DOUGH:					
Fat		7 oz.			
Sugar		8 oz.			
Eggs	2				
Milk	1 qt.				
Flour		2 lb. 4 oz.			
Baking powder, S.A.S.-phosphate type . .	6 tbsp.				
Salt	2 tsp.				
SAUCE:					
Flour		3 oz.			
Brown sugar		5 lb. 7 oz.			
Heavy sour cream . .	2½ qt.				
Sour milk	1¼ qt.				

Cream the fat and the sugar, add the beaten eggs and alternate the milk with the mixed and sifted dry ingredients. Divide the dough into two parts and place in the bottom of two deep steam-table or baking pans, about 9″ × 15″. Mix the brown sugar and the flour together and mix well with the sour cream and milk. Pour over the dough. Bake in a moderate oven about forty-five minutes. As the pudding bakes, the dough will come to the top of the pans, and the caramel sauce will go to the bottom. Serve hot with whipped cream.

Total Weight: 15 lb., after baking.
Yield: 60 servings, 4 oz. each.
Per Serving: Cost_____   Selling Price_____   Calories_____

STEAMED FIG PUDDING

Ingredients	Amount	Weight	Multiple	Unit Cost	Total Cost
Suet		9 oz.			
Molasses	2 c.				
Eggs	4				
Flour		2 lb.			
Soda	4 tsp.				
Cinnamon	2 tsp.				
Cloves	½ tsp.				
Nutmeg	½ tsp.				
Milk	2 c.				
Figs, layer		2 lb.			
Nuts		4 oz.			

Chop or grind the suet and mix with the molasses and the well-beaten eggs. Mix and sift the dry ingredients and add alternately with the milk. Chop the figs and the nuts and add to the mixture. Mix well. Pour into greased pans or brown-bread cans and steam, covered, about three hours or until done. Serve hot with a hard, foamy or vanilla sauce.

Total Weight: 7 lb. 8 oz.
Yield: 45 servings, 2⅔ oz. each.
Per Serving: Cost_____   Selling Price_____   Calories_____

STEAMED MOLASSES PUDDING

Ingredients	Amount	Weight	Multiple	Unit Cost	Total Cost
Eggs	6				
Molasses, medium dark .	1½ qt.				
Salt	2 tsp.				
Boiling water	1 qt.				
Flour		2 lb. 9 oz.			
Soda	2 tbsp.				

Beat the eggs and mix with the molasses, salt and water. Add the flour and soda and mix. This makes a very thin batter. Pour into well-greased pans, cover and steam from one to one and one half hours. Serve with a foamy sauce. If the molasses is very dark and strong use one half molasses and one half corn syrup. This may be steamed in brown-bread tins, allowing one pound of batter for each tin. It may also be steamed in individual molds.

Total Weight: 9 lb. 3 oz.
Yield: 50 servings, approximately 3 oz. each.
Per Serving: Cost_____ Selling Price_____ Calories_____

BAKING POWDER BISCUIT SHORTCAKES

INGREDIENTS	AMOUNT	WEIGHT	MULTIPLE	UNIT COST	TOTAL COST
Flour		3 lb.			
Baking powder, S.A.S.- phosphate type . . .	5⅓ tbsp.				
Salt	3 tsp.				
Sugar	2⅔ tbsp.				
Shortening		1 lb. 2 oz.			
Milk	2⅔–4 c.				
Melted butter		2⅔ oz.			

Mix and sift the dry ingredients. Rub in the shortening lightly with the tips of the fingers. Add the milk gradually, mixing to a soft dough lightly with a wire spoon. The amount of milk may vary due to differences in the flour. Put one half of the dough on a board at a time, knead lightly for a few seconds and roll out to about one-fourth-inch thickness. Cut out, using a cutter two and five eighths inches in diameter. Brush half of the biscuits with melted butter and place the unbrushed biscuit on top. Bake in a hot oven, 425 degrees F. Break open and serve with fruit between the halves and on the top.

Total Weight: 6 lb. 4 oz.
Yield: 50 shortcakes, 2 oz. each.
Per Serving: Cost_____ Selling Price_____ Calories_____

PRUNECOT SHORTCAKE

Ingredients	Amount	Weight	Multiple	Unit Cost	Total Cost
Prunes, cooked		3 lb.			
Dried apricots, cooked .		3 lb.			
Prune and apricot juice .	2 c.				
Sugar		2 lb. 13 oz.			
Lemon juice	9 tbsp.				
Shortcakes (see page 261)	50				

Seed the cooked prunes and mix with the cooked apricots. Chop slightly. Add the sugar to the prune and apricot juice and bring to a boil to dissolve the sugar. Pour over the apricots and prunes. Add the lemon juice. Bake the shortcakes. Split and fill with the prunecot filling. Serve with whipped cream.

Total Weight: 9 lb. 6 oz. of filling.
Yield: 50 servings, 3 oz. filling each (approximately ⅓ c.); one 2-oz. shortcake biscuit.
Per Serving: Cost___   Selling Price___   Calories___

STRAWBERRY SHORTCAKE

Ingredients	Amount	Weight	Multiple	Unit Cost	Total Cost
Strawberries	9 qt.				
Sugar		1½–2 lb.			
Shortcake biscuits (see page 261)	50				

Hull the strawberries and wash them in a colander. Crush slightly or cut in quarters, add the smaller amount of sugar and taste for sweetness. Let stand half an hour or until the sugar has dissolved. Serve between halves of the shortcake biscuit and cover with whipped cream. A mixture of creamed brown sugar and butter spread over the biscuit before adding the strawberries gives a good flavor and is a pleasing variation. Serve with whipped cream.

Since strawberries are now being quick frozen at the period when they are ripest and best flavored, it may prove more satisfactory to substitute them for the fresh berries, except in the height of the season.

Yield: 50 servings, 4 oz. filling each (approximately ½ c.) ; one 2-oz. shortcake biscuit.
Per Serving: Cost____   Selling Price____   Calories____

FIG AND NUT TAPIOCA

Ingredients	Amount	Weight	Multiple	Unit Cost	Total Cost
Pearl tapioca		1 lb. 4 oz.			
Water, boiling	4 qt.				
Brown sugar		2 lb. 15 oz.			
Layer figs		2 lb.			
Salt	1⅓ tsp.				
Vanilla	¼ c.				
Nut meats, chopped . .		8 oz.			
Mapeline	2 tsp.				

Soak the tapioca in cold water overnight. Drain and add to the rapidly boiling water and cook until clear. Remove from the fire and add the sugar, chopped figs, nuts, vanilla, mapeline and salt. Serve cold with whipped cream.

Total Weight: 14 lb. 1 oz.
Yield: 50 servings, 4½ oz. each (approximately ½ c.).
Per Serving: Cost____   Selling Price____   Calories____

TAPIOCA CREAM WITH QUICK-COOKING TAPIOCA

Ingredients	Amount	Weight	Multiple	Unit Cost	Total Cost
Quick-cooking tapioca .		5 oz.			
Milk	1 gal.				
Eggs	10				
Sugar		15 oz.			
Salt	½ tsp.				
Vanilla	1 tbsp.				

Scald the milk, add the tapioca and cook until the tapioca is clear. Beat the eggs and the sugar. Add to the tapioca slowly, stirring with a wire spoon, and cook for a few minutes until thickened and creamy in consistency. Remove from the fire and add the salt and vanilla.

Total Weight: 10 lb.
Yield: 40 servings, 4 oz. each (approximately ½ c.).
Per Serving: Cost_____   Selling Price_____   Calories_____

TAPIOCA CREAM (WITH PEARL TAPIOCA)

Ingredients	Amount	Weight	Multiple	Unit Cost	Total Cost
Pearl tapioca		11 oz.			
Milk	1 gal.				
Eggs	10				
Sugar		15 oz.			
Salt	½ tsp.				
Vanilla	1 tbsp.				

Soak the tapioca overnight. Drain and cook in the scalded milk until clear. Beat the eggs and the sugar and add to the tapioca mixture slowly, stirring with a wire spoon. Cook for a few minutes until thick and creamy. Remove from the fire and add the salt and vanilla.

Total Weight: 10 lb.
Yield: 40 servings, 4 oz. each (approximately ½ c.).
Per Serving: Cost_____   Selling Price_____   Calories_____

DRIED APRICOT SAUCE

Ingredients	Amount	Weight	Multiple	Unit Cost	Total Cost
Apricots, dried		3 lb.			
Water	6 qt.				
Sugar		1 lb. 7 oz.			

Wash the apricots. Cover with the cold water and soak thirty-six to forty-eight hours. Do not drain. Cook slowly until tender. Do not stir. Add the sugar and cook only until the sugar is dissolved. Pour into a shallow pan, from which they may be dished without breaking.

The old-fashioned method of soaking dried fruit "overnight" does not give comparable results with the longer period given above. The longer soaking for both prunes and apricots gives a more tender, plumper, fresher appearing fruit.

Total Weight: 15 lb.
Yield: 60 servings, 4 oz. each (approximately ½ c.).
Per Serving: Cost_____ Selling Price_____ Calories_____

CRANBERRY JELLY

Ingredients	Amount	Weight	Multiple	Unit Cost	Total Cost
Cranberries		2 lb.			
Water	3½ c.				
Sugar		2 lb. 4 oz.			

Wash and drain the cranberries. Add the water and bring to the boiling point. When the cranberries are tender run through a purée sieve or china cap. Add the sugar, bring to a boil and pour into wet pans or individual molds to set.

Total Weight: 5 lb. 1 oz.
Yield: 54 servings, 1½ oz. each or 3 tbsp.
Per Serving: Cost_____ Selling Price_____ Calories_____

STRAINED CRANBERRY SAUCE

Ingredients	Amount	Weight	Multiple	Unit Cost	Total Cost
Cranberries		4 lb. 12 oz.			
Water	2½ qt.				
Sugar		3 lb. 2 oz.			

Look over and wash the cranberries. Add the water and cook until the berries are soft. Rub through a sieve. Add the sugar and bring to the boiling point. Chill thoroughly before serving.

Total Weight: Approximately 10 lb.
Yield: 40 servings, 4 oz. each.
Per Serving: Cost_____ Selling Price_____ Calories_____

UNSTRAINED CRANBERRY SAUCE

Ingredients	Amount	Weight	Multiple	Unit Cost	Total Cost
Cranberries		3 lb. 12 oz.			
Sugar		3 lb. 12 oz.			
Water	2 qt.				

Look over and wash the cranberries. Add the water and cook until the berries are soft. Add the sugar and bring to a boil. Chill thoroughly before serving.

Total Weight: Approximately 10 lb. 8 oz.
Yield: 42 servings, 4 oz. each.
Per Serving: Cost_____ Selling Price_____ Calories_____

DRIED PRUNE SAUCE

Ingredients	Amount	Weight	Multiple	Unit Cost	Total Cost
Prunes, 40–50 size . . .		4 lb.			
Water	4 qt.				
Sugar		1 lb. 12 oz.			

Wash the prunes. Cover with cold water and soak thirty-six to forty-eight hours. Cook slowly until tender. Add the sugar and cook until the sugar has dissolved. Soaking only overnight does not plump the prunes sufficiently. They are markedly improved in flavor, texture and appearance by a two-day soaking period.

Total Weight: 12 lb. 15 oz.
Yield: 46 servings, 4½ oz. each (4 prunes and 2 tbsp. of juice).
Per Serving: Cost_____ Selling Price_____ Calories_____

CHOCOLATE SAUCE FOR PUDDINGS

INGREDIENTS	AMOUNT	WEIGHT	MULTIPLE	UNIT COST	TOTAL COST
Sugar		1 lb. 14 oz.			
Cocoa		5 oz.			
Cornstarch		2 oz.			
Salt	1 tsp.				
Water	2 qt.				
Fat		12 oz.			
Vanilla	1 tbsp.				

Mix the dry ingredients. Add to the boiling water, stirring constantly. Cook until thickened, about five to seven minutes. Add the fat and the vanilla.

Total Weight: 6 lb. 12 oz.
Yield: 48 servings, 2¼ oz. each (approximately ¼ c.).
Per Serving: Cost_____ Selling Price_____ Calories_____

CUSTARD SAUCE

INGREDIENTS	AMOUNT	WEIGHT	MULTIPLE	UNIT COST	TOTAL COST
Cornstarch	3 tbsp.				
Sugar		10 oz.			
Milk	2½ qt.				
Egg yolks	⅔ c.				
Salt	⅓ tsp.				
Vanilla	1⅓ tbsp.				

Mix the cornstarch and the sugar and add to the scalded milk. Cook seven to ten minutes. Add the thoroughly beaten egg yolks, which have been blended with some of the thickened mixture, and cook for a few minutes. Remove from the fire and add the salt and vanilla.

Total Weight: 5 lb. 3 oz.

Yield: 50 servings, 1⅔ oz. each (approximately ¼ c.).

Per Serving: Cost_____ Selling Price_____ Calories_____

HARD SAUCE

Ingredients	Amount	Weight	Multiple	Unit Cost	Total Cost
Butter		1 lb.			
Powdered sugar. . . .		2 lb. 6 oz.			
Vanilla.	9 tbsp.				

Cream the butter and add the sugar and the vanilla gradually. Put the mixture into the refrigerator to harden. If desired, sprinkle with nutmeg before serving.

Uniform-sized servings may be obtained by spreading the mixture evenly on shallow pans about one-third-inch thick, sprinkling with nutmeg and hardening in the ice box. Cut in squares (54) to serve.

Total Weight: 3 lb. 6 oz.

Yield: 54 servings, 1 oz. each (approximately 2⅓ tbsp.).

Per Serving: Cost_____ Selling Price_____ Calories_____

LEMON SAUCE

Ingredients	Amount	Weight	Multiple	Unit Cost	Total Cost
Sugar		2 lb. 5 oz.			
Cornstarch		4 oz.			
Salt	1 tsp.				
Water	2 qt.				
Lemon juice	⅞ c.				
Grated rind of lemon . .	1 tbsp.				
Egg yolks	⅓ c.				
Fat		7 oz.			

Mix the sugar, cornstarch and salt thoroughly and add to the boiling water, stirring with a wire whip.   Cook until thickened.   Add the lemon juice, grated rind and egg yolks beaten together and remove from the fire.   Add the fat and serve hot.

Total Weight: 6 lb.
Yield: 48 servings, 2 oz. each (approximately ¼ c.).
Per Serving: Cost____   Selling Price____   Calories____

VANILLA SAUCE

Ingredients	Amount	Weight	Multiple	Unit Cost	Total Cost
Salt	1 tsp.				
Cornstarch		3 oz.			
Sugar		2 lb. 6 oz.			
Water	2 qt.				
Egg yolks	¼ c.				
Fat		12 oz.			
Vanilla	⅛ c.				

Mix the salt, cornstarch, and one half of the sugar thoroughly and add to the boiling water, stirring rapidly. Cook seven to ten minutes.   Beat the egg yolks and mix with the remaining sugar.   Add to the above mixture slowly, stirring constantly.   Remove from the fire and add the fat and the vanilla.

Total Weight: 6 lb.
Yield: 48 servings, 2 oz. each (approximately ¼ c.).
Per Serving: Cost____   Selling Price____   Calories____

CHAPTER XIII

Butter Cakes: Aims and Methods

In Cake Making It Is Important to Establish a Standard.
The aim in making butter cakes should be to produce a
fine-textured, soft, velvety cake with good lift, superior
flavor and good keeping quality.

There Are Four Essentials to Good Cake Making: 1. A
properly balanced formula. 2. Correct temperature of
ingredients. 3. Proper mixing of ingredients, especially
the combining of fat and sugar. 4. Attention to correct
oven temperature and baking time.

Cake Formulas Must Be "Balanced." A properly balanced formula which will produce a cake that is tender, moist and of superior keeping quality provides for approximately 50 per cent. as much fat as flour by weight.
Using flour as 100 per cent., the sugar may range from
120–140 per cent., the milk may equal or slightly exceed
the weight of the flour and the eggs may be 50–55 per cent.
of the flour by weight. The leavening will be determined
by whether it is a combination of soda and baking powder
or baking powder alone. In the latter case it may be
about 4–5 per cent. of the flour, if an S.A.S.-phosphate-
type baking powder is used. In figuring on soda, allow
one half teaspoon per cup of sour milk. An excess is
usually used to produce a red chocolate cake, since a
strongly alkaline reaction seems to be necessary to produce
this color.

The Temperature of Ingredients Is Important. The ingredients should be of a uniform temperature around
seventy to seventy-five degrees F. That means that eggs,

milk and the fat should not be used at once on coming out of the refrigerator. On the other hand, in hot weather they should not be left out to get overheated. Warm, oily fat will not cream satisfactorily, will not incorporate air and build up a smooth creamy mass and will produce a coarse-textured cake.

The Creaming Process Is of Prime Importance in Cake Making. Unless the creaming process is adequate and the fat evenly distributed over the sugar granules, and air thus enclosed, a good quality cake is not obtained. Creaming by power machine should be done on low speed for fifteen to twenty minutes. Shorter creaming periods, while they may produce satisfactory cakes, do not produce cakes of such good keeping quality. If the eggs are to be added directly to the fat and sugar, they may be added during the last half of the creaming time and the speed may be increased for the remainder of the period. Some flour should be added and thoroughly creamed before the addition of the liquid and the remaining dry ingredients.

There Are Two Satisfactory Methods of Combining Ingredients. In the experience of the authors, equally good cakes may be made by either of these methods. The method most often followed in making butter cakes is to cream the fat and sugar thoroughly, alternate the dry and liquid ingredients and fold in the beaten egg whites last. This produces a cake of fine texture and good lift with better than average keeping qualities. The dough may be held from day to day if it is kept covered in the cooler. The average mixing time by this method is twenty-five minutes to one half hour.

A second method of mixing involves creaming the fat and sugar eight to ten minutes and adding unbeaten whites and beating on second speed for another eight to ten minutes. The mixed and sifted dry ingredients and liquid are added alternately to finish. This method produces a satisfactory dough of good keeping quality and a fine-grained cake with good lift and excellent flavor.

An Excellent Dough May Be Spoiled by an Incorrect Oven Temperature. If the oven temperature is too low, a coarse, harsh-textured, quick-staling cake is produced. The shape of the layer will be level on top or slightly depressed in the center. If too high a temperature is used, the texture may be good but the cake compact, crusty, the edges hard and the center too high. A proper temperature, around 380–400 degrees F., will produce from a good dough a cake of fine texture, good volume, velvety crumb and appealing flavor. Overbaking should be avoided. Most cakes require from twenty-five to thirty minutes in the oven, at which time they spring back when touched lightly. Beyond that time the cake shrinks and dries and the texture is impaired accordingly.

There Appears to Be a Relationship between the Amount of Dough and the Size of the Pan. If too little dough is used in too large a pan the same lift is not produced as when it is scaled so that the dough just fills the tin when baked.

Paper Liners for Cake Pans Save Time and Give More Lift. These commercial cake liners peel off readily, prevent the use of too much grease and flour in preparing cake tins, and provide a side wall to which the dough may adhere when coming up in the oven. The liners are an economy, since there is a tendency for employees to feel that if a little grease in the pans is good, a lot is better, with consequent waste and poor quality of cake.

Cakes Should Be Left in the Pans Until Cool. This will require about twenty minutes. This allows them time to set and become firm so they will not lose shape when iced.

In Icing a Number of Cakes a System Should Be Established to Promote Speed. Icings, such as butter icings kept in the refrigerator, should have been removed from the ice-box and allowed to reach room temperature to facilitate spreading without tearing a delicate cake.   Fillings, nuts, cocoanut, coloring or decorating equipment should be at hand.   All cakes of one kind should be finished at once and the various steps in the frosting process carried through at one time.   For instance, the cakes should all be taken from the pans; filling weighed onto all bottom layers; second layers placed on top (if they are to be two-layer cakes); a given weight of frosting put on top of each; and, working quickly, the frosting spread over the tops and sides.   They may then be decorated if and as desired.   This general procedure may vary with different kinds of cake, but some such system is necessary.   It is wasteful of labor to complete one cake at a time.   Cakes may be placed on a cardboard and then on a revolving cake icer for frosting, or they may be placed on the inverted cake tin in which they were baked and that tin simply turned on the hand during the frosting.   Broad-bladed knives, spoons or spatulas may be used, depending on which the worker finds easiest or with which the best technique and results are obtained.

ANGEL FOOD

Ingredients	Amount	Weight	Multiple	Unit Cost	Total Cost
Egg whites		5 lb. 10 oz.			
Salt	1 tsp.				
Cream of tartar. . . .	3 tbsp.				
Sugar		6 lb. 6 oz.			
Vanilla.	5 tbsp.				
Flour		2 lb.			

Bring the egg whites to about 70 degrees F.   Beat on second speed on a mixing machine until frothy.   Add the salt, cream of tartar and four pounds six ounces of sugar, which has been sifted.   Continue beating until a soft wet peak is formed.   Add the vanilla and change to first speed.

Add the remaining two pounds of sugar and the flour, which have been sifted together three or four times immediately before using. Remove from the machine and continue mixing by hand, removing any sugar and flour lumps in the dough. Handle as little as possible to mix. Scale into standard-size angel-food cake pans, allowing one pound twelve ounces per cake.

Bake the cakes fifteen to twenty minutes at 300–325 degrees F. Gradually raise the temperature to 340 degrees F. and bake twenty-five to thirty minutes longer, or a total of forty-five to fifty minutes in all. The cake should spring back when the top is pressed gently with the finger. When the cake comes out of the oven, invert the pan until the cake is cool.

Angel-food cakes keep fresh longer if left in the cake pans until they are used.

To be standard, an angel food should be of good volume; generous in appearance; the texture should be fine and even in grain; the cake moist, not dry and "feathery"; it should have a pleasing flavor. There is a popular tendency to regard an angel food possessing the first requirement as satisfactory, when actually all of the above requirements must be met if the cake is to be of high standard.

Angel food tins should be carefully washed and never have any grease on them. Unless clean, the cake fails to adhere to the pan and when taken from the oven shrinks before it cools.

Total Weight: 14 lb.
Yield: 8 cakes weighing 1 lb. 12 oz. before baking.
Per Serving: Cost_____   Selling Price_____   Calories_____

APPLE-SAUCE CAKE

Ingredients	Amount	Weight	Multiple	Unit Cost	Total Cost
Sugar		1 lb. 14 oz.			
Fat		1 lb.			
Apple sauce	1½ qt.				
Flour, pastry		2 lb.			
Nutmeg	1 tsp.				
Cinnamon	2 tsp.				
Cloves	2 tsp.				
Salt	2 tsp.				
Soda	4 tsp.				
Raisins		1 lb. 9 oz.			

Cream the fat and the sugar. Add the apple sauce, then the dry ingredients and the raisins. Bake about one hour in a slow 325-degree F. oven in loaf or sheet pans. A popular frosting with this cake is white boiled icing over which melted chocolate is poured. This cake is excellent when baked as needed and served hot, right from the oven.

Total Weight: 9 lb. 12 oz.
Yield: 48 servings; 6 pans, 8″ × 8″, with 1 lb. 10 oz. per pan.
Per Serving: Cost____ Selling Price____ Calories____

CARAMEL CAKE

Ingredients	Amount	Weight	Multiple	Unit Cost	Total Cost
Shortening		1 lb. 13 oz.			
Sugar		6 lb.			
Water	2 c.				
Milk	1¾ qt.				
Pastry flour		4 lb. 12 oz.			
Salt	2 tbsp.				
Baking powder, S.A.S.-phosphate type . . .		3¾ oz.			
Egg whites, unbeaten . .		2 lb. 6 oz.			

Caramelize two cups of the sugar to a fairly dark brown color. Add the two cups of water and cook until the caramelized sugar is dissolved. Cool. The remaining ingredients should be of average room temperature, approximately 70–75 degrees F. Cream the fat and the remaining sugar fifteen minutes on low speed. Scrape the bowl and beater three or four times during the creaming process to prevent any unmixed fat or sugar adhering to the bowl.

Add one pound of flour and the mixed and sifted dry ingredients and beat two or three minutes. Add the milk, the caramelized sugar syrup and the remaining dry ingredients alternately and quickly, being careful to keep the dough smooth and of an even consistency. Scrape down the bowl and beater with the hands or a spatula two or three times during this process. Add the unbeaten whites and beat two minutes on second speed. Scrape down the bowl and beater and remove from the machine. Scale into paper-lined cake tins, allowing one pound of dough for eight-inch square tins. Bake in a moderately hot oven about 375 degrees F. for twenty-five to thirty minutes.

While cakes baked immediately have greater lift, if the dough is put into the cooler immediately it will hold to give very satisfactory results with little loss of leavening, provided an S.A.S.-phosphate type of baking powder is used.

Total Weight: Approximately 19 lb. 3 oz.
Yield: Approximately 19 8-inch square layers (1 lb. each).
Per Serving: Cost_____ Selling Price_____ Calories_____

CHOCOLATE CAKE

Ingredients	Amount	Weight	Multiple	Unit Cost	Total Cost
Fat		1 lb. 14 oz.			
Sugar		6 lb. 8 oz.			
Egg yolks	1¾ c.				
Chocolate		1 lb. 2 oz.			
Flour, pastry		4 lb. 4 oz.			
Salt	1 tbsp.				
Buttermilk	1¼ qt.				
Soda	4 tbsp.				
Water	1 qt.				
Egg whites	2⅔ c.				
Vanilla	¼ c.				

Place the fat and the sugar in the bowl of a mixing machine and cream twenty minutes on first speed. Scrape down the bowl and the paddle three to four times during this creaming period with hands or spatula.

Add the egg yolks and melted chocolate and scrape down the bowl and paddle.

Add one half of the sifted flour and dry ingredients and the buttermilk alternately to the creamed mixture. Mix and scrape down the bowl and beater. Add the remainder of the dry ingredients with enough of the water, to which the soda has been added, to keep the batter of an even consistency. Scrape down the sides of the bowl and the beater. Add the remainder of the water and soda gradually.

Add the unbeaten egg whites and beat two minutes on second speed.

Weigh into 8″ × 8″ cake pans, allowing one pound of dough per pan.

Bake twenty-five to thirty minutes in a 375–380-degree (F.) oven.

Total Weight: Approximately 20 lb. dough.
Yield: 20 single layers, 8″ × 8″, one pound each.
Per Serving: Cost____ Selling Price____ Calories____

FRUIT CAKE

Ingredients	Amount	Weight	Multiple	Unit Cost	Total Cost
Chopped pineapple, candied		2 lb.			
Chopped cherries, candied		2 lb.			
Chopped citron		8 oz.			
Raisins, white		4 lb.			
Fruit juice	¼ c.				
Lemon juice	¼ c.				
Coffee	1 c.				
Fat		1 lb.			
Sugar, brown		1 lb.			
Eggs, yolks	1 c.				
whites	1½ c.				
Flour, pastry		1 lb. 4 oz.			
Soda	1 tsp.				
Baking powder	1 tsp.				
Cinnamon	2 tsp.				
Cloves, ground	1 tsp.				
Nutmeg, grated . . .	2 tsp.				
Salt	¼ tsp.				
Chopped pecans . . .		1 lb.			
Chopped almonds . . .		1 lb. 8 oz.			

Soak the fruit in the fruit juice, lemon juice and coffee three hours. Do not drain. Cream the fat and sugar until light. Beat the eggs until light and add to the creamed mass alternately with the sifted flour, soda, baking powder and spices. Lastly, add the fruit and nuts and mix only enough to distribute the fruit evenly through the batter. Weigh into paper-lined pans and bake in a slow 325-degree (F.) oven for one and one fourth to one and one half hours. If a large three- to five-pound cake is being baked, a longer time in the oven will be necessary. During the last half hour of cooking the cakes should be covered. A damp cloth or greased paper may be used. Care should be taken not to tear the top of the cake when removing it.

Fruit cakes produced for sale commercially must present

the maximum of eye appeal. This is achieved through decoration, through variety in size and shape and through attractive containers. In decorating fruit cakes blanched almonds, whole cherries, glacéed fruits, citron or angelica may be used. They should be put on in a design.

Total Weight: 16 lb.
Yield: 15 loaves, 1 lb. 1 oz. per loaf, before baking.
Per Serving: Cost_____   Selling Price_____   Calories_____

JAM CAKE

INGREDIENTS	AMOUNT	WEIGHT	MULTIPLE	UNIT COST	TOTAL COST
Fat		1 lb. 13 oz.			
Brown sugar		3 lb. 8 oz.			
Jam	1½ qt.				
Eggs	18				
Flour, pastry		4 lb. 12 oz.			
Cinnamon	3½ tbsp.				
Nutmeg	3 tbsp.				
Cloves	4 tsp.				
Soda	2 tbsp.				
Salt	2 tbsp.				
Baking powder, S.A.S.-phosphate type . . .	2 tbsp.				
Molasses	1 c.				
Milk	1½ qt.				

Cream the fat and the sugar for fifteen minutes on first speed. Scrape down the bowl and beater three or four times during the creaming period. Add the egg yolks and the jam. Add one pound of the sifted flour and dry ingredients. Beat two to three minutes. Scrape down the bowl and beater with the hands or a spatula. Add the remaining dry ingredients alternately with milk and molasses, keeping dough uniform in consistency. Scrape down the bowl and beater. Add the unbeaten egg whites and beat for two minutes at second speed. Scale into paper-lined pans, allowing one pound of dough to an 8″ × 8″ pan. Bake twenty-five to thirty minutes in a 375-degree (F.) oven.

Total Weight: 20 lb.
Yield: 16 8-inch square layers, 1 lb. 4 oz. per layer.
Per Serving: Cost_____   Selling Price_____   Calories_____

MAPLE NUT CAKE

Ingredients	Amount	Weight	Multiple	Unit Cost	Total Cost
Fat		1 lb. 13 oz.			
Sugar		6 lb.			
Mapeline	5 tsp.				
Pastry flour		4 lb. 12 oz.			
Salt	2 tbsp.				
Baking powder, S.A.S.-phosphate type . . .		3¾ oz.			
Milk	2¼ qt.				
Egg whites, unbeaten . .		2 lb. 6 oz.			
Nut meats		1 lb. 4 oz.			

The ingredients should be of average room temperature, approximately 70–75 degrees F. Cream the fat and sugar fifteen minutes on low speed. Scrape the bowl and beater three or four times during the creaming process to prevent any unmixed fat or sugar adhering to the bowl. Add the mapeline.

Add one pound of flour and the mixed and sifted dry ingredients and beat two or three minutes. Add the milk and the remaining dry ingredients alternately and quickly, being careful to keep the dough smooth and of an even consistency. Scrape down the bowl and beater with the hands or a spatula two or three times during this process. Add the unbeaten whites and beat two minutes on second speed. Scrape down the bowl and beater and remove from the machine. Fold in the nuts. Scale into paper-lined cake tins, allowing one pound of dough for eight-inch square tins. Bake in a moderately hot oven about 375–380 degrees F. for twenty-five to thirty minutes.

While cakes baked at once have greater lift, if the dough is put into the cooler immediately it will hold to give very satisfactory results with little loss of leavening, provided an S.A.S.-phosphate type of baking powder is used.

Total Weight: 20 lb. 12 oz.
Yield: Approximately 20 single layers, 1 lb. each.
Per Serving: Cost_____ Selling Price_____ Calories_____

MOCHA NUT CAKE

INGREDIENTS	AMOUNT	WEIGHT	MULTIPLE	UNIT COST	TOTAL COST
Fat		1 lb. 13 oz.			
Sugar		6 lb.			
Vanilla.	¼ c.				
Flour, pastry		4 lb. 12 oz.			
Baking powder, S.A.S.-phosphate type . . .		3¾ oz.			
Salt	2 tbsp.				
Milk	1 qt.				
Coffee, strong	1¼ qt.				
Egg whites	4½ c.				
Nuts, pecans.		10 oz.			

Cream the fat and the sugar for fifteen minutes on first speed of a mixing machine. Scrape down the bowl and beater three or four times during the creaming period. Add the vanilla.

Add one pound of flour and the mixed and sifted dry ingredients and beat two or three minutes. Add the milk and coffee and the remaining dry ingredients alternately and quickly, being careful to keep the dough smooth and of an even consistency. Scrape down the bowl and beater with the hands or a spatula two or three times during this process. Add the unbeaten whites and beat two minutes on second speed. Add the nut meats. Scrape down the bowl and beater and remove from the machine. Scale into paper-lined cake tins, allowing one pound of dough for eight-inch square tins. Bake in a moderately hot oven about 375 degrees F. for twenty-five to thirty minutes.

While cakes baked immediately have greater lift, if the dough is put into the cooler immediately it will hold to give very satisfactory results with little loss of leavening, provided an S.A.S.-phosphate type of baking powder is used.

Total Weight: 20 lb.
Yield: 20 layers, 8 inches square (1 lb. dough per layer).
Per Serving: Cost_____   Selling Price_____   Calories_____

ORANGE AND RAISIN CUP CAKES

Ingredients	Amount	Weight	Multiple	Unit Cost	Total Cost
Fat		14 oz.			
Sugar		3 lb.			
Egg yolks	$\frac{7}{8}$ c.				
Flour, pastry		2 lb. 6 oz.			
Baking powder, S.A.S.- phosphate type . . .	4 tbsp.				
Salt	1 tbsp.				
Whole oranges		2 lb. 4 oz.			
Liquid:					
Orange juice and milk .	1 qt.				
Raisins		1 lb.			
Egg whites	$1\frac{1}{2}$ c.				

Cream the fat and sugar fifteen minutes on low speed. Scrape the bowl and beater three or four times during the creaming process to prevent any mixed fat and sugar adhering to the bowl. Add the egg yolks and continue beating two or three minutes. Add twelve ounces of the flour and beat two minutes more.

Wash, halve and remove the seeds from the oranges. Squeeze out the juice and chop the rind fine. Measure the juice and add milk sufficient to make one quart of liquid. Alternate, adding the remaining mixed and sifted dry ingredients with the one quart of liquid, being careful to keep the dough smooth and of an even consistency. Scrape down the bowl and beater with a spatula or hands. Add the raisins and chopped oranges and scrape down the bowl. Add the unbeaten egg whites and beat two minutes on second speed.

Use a number-sixteen or a number-forty scoop and fill lined or greased cup-cake pans. Bake in a 350–360-degree (F.) oven twenty-five to thirty minutes. The size scoop depends on whether small or large cup cakes are desired.

Total Weight: 11 lb. 7 oz.
Yield: 88 cup cakes, No. 16 scoop (approximately 2 oz. each);
220 cup cakes, No. 40 scoop (approximately ¾–1 oz. each).
Per Serving: Cost____   Selling Price____   Calories____

PLAIN CAKE

INGREDIENTS	AMOUNT	WEIGHT	MULTIPLE	UNIT COST	TOTAL COST
Sugar		2 lb. 5 oz.			
Fat		12 oz.			
Eggs	7				
Vanilla	1 tbsp.				
Salt	1½ tsp.				
Baking powder, S.A.S.-phosphate type . . .	4 tbsp.				
Flour, pastry		2 lb. 8 oz.			
Milk	5 c.				

Cream the fat and the sugar in a mixer on low speed for about fifteen minutes. Scrape down the sides of the bowl and paddle with the hand or a spatula two to three times

during this period. Add the egg yolks and vanilla. Mix
and sift the dry ingredients and add alternately with the
milk. Keep the paddle and sides of the bowl free of
unmixed dough by scraping down with hands or spatula.
Fold in the well-beaten whites quickly. Using fourteen
and one half ounces per pan, fill cake tins and bake in a
375-degree (F.) oven twenty to twenty-five minutes. This
is a good inexpensive cake to use when cake is to be eaten
fresh.

Total Weight: 9 lb. 1 oz. dough.
Yield: 10 8-inch round pans.
Per Serving: Cost_____ Selling Price_____ Calories_____

SPICE CAKE

Ingredients	Amount	Weight	Multiple	Unit Cost	Total Cost
Fat		1 lb. 13 oz.			
Sugar		5 lb. 8 oz.			
Molasses	2½ c.				
Vanilla.	2 tbsp.				
Milk	2¼ qt.				
Pastry flour		4 lb. 12 oz.			
Salt	2 tbsp.				
Baking powder, S.A.S.- phosphate type . . .		3¾ oz.			
Cinnamon	5 tbsp.				
Nutmeg	2½ tbsp.				
Allspice	1½ tbsp.				
Cloves	⅛ tsp.				
Raisins		1 lb. 10 oz.			
Egg whites		2 lb. 6 oz.			

The ingredients should be of average room temperature,
approximately 70–75 degrees F. Cream the fat and sugar
fifteen minutes on low speed. Scrape the bowl and beater
three or four times during the creaming process to prevent
any unmixed fat or sugar adhering to the bowl. Add the
molasses and vanilla.

Add one pound of flour and the mixed and sifted dry ingredients and beat two or three minutes. Add the milk and the remaining dry ingredients alternately and quickly, being careful to keep the dough smooth and of an even consistency. Reserve a small amount of the flour to mix with the raisins. Scrape down the bowl and beater with the hands or a spatula two or three times during this process. Add the unbeaten whites and beat two minutes on second speed. Add the floured raisins. Scrape down the bowl and beater and remove from the machine. Scale into paper-lined cake tins, allowing one pound of dough for eight-inch square tins. Bake in a moderately hot oven, about 375 degrees F., for twenty-five to thirty minutes.

While cakes baked immediately have greater lift, if the dough is put into the cooler immediately it will hold to give very satisfactory results with little loss of leavening, provided an S.A.S.-phosphate type of baking powder is used.

Total Weight: 22 lb. 12 oz.
Yield: Approximately 22 single layer cakes, scaling 1 lb. each.
Per Serving: Cost____ Selling Price____ Calories____

WASHINGTON PIE

Ingredients	Amount	Weight	Multiple	Unit Cost	Total Cost
Plain cake	10 layers				
(See page 283)					
Filling:					
Sugar		2 lb. 5 oz.			
Cocoa		6 oz.			
Flour		6¾ oz.			
Salt	½ tbsp.				
Water	2 qt.				
Egg yolks	1 c.				
Fat		6 oz.			
Vanilla	2 tbsp.				

Split the round plain-cake layers in half and spread with one and one fourth cups filling. Sift powdered sugar over the top. Cut in pie-shaped wedges to serve. For the filling, mix the sugar, cocoa, flour and salt together and sift into the boiling water, stirring constantly. Cook seven to ten minutes. When thick add the well-beaten yolks and cook a few minutes. Add the fat and the vanilla.

Total Weight: 6 lb. 14 oz. filling.
Yield: 10 pies cutting 6–7 servings each; 11 oz. filling or 1¼ c. filling per pie.
Per Serving: Cost_____   Selling Price_____   Calories_____

WHITE CAKE

INGREDIENTS	AMOUNT	WEIGHT	MULTIPLE	UNIT COST	TOTAL COST
Shortening		15 oz.			
Butter		14 oz.			
Sugar		6 lb.			
Vanilla		2 oz.			
Pastry flour		4 lb. 12 oz.			
Salt	2 tbsp.				
Baking powder, S.A.S.-phosphate type . . .		3¾ oz.			
Milk	2¼ qt.				
Egg whites, unbeaten . .		2 lb. 6 oz.			

The ingredients should be of average room temperature, approximately 70–75 degrees F. Cream the fat and sugar twenty minutes on low speed. Scrape the bowl and beater three or four times during the creaming process to prevent any unmixed fat or sugar adhering to the bowl. Add the vanilla.

Add one pound of flour and the mixed and sifted dry ingredients and beat two or three minutes. Add the milk and the remaining dry ingredients alternately and quickly, being careful to keep the dough smooth and of an even consistency. Scrape down the bowl and beater with the hands or a spatula two or three times during this process. Add the unbeaten whites and beat two minutes on second speed. Scrape down the bowl and beater and remove from the machine. Scale into paper-lined cake tins, allowing one pound of dough for 8-inch square tins. Bake in a moderately hot oven, about 375–380 degrees F., for twenty-five to thirty minutes.

While cakes baked immediately have greater lift, if the dough is put into the cooler immediately it will hold to give very satisfactory results with little loss of leavening, provided an S.A.S.-phosphate type of baking powder is used.

Total Weight: 19 lb. 12 oz.
Yield: Approximately 19 8″ × 8″ single layers, 1 lb. dough per pan.
Per Serving: Cost____   Selling Price____   Calories____

BOILED ICING

Ingredients	Amount	Weight	Multiple	Unit Cost	Total Cost
Cornstarch		2 oz.			
Granulated sugar . . .		5 lb. 10 oz.			
Glucose		12 oz.			
Water	1 qt.				
Egg whites	1 qt.				
Vanilla	¼ c.				
Salt	¼ tsp.				

Weigh the cornstarch, sugar and glucose into a kettle and mix together. Cover with the water and stir only until the sugar is dissolved, and do not stir again. Place a sugar thermometer in the kettle so that the bulb is covered and it can be read without moving. Boil rapidly to 246 degrees F. Pour in a fine stream over the stiffly beaten whites (do not scrape kettle) and beat seven to nine minutes on high speed. Do not beat until it begins to lose its gloss.

Note: In making frostings the same sized kettle with the same evaporating surface should always be used, or there will be wide variation in results due to the difference in the length of time necessary to reach the required temperature and the consequent variation in the amount of inversion of the sugar produced.

Use twelve ounces of frosting for each two-layer cake, 8″ × 8″; use six ounces of frosting for each dozen large cup cakes, muffin-tin size. When frosting a number of cakes at one time the most efficient method is to carry through each process to completion on the total number of cakes. This saves time over the method of completing cakes one at a time.

Use a spatula or large spoon to spread or swirl the frosting. Swirling the frosting, when well done, adds to the attractiveness of the cakes and makes the amount of frosting appear generous.

Total Weight: 8 lb.
Per Serving: Cost_____ Selling Price_____ Calories_____

CHOCOLATE BOILED ICING

INGREDIENTS	AMOUNT	WEIGHT	MULTIPLE	UNIT COST	TOTAL COST
White boiled icing . . .		8 lb.			
Melted chocolate . . .		2 lb.			

Scale the melted chocolate into the white boiled icing and mix thoroughly. This will yield icing sufficient for approximately ten two-layer 8″ × 8″ cakes, allowing fifteen ounces of icing per cake. Allow seven and one half ounces for each dozen of large-sized cup cakes to be iced.

Total Weight: 10 lb.
Per Serving: Cost_____ Selling Price_____ Calories_____

BUTTER CREAM ICING

Ingredients	Amount	Weight	Multiple	Unit Cost	Total Cost
Butter		2 lb. 8 oz.			
Powdered sugar		18 lb. 10 oz.			
Honey, strained		1 lb. 14 oz.			
Egg whites	1⅓ c.				
Egg yolks	1 c.				
Vanilla	½ c.				
Salt	¼ tsp.				
Water	3 c.				

Pour the sugar and the fat into the bowl of a mixing machine and beat until blended. Add the remainder of the ingredients and continue mixing until smooth and creamy. This icing may be stored in covered cans in the refrigerator until needed. To facilitate spreading, bring the amount to be used to room temperature. Allow four ounces of icing per dozen cup cakes, number-forty-scoop size; fourteen ounces icing per two-layer cake, eight inches square, and nine ounces icing per dozen cup cakes, number-sixteen-scoop size.

Total Weight: 25 lb. 14 oz.
Per Serving: Cost____ Selling Price____ Calories____

CHOCOLATE BUTTER CREAM ICING

Ingredients	Amount	Weight	Multiple	Unit Cost	Total Cost
Butter		4 lb.			
Egg yolks	1⅓ c.				
Egg whites	2⅔ c.				
Honey		2 lb.			
Powdered sugar		25 lb.			
Cocoa		6 lb. 10 oz.			
Salt	2⅔ tbsp.				
Scalded milk	3 qt.				
Vanilla	⅔ c.				

Beat the fat, yolks, whites and honey until smooth and fluffy. Add the mixed powdered sugar, cocoa and salt gradually. If the mixture gets too stiff add a little of the hot milk. When the above mixture is smooth pour in the scalded milk. Add the vanilla. Beat at high speed and pour into containers and cover well to hold until used. In summer it may be necessary to reduce the liquid; in winter, to increase it slightly if the icing is too stiff. Allow fourteen ounces of icing per two-layer cake, eight inches square; nine ounces icing per dozen cup cakes, number-sixteen-scoop size; and four ounces of icing per dozen cup cakes, number-forty-scoop size.

Total Weight: 45 lb. 10 oz.
Per Serving: Cost_____   Selling Price_____   Calories_____

ORANGE ICING

INGREDIENTS	AMOUNT	WEIGHT	MULTIPLE	UNIT COST	TOTAL COST
Butter		4 lb.			
Egg yolks	2 c.				
Egg whites	1⅓ c.				
Honey		2 lb.			
Powdered sugar. . . .		22 lb.			
Salt	1 tbsp.				
Orange juice	1 qt.				
Ground or chopped fresh orange peel		3 lb.			

Beat the fat, egg yolks, whites and honey until smooth and fluffy. Add the powdered sugar and salt. Continue mixing. Add the orange juice and chopped or ground fresh orange peel. Beat at high speed for a few minutes and put into covered containers to hold until used. In winter, when ingredients are all colder, it may be necessary to add more orange juice if the icing is too stiff. Whatever amount of icing is needed should be taken out of the refrigerator and brought up to room temperature before using.

Allow fourteen ounces of icing per two-layer cake, eight inches square; nine ounces of icing per dozen cup cakes, number-sixteen-scoop size; and four ounces of icing per dozen cup cakes, number-forty-scoop size.

Total Weight: 34 lb. 10 oz.
Per Serving: Cost_____ Selling Price_____ Calories_____

CHOCOLATE BROWNIES

Ingredients	Amount	Weight	Multiple	Unit Cost	Total Cost
Shortening		1 lb. 4 oz.			
Sugar		2 lb. 8 oz.			
Chocolate		12 oz.			
Eggs, whole	10				
Vanilla	4 tsp.				
Pastry flour		1 lb.			
Salt	2 tsp.				
Pecans or walnuts . . .		1 lb. 4 oz.			

Melt the shortening and chocolate together over hot water and add to the sugar, eggs and vanilla, which have been mixed together. Add the flour, salt and nuts. Scale into seven well-greased and floured pans 10″ × 10″. Bake in a slow oven, 325 degrees F., for twenty to twenty-five minutes. Cut while still warm (4 × 4) to form squares. These brownies should have a shiny top and a fudge-like center. If stored in tight containers they will keep several days.

Total Weight: 7 lb. 14 oz.
Yield: 7 pans, approximately 1 lb. 2 oz. each, or 112 brownies.
Per Serving: Cost_____ Selling Price_____ Calories_____

CHOCOLATE FILBERT COOKIES

Ingredients	Amount	Weight	Multiple	Unit Cost	Total Cost
Light-brown sugar . .		2 lb. 3 oz.			
Fat		1 lb. 5 oz.			
Egg yolks	½ c.				
Egg whites	½ c.				
Melted chocolate . . .		6 oz.			
Salt	1⅓ tsp.				
Soda	2 tsp.				
Pastry flour		1 lb. 8 oz.			
Chopped filberts . . .		12 oz.			

Cream the sugar and the fat. Add the yolks and unbeaten whites and continue creaming. Add the melted chocolate. Sift the salt, soda and flour and add with the nuts. Drop with a number-forty scoop onto a well-greased and floured cooky sheet. Flatten and glaze the cookies by pressing with the end of a wooden potato masher which is dipped in beaten whole eggs. Bake ten to twelve minutes at about 350 degrees F.

Total Weight: 6 lb. 10 oz.
Yield: 11 dozen cookies, approximately 20 per pound of dough.
Per Serving: Cost____ Selling Price____ Calories____

CHOCOLATE PINWHEEL COOKIES

Ingredients	Amount	Weight	Multiple	Unit Cost	Total Cost
Butter		1 lb.			
Sugar		15 oz.			
Egg yolks, unbeaten . .	⅓ c.				
Milk	¾ c.				
Vanilla	4 tsp.				
Bread flour		1 lb. 11 oz.			
Baking powder, S.A.S.-phosphate type . . .	2 tsp.				
Salt	½ tsp.				
Chocolate, melted . . .		4 oz.			

Cream the butter and sugar. Add the egg yolks, milk, vanilla and the sifted flour, baking powder and salt. To one half of the dough add the melted chocolate. Chill both the white and chocolate doughs. On a floured pastry canvas roll each to rectangles of equal size. Place one rectangle on top of the other, being careful to see there is no flour on either surface or the chocolate and white layers will not adhere. Roll up tightly like a jelly roll. Chill thoroughly or place in the icebox overnight. This will make four rolls weighing seventeen and one half ounces each. Cut in very thin slices, sixty per roll. Bake in a 350–375-degree (F.) oven.

Total Weight: 4 lb. 6 oz.
Yield: 20 dozen cookies, approximately 54 per lb. of dough.
Per Serving: Cost_____ Selling Price_____ Calories_____

CHOCOLATE ROCKS

Ingredients	Amount	Weight	Multiple	Unit Cost	Total Cost
Fat		12 oz.			
Sugar		1 lb. 7 oz.			
Chocolate, melted . . .		6 oz.			
Vanilla.	1 tbsp.				
Eggs	3				
Flour, pastry		1 lb. 8 oz.			
Salt	1½ tsp.				
Soda	1½ tsp.				
Sour milk	1½ c.				
Raisins, chopped . . .		9 oz.			
Pecans or walnuts, chopped		6 oz.			

Cream the fat and the sugar. Add the melted chocolate, vanilla and the beaten eggs. Alternate the well-mixed and sifted dry ingredients with the sour milk. Add the chopped raisins and nuts. Using a number-forty scoop, drop on a well-greased and floured baking sheet. Bake at 350 degrees F. for approximately ten minutes. Frost these cookies with a powdered-sugar chocolate icing.

Total Weight: 6 lb.

Yield: 10 dozen, 20 cookies per lb. of dough (approximately $\frac{3}{4}$ oz. each).

Per Serving: Cost____   Selling Price____   Calories____

DATE SANDWICH COOKIES

Ingredients	Amount	Weight	Multiple	Unit Cost	Total Cost
Filling:					
Dates		2 lb. 4 oz.			
Milk	1 qt.				
Orange juice	3 tbsp.				
Fat	3 tbsp.				
Dough:					
Sugar		1 lb. 4 oz.			
Flour, pastry		10 oz.			
Oatmeal		14 oz.			
Salt	1½ tsp.				
Light sweet crumbs .		8 oz.			
Fat		10 oz.			

Steam the dates to soften and cook with the milk, orange juice and three tablespoons of fat to a smooth paste.

Mix the sugar, flour, oatmeal, salt and crumbs. Rub in the fat lightly with the tips of the fingers.

Spread one half of the crumbs evenly on the bottom of two pans about 9" × 20" and pat smooth. Cover with the paste and spread the remainder of the crumb mixture evenly on top of the paste. Bake twenty to twenty-five minutes at 275 degrees F. When cool cut pans five by twelve.

Yield: 10 dozen cookies.

Per Serving: Cost____   Selling Price____   Calories____

FILLED COOKIES

Ingredients	Amount	Weight	Multiple	Unit Cost	Total Cost
Cooky Dough:					
Sugar		1 lb.			
Fat		1 lb.			
Eggs	2				
Vanilla	2 tsp.				
Milk	1 c.				
Flour		1 lb. 12 oz.			
Baking powder, S.A.S.-phosphate type . .	2 tbsp.				
Filling:					
Flour	4 tbsp.				
Sugar		1 lb.			
Water	2 c.				
Figs, chopped . . .		10 oz.			
Raisins, chopped . .		12 oz.			
Nuts, chopped . . .		4 oz.			
Lemon juice	¼ c.				

Cream the fat and the sugar. Add the eggs and vanilla, and alternate the milk with the mixed and sifted flour and baking powder. Chill the dough and, removing only a part from the icebox at one time, roll on a lightly floured pastry canvas to about one sixteenth inch in thickness. Cut out cookies two and seven eighths to three inches in diameter. Make the filling by mixing the flour and the sugar and adding to the boiling water. When this thickens add the chopped fruit, nuts and lemon juice. Cool. This makes four and two thirds cups of filling. Allowing about one and one third teaspoons of filling per cooky, place on the center of the cut cookies and with the blade of a knife fold the cooky over to form a semicircle. Press down the edges lightly. Bake in a moderate oven until done.

Total Weight: Dough, 4 lb. 8 oz.; filling, 3 lb.
Yield: 13½ dozen (36 cookies to one pound of dough).
Per Serving: Cost____   Selling Price____   Calories____

GERMANTOWN OR PENNSYLVANIA DUTCH COOKIES

Ingredients	Amount	Weight	Multiple	Unit Cost	Total Cost
Bread flour		1 lb.			
Sugar		15 oz.			
Salt.	¾ tsp.				
Cinnamon	2 tsp.				
Cloves	2 tsp.				
Baking powder, S.A.S.-phosphate type . . .	¼ tsp.				
Shortening		9 oz.			
Molasses, light	1 c.				
Sour milk or buttermilk .	¼ c.				

Mix the dry ingredients and mix in fat lightly as in making pie crust. Add the molasses and the sour milk gradually. Chill the dough until firm enough to handle. Roll to paper thickness on a lightly floured pastry canvas. Cut with a round cooky cutter three inches in diameter. Bake in a 350–375-degree (F.) oven. Loosen from the pan at once after removing from the oven to prevent sticking. These should be thin and crisp and almost transparent when held to the light.

Total Weight: 3 lb. 4 oz.

Yield: 9¾ dozen cookies, 36 cookies per lb. of dough.

Per Serving: Cost____ Selling Price____ Calories____

GINGER COOKIES

Ingredients	Amount	Weight	Multiple	Unit Cost	Total Cost
Shortening		1 lb.			
Sugar		1 lb.			
Eggs	4				
Dark molasses	2 c.				
Soda	4 tsp.				
Cinnamon	2 tsp.				
Ginger	2 tbsp.				
Cloves	1 tsp.				
Bread flour		2 lb. 4 oz.			

Cream the shortening and sugar. Add the well-beaten eggs, molasses and mixed and sifted dry ingredients. Chill the dough. Roll about one eighth inch in thickness on a lightly floured pastry canvas. Cut with a $2\frac{7}{8}$-inch cooky cutter. Bake ten to twelve minutes in a 350–375-degree (F.) oven. Cool and remove from pan by loosening with a spatula.

Total Weight: 6 lb. dough.
Yield: 12 dozen cookies, 24 cookies per lb. of dough.
Per Serving: Cost____   Selling Price____   Calories____

HAZELNUT BARS

INGREDIENTS	AMOUNT	WEIGHT	MULTIPLE	UNIT COST	TOTAL COST
Egg whites	$1\frac{1}{4}$ c.				
Sugar		1 lb. 4 oz.			
Glucose	$\frac{1}{4}$ c.				
Flour	1 tbsp.				
Hazelnuts, medium fine .		1 lb. 4 oz.			

Beat the egg whites until light. Add the sugar and glucose and continue beating. Fold in the flour and the nuts and pour into paper-lined pans. This will fill three 10″ × 10″ pans. Bake in a 350-degree F. oven for twenty-five to thirty minutes. Cut pans four by six to make twenty-four bars. Invert on a tray and moisten the paper to make it remove easily. Put the bars together with butter cream, using either hazelnut or chocolate flavors.

Total Weight: 3 lb. 4 oz.
Yield: 36 cookies.
Per Serving: Cost____   Selling Price____   Calories____

CHOCOLATE-COCOANUT MACAROONS

Ingredients	Amount	Weight	Multiple	Unit Cost	Total Cost
Almond paste		9 oz.			
Powdered sugar. . . .		1 lb. 8 oz.			
Egg whites	1 c.				
Cocoanut		1 lb. 4 oz.			
Chocolate, melted . . .	3 tbsp.				
Vanilla	1½ tsp.				

Blend the almond paste and the powdered sugar with the hands until fine and of an even texture. Beat the whites to a wet peak and fold in the blended almond paste and sugar. Add the cocoanut, the melted chocolate and vanilla. Using a number-forty scoop, drop onto a well-greased paper-lined cooky sheet and bake in a 325–350-degree F. oven twenty to twenty-five minutes. Remove from the paper as soon as possible on coming out of the oven.

Total Weight: 3 lb. 12 oz.
Yield: 6 dozen, ⅚ oz. each.
Per Serving: Cost_____ Selling Price_____ Calories_____

COCOANUT MACAROONS

Ingredients	Amount	Weight	Multiple	Unit Cost	Total Cost
Almond paste		9 oz.			
Powdered sugar. . . .		1 lb. 8 oz.			
Egg whites	1 c.				
Cocoanut		1 lb. 4 oz.			
Vanilla	1½ tsp.				

Blend the almond paste and the powdered sugar with the hands until fine and of an even texture. Beat the whites to a wet peak and fold in the blended almond paste and sugar, together with the cocoanut, by hand. Add the vanilla. Using a number-forty scoop, drop onto a well-greased paper-lined cooky sheet and bake in a 325–350-degree (F.) oven twenty to twenty-five minutes until brown. Remove from the paper as soon as possible on coming out of the oven.

Total Weight: 3 lb. 12 oz.
Yield: 6 dozen, $\frac{5}{6}$ oz. each.
Per Serving: Cost____ Selling Price____ Calories____

OATMEAL ROCKS

INGREDIENTS	AMOUNT	WEIGHT	MULTIPLE	UNIT COST	TOTAL COST
Sugar		1 lb. 3 oz.			
Fat		8 oz.			
Eggs	3				
Sour cream	1½ c.				
Lemon juice	1½ tbsp.				
Mapeline	1 tsp.				
Flour, pastry		14 oz.			
Light sweet crumbs . .		6½ oz.			
Oatmeal		10 oz.			
Salt	½ tbsp.				
Soda	½ tbsp.				
Cinnamon	1 tbsp.				
Raisins		1 lb. 3 oz.			
Nuts		2 oz.			

Cream the fat and sugar. Add the eggs, sour cream, lemon juice, mapeline and the well-mixed dry ingredients, to which the nuts and raisins have been added. Drop onto a greased and floured pan, using a number-forty scoop, and bake in a 350-degree (F.) oven ten to fifteen minutes. This mixture may be spread out on a sheet pan and when baked cut in squares or bars.

Total Weight: 6 lb. dough.
Yield: 9 dozen cookies, 18 cookies per lb. of dough.
Per Serving: Cost____ Selling Price____ Calories____

DOUGHNUTS

Ingredients	Amount	Weight	Multiple	Unit Cost	Total Cost
Egg yolks	1½ c.				
Sugar		2 lb.			
Fat, melted		4 oz.			
Potato, mashed		2 lb.			
Flour, pastry		2 lb.			
Flour, bread		1 lb. 8 oz.			
Baking powder, S.A.S.-phosphate type . . .	5 tbsp.				
Salt	1¼ tbsp.				
Nutmeg	2⅔ tbsp.				
Mace	4 tsp.				
Milk	2½ c.				

Beat the egg yolks. Add the sugar gradually and the melted fat. Put the cold mashed potatoes through a sieve or a china cap and add to the beaten eggs, fat and sugar. Add the remaining mixed and sifted dry ingredients alternately with the milk. Mix to a smooth dough. Roll out one fourth inch thick on a floured board and cut out with a floured cutter. Weigh first three doughnuts. They should weigh four ounces if a yield of ten dozen is to be obtained. Cut out the remainder and lift carefully with fingers or a broad bladed knife and drop into the fat, which should be maintained at 350 degrees F. The doughnuts should be rolled out in close proximity to the frying kettle to eliminate carrying and handling. If a crusty doughnut is desired, try out suet and add one part to every three parts of fat when filling the fry kettle. After each frying the fat should be strained through a cloth.

Total Weight: 10 lb.

Yield: 10 dozen doughnuts weighing approximately 16 oz. per dozen before frying and approximately 18–20 oz. per dozen after frying.

Per Serving: Cost_____   Selling Price_____   Calories_____

CHAPTER XIV

Pies

A Reputation for Good Pies Is Worth Every Effort. As everyone knows, pie is the favorite dessert of the American people. It is "Pie American'" which contributes to the homesickness of the exile and traveler. It outsells any other single kind of dessert, and this is true even when the cakes and puddings are of equally high standard. Good pie, as well as good coffee, goes a long way toward making a restaurant famous.

It Is Therefore Necessary to Establish a Standard for Good Pies. Good pie crust must be short, flaky, delicately browned, not too thick nor too thin and must have a good flavor. Especial attention must be given to the fat. It should be firm, not mealy, and it must be sweet in taste. The filling must be of appetizing color and pleasing flavor. It should not be too stiff. A fruit pie should be sufficiently juicy to run slightly. A cream-filled pie should just hold its shape when cut and that is all. A good pie is in a sense a confection, which means it should be rich in fat and in sugar.

Apple Pie Is Usually the Most Popular of All Pies. Its tart, sweet, spicy richness is not maintained without constant attention to the quality of the apples, which varies with the kind purchased and also with the season. The amount of sugar must be increased when the apples are very tart and decreased when less so, as is apt to be the case when using apples from storage in the late spring. The amount of thickening, too, must be adjusted, as well as the length of the baking time. There are many good canned apples in the market which will make pies that are hard to distinguish from those made with fresh apples. However, in the average restaurant the customer is predisposed in favor of a pie made of what he calls "green apples."

Lemon and Pumpkin Pie Probably Tie for Second Place in Popularity. Lemon pie appears to be more acceptable to the public when it is quite strong with lemon, rich in fat and quite sweet. A meringue which is piled rather high also adds to the popularity. The standard for spices in pumpkin pie varies with the individual but experience seems to show that a golden pie not so full of spice as to cover the pumpkin flavor pleases the majority of customers.

Quick Frozen Fruit Promotes Variety in the Pie Menu. With the excellent frozen fruits now in the market, the institution operating on even a limited budget may afford fresh fruit for pies. It has been the experience of the authors that the frozen fruit is often of better quality than the same fruit bought in season in their markets.

Pies Have a High Food Cost. Compared to all other desserts, such as puddings, cakes and icecreams, pies have a high average food cost. Since this is true, careful planning to the end that there are few left over is essential to good management.

Small Pies Require As Much Labor As Large. Each institution, commercial or otherwise, should make a pie of the size best suited to its needs. In a bake shop the smaller pies are best, for customers usually wish to buy not more than four to five portions. However, the average restaurant finds the pie cutting six or seven pieces most economical, for it takes no longer to make and bake a large pie than a small one.

INEXPENSIVE PIE CRUST

INGREDIENTS	AMOUNT	WEIGHT	MULTIPLE	UNIT COST	TOTAL COST
Flour		15 lb.			
Lard		7 lb. 8 oz.			
Salt	⅔ c.				
Iced water	1¼–1½ qt.				

Weigh the fat and the flour. Add the salt and work the fat into the flour lightly, using the tips of the fingers. Add the iced water a little at a time, being careful to distribute the water evenly through the mixture. As one becomes expert and used to the manipulation, the total amount of water needed can be estimated and poured over all at once and mixed lightly. Avoid getting the dough too wet. For this amount, about one and one fourth to one and one half quarts of water will be sufficient.

This amount will make fifty to fifty-five pie shells, using pie tins ten and three fourths inches in diameter, or it will make twenty-six to thirty two-crust pies of the same size. It will require about eight ounces of dough for each top or bottom. If the dough is to be used the same day it is made, less water will be required than if it is to be held over in the refrigerator. It is almost impossible to mix pie crust on a machine without developing gluten and consequently a tough crust. Hand mixing gives a superior product and even in large quantities may be done quickly, as the worker becomes expert.

Total Weight: 26 lb. of dough.
Yield: Approximately 26 two-crust pies; 52 one-crust pies (8 oz. of dough for each top or bottom).
Per Serving: Cost____   Selling Price____   Calories____

RICH PIE CRUST

INGREDIENTS	AMOUNT	WEIGHT	MULTIPLE	UNIT COST	TOTAL COST
Flour		15 lb.			
Lard		10 lb. 8 oz.			
Salt	¾ c.				
Iced water	1½–1¾ qt.				

Weigh the fat and the flour. Add the salt and work the fat into the flour lightly using the tips of the fingers. Add the iced water a little at a time, being careful to distribute the water evenly through the mixture. As one becomes expert, the iced water may be poured over at once and mixed lightly. See recipe for inexpensive pie crust for further discussion.

Total Weight: 28 lb. 14 oz.
Yield: 28–29 two-crust pies, approximately 1 lb. each.
Per Serving: Cost____ Selling Price____ Calories___

MERINGUE

INGREDIENTS	AMOUNT	WEIGHT	MULTIPLE	UNIT COST	TOTAL COST
Glucose		1 lb. 8 oz.			
Granulated sugar . . .		8 oz.			
Powdered sugar		6 oz.			
Cream of tartar	½ tsp.				
Egg whites	2 c.				

Weigh the glucose into the bowl of a mixing machine and add the remainder of the ingredients. Beat on high speed five to eight minutes. Spread on pie filling or pudding in swirls and brown in a hot oven for about three to four minutes. To insure uniformity in amount, an icecream dipper may be used in putting the meringue on the pies. A 10¾-inch pie will require four number-eight scoops of

meringue.   This meringue will hold up throughout the day
if kept in the refrigerator.

Total Weight: 3 lb. 2 oz.

Yield: Meringue for twelve 10¾-inch pies, approximately 4 oz.
 per pie.

Per Serving: Cost____   Selling Price____   Calories____

APPLE PIE

INGREDIENTS	AMOUNT	WEIGHT	MULTIPLE	UNIT COST	TOTAL COST
Apples, peeled and sliced .		12 lb.			
Cinnamon	1 tbsp.				
Sugar		5 lb. 10 oz.			
Nutmeg	1 tsp.				
Butter		1 lb.			
Salt	1 tbsp.				

Put the apples in a heavy-bottomed kettle and pour the
fat and the mixed sugar, salt and spices over them.   Cook
until the apples are heated through and just beginning to
get tender.   Avoid cooking beyond this point to prevent
the apples from losing shape.   Stir carefully to avoid
breaking up the fruit.   A little water may be added if the
apples are dry; this is especially necessary as the season
advances and the apples are lacking in juice.   Lemon
juice may be added to taste if the apples are lacking in
flavor.   Measure three and one half cups or two pounds of
filling into each bottom crust.   Cover with a top crust,
being careful to wet the edge of the bottom crust, and press
down firmly.   Bake in a 375-degree F. oven about forty-
five minutes.   If the pie is lacking in juice, a syrup
(made by cooking the apple skins in a small amount of
water and adding sugar) may be kept on hand and a spoonful placed around each piece of pie as it is cut.

Total Weight: 18 lb.

Yield: Nine 10¾-inch pies, 3½ c. or 2 lb. filling for each pie.

Per Serving: Cost____   Selling Price____   Calories____

DRIED-APRICOT PIE

Ingredients	Amount	Weight	Multiple	Unit Cost	Total Cost
Apricots, dried		3 lb. 2 oz.			
Water	6¼ qt.				
Sugar		5 lb. 10 oz.			
Cornstarch		5 oz.			
Lemon juice	2½ tbsp.				
Fat		10 oz.			

Soak the apricots thirty-six to forty-eight hours in the six and one fourth quarts of water and cook in the water in which they have been soaked. When the apricots are soft, strain out the fruit and thicken the juice by adding the well-mixed sugar and cornstarch, stirring vigorously with a wire whip. Cook until the mixture is thick, about seven to ten minutes. Add the lemon juice and fat and pour over the apricots. Fill 10$\frac{3}{4}$-inch unbaked shells, using three and one half cups per pie. A latticed top makes an attractive variation. Bake about one hour in a moderate 375–400-degree (F.) oven.

Total Weight: 20 lb.
Yield: Ten 10¾-inch pies, 3½ c. or 2 lb. filling each.
Per Serving: Cost_____ Selling Price_____ Calories_____

CANNED BLACKBERRY PIE

Ingredients	Amount	Weight	Multiple	Unit Cost	Total Cost
Berries, #10 cans . . .	2				
Sugar		7 lb. 8 oz.			
Cornstarch		8 oz.			
Lemon juice	½ c.				
Fat		1 lb.			
Salt	2 tbsp.				

Drain the fruit into a colander. Heat the juice to the boiling point and add the well-mixed cornstarch and sugar, stirring constantly. Cook seven to ten minutes. Add the fat, lemon juice and salt. Add the berries, stirring as little as possible. Fill the unbaked pie shells, using three and one half cups of filling per pie. Wet the edge of the bottom crust and cover with a top crust, pressing down carefully. Bake about forty-five minutes in a 400-degree F. oven until brown.

Total Weight: 22 lb.

Yield: Eleven 10¾-inch pies, approximately 3½ c. or 2 lb. filling per pie.

Per Serving: Cost_____ Selling Price_____ Calories_____

CANNED BLUEBERRY PIE

INGREDIENTS	AMOUNT	WEIGHT	MULTIPLE	UNIT COST	TOTAL COST
Blueberries, #10 cans . .	2				
Sugar		7 lb. 8 oz.			
Cornstarch		8 oz.			
Lemon juice	½ c.				
Fat		1 lb.			

Drain the berries and heat the juice to boiling. Mix the sugar and cornstarch and sift into the boiling juice, stirring vigorously with a wire whip. Cook seven to ten minutes. When thickened add the berries, lemon juice and fat. Fill the 10¾-inch unbaked pie shells, using three and one half cups of filling per pie. Wet the edge of the crust, cover with the top crust and press down carefully. Bake at 375-400 degrees F. for about forty-five minutes to an hour.

Total Weight: 22 lb.

Yield: Eleven 10¾-inch pies, approximately 3½ c. or 2 lb. filling per pie.

Per Serving: Cost_____ Selling Price_____ Calories_____

FRESH BLUEBERRY PIE

Ingredients	Amount	Weight	Multiple	Unit Cost	Total Cost
Fresh blueberries . . .		9 qt.			
Sugar		5 lb. 4 oz.			
Salt	1 tbsp.				
Flour		7 oz.			
Fat		9 oz.			
Lemon juice	1 c.				

Look over the blueberries carefully to remove stems and leaves. Pour into a colander and wash. Drain carefully. Mix the sugar, salt and the flour thoroughly and pour over the berries. Stir through, being very careful not to crush the berries. Measure four and one half cups into an unbaked pie shell. Dot with one ounce of fat per pie and add one and one half tablespoons of lemon juice per pie. Moisten the edges of the lower crust and cover with a top crust, pressing the edges down carefully. Bake in a 400-degree (F.) oven about one hour.

Total Weight: 18 lb.
Yield: Nine 10¾-inch pies, 4½ c. or 2 lb. filling per pie.
Per Serving: Cost____ Selling Price____ Calories____

BUTTERSCOTCH PIE

Ingredients	Amount	Weight	Multiple	Unit Cost	Total Cost
Milk, scalded	6 qt.				
Brown sugar		6 lb. 4 oz.			
Flour		1 lb. 1 oz.			
Cornstarch		6 oz.			
Salt	1½ tbsp.				
Egg yolks	¾ qt.				
Fat		1 lb. 8 oz.			
Vanilla	¼ c.				
Pie shells, 10¾-inch . .	11				

Mix the flour, cornstarch and brown sugar thoroughly and add to the scalded milk, stirring constantly with a wire whip. Cook seven to ten minutes. When the mixture has thickened add the fat, salt and egg yolks, which have been mixed with a small amount of the thickened mixture, and cook for a few minutes. Remove from the fire and add the vanilla. This will make filling for eleven baked shells, ten and three fourths inches in diameter and using three and one half cups per shell. Spread whipped cream or meringue on top.

Total Weight: 22 lb.
Yield: Eleven 10¾-inch pies, 3½ c. or 2 lb. filling per pie.
Per Serving: Cost_____   Selling Price_____   Calories_____

FRESH FROZEN CHERRY PIE

Ingredients	Amount	Weight	Multiple	Unit Cost	Total Cost
Fresh frozen cherries . .		30-lb. can			
Sugar		9 lb.			
Cornstarch		10 oz.			
Fat		1 lb. 14 oz.			
Water	4 qt.				

Thaw the fresh frozen cherries. This may be done by allowing them to stand at room temperature or, if time permits, by leaving in the refrigerator until thawed.

Mix the sugar and cornstarch thoroughly and mix with the cherries. Add the melted fat and water. Scale into unbaked pie shells, wet the edge of the crust and cover with a crust or latticed top. Bake in a 375–400-degree (F.) oven for forty-five minutes to an hour.

This recipe is based on a thirty-pound can, since that is an economical unit in which to buy quick frozen fruit.

A smaller can is obtainable but a premium is paid for its use. The filling will hold satisfactorily for several days.

Total Weight: Approximately 50 lb.
Yield: 25 pies, 10¾ inches in diameter (approximately 2 lb. filling per pie).
Per Serving: Cost____ Selling Price____ Calories____

CHOCOLATE PIE

INGREDIENTS	AMOUNT	WEIGHT	MULTIPLE	UNIT COST	TOTAL COST
Cocoa		13 oz.			
Flour		1 lb. 3 oz.			
Salt	4 tsp.				
Sugar		6 lb. 11 oz.			
Water	5¾ qt.				
Egg yolks	¾ qt.				
Fat		1 lb. 8 oz.			
Vanilla	4 tbsp.				
Pie shells, 10¾-inch . .	10				

Mix the cocoa, flour, salt and sugar together thoroughly. Sift into the boiling water, stirring constantly. Cook seven to ten minutes. When the mixture has thickened add the well-beaten egg yolks carefully and cook three or four minutes. Add the fat and the vanilla. Fill the pie shells and cover with meringue or whipped cream. Grated chocolate or chopped nuts may be sprinkled over the top of the whipped cream, if desired.

Total Weight: 20 lb.
Yield: Ten 10¾-inch pies (approximately 3½ c. or 2 lb. filling per pie).
Per Serving: Cost____ Selling Price____ Calories____

CREAM PIE

Ingredients	Amount	Weight	Multiple	Unit Cost	Total Cost
Milk	5¾ qt.				
Sugar		6 lb. 4 oz.			
Cornstarch		6 oz.			
Flour		1 lb. 2 oz.			
Egg yolks	⅔ qt.				
Fat		1 lb. 8 oz.			
Salt	4 tsp.				
Vanilla	¼ c.				
Pie shells, 10¾-inch . .	11				

Scald the milk. Mix the sugar, cornstarch and flour and add to the scalded milk, stirring rapidly with a wire whip. Cook seven to ten minutes. When thickened add the well-beaten egg yolks, which have been mixed with a small amount of the thickened mixture, the fat, salt and vanilla, stirring vigorously. Remove from the fire when the eggs are cooked. Fill the pie shells, using three and one half cups per pie or two pounds of filling, and cover with meringue or whipped cream. To make meringue see page 304.

Total Weight: 22 lb. 2 oz.

Yield: 11 pies, 10¾ inches in diameter, approximately 3½ c. or 2 lb. filling per pie.

Per Serving: Cost_____ Selling Price_____ Calories_____

CUSTARD PIE

Ingredients	Amount	Weight	Multiple	Unit Cost	Total Cost
Milk	8 qt.				
Sugar		3 lb. 8 oz.			
Flour		3½ oz.			
Salt	1 tbsp.				
Eggs, whole	30				
Egg yolks	1¼ c.				
Vanilla	¼ c.				
Nutmeg	2 tbsp.				

Scald the milk and add the mixed sugar, flour and salt. Add to the well-beaten eggs and vanilla. Fill the pie shells with four cups of the custard mixture for each $10\frac{3}{4}$-inch pie and sprinkle nutmeg over the top. Bake in a hot oven (400 degrees F.) for ten minutes; then decrease the temperature to 300 degrees F. and bake until the custard is set. The shell should be crimped high along the edge to make a standing rim. This increases the capacity of the shell and tends to prevent spilling in the oven. It may be easier to fill the shells on the oven shelf to facilitate handling them. Let the pies cool and set before attempting to cut them. In this recipe a little flour is used to insure the custard against breaking. A good custard pie should just hold its shape, should be satiny when cut, should not "whey" on standing, and the crust should not be soaked.

Total Weight: Approximately 24 lb.
Yield: Ten $10\frac{3}{4}$-inch pies, approximately 4 cups per pie.
Per Serving: Cost_____   Selling Price_____   Calories_____

GOOSEBERRY AND RAISIN PIE

Ingredients	Amount	Weight	Multiple	Unit Cost	Total Cost
Gooseberries, #10 cans .	2				
Raisins		2 lb.			
Sugar		4 lb.			
Cornstarch		$7\frac{1}{2}$ oz.			
Gooseberry juice,					
or					
Gooseberry juice and					
water	$2\frac{1}{2}$ qt.				
Fat		12 oz.			

Drain the gooseberries. Measure the juice and add water, if necessary, to make two and one half quarts of liquid. Heat the juice and when it reaches the boiling

point add the well-mixed sugar and cornstarch, stirring
constantly with a wire whip. Cook seven to ten minutes.
When the mixture has thickened add the gooseberries.
Add the raisins which have been plumped in the steamer.
Add the fat. Fill 10¾-inch uncooked pie shells, using
approximately three and one half cups of filling per pie.
Wet the edge of the crust, cover with the top crust and
press the edges down carefully. Bake forty-five minutes
at 375–400 degrees F.

Total Weight: 20 lb.
Yield: Ten 10¾-inch pies with approximately 2 lb. filling or 3½
c. per pie.
Per Serving: Cost_____ Selling Price_____ Calories_____

ORANGE TARTS

INGREDIENTS	AMOUNT	WEIGHT	MULTIPLE	UNIT COST	TOTAL COST
Water	2¼ qt.				
Sugar		5 lb. 10 oz.			
Cornstarch		8 oz.			
Flour		1 lb. 4 oz.			
Salt	⅜ tsp.				
Egg yolks	2 c.				
Fat		8 oz.			
Orange juice	1½ qt.				
Grated orange rind . .	6 tbsp.				
Lemon juice	¾ c.				
Tart shells	56				

Mix the sugar, cornstarch, flour and salt and add to the
rapidly boiling water, stirring rapidly with a wire whip.
Cook from seven to ten minutes. This should be cooked
in a heavy-bottomed kettle, because it will be quite thick
until the orange and lemon juice are added and will
scorch easily. Beat the egg yolks and add to the thickened mixture. Continue stirring until the egg yolks are

cooked. Add the fat, orange juice, grated orange rind and lemon juice. Pour the filling into the individual pie shells. Cover with a meringue and brown in a 350-degree (F.) oven. Whipped cream may be substituted for the meringue, if preferred.

Total Weight: 16 lb.
Yield: 56 individual pies, 4½ oz. filling (approximately ½–⅔ c. per pie).
Per Serving: Cost____ Selling Price____ Calories____

FRESH PEACH PIE

INGREDIENTS	AMOUNT	WEIGHT	MULTIPLE	UNIT COST	TOTAL COST
Sugar		6 lb.			
Cornstarch		4 oz.			
Nutmeg	1 tbsp.				
Salt	1 tbsp.				
Peaches, peeled and sliced		10 lb.			
Lemon juice	½ c.				
Fat, melted		12 oz.			

Mix the sugar, cornstarch, nutmeg and salt together and add to the sliced peaches. Add the lemon juice and melted fat. Mix thoroughly and divide between ten 10¾-inch unbaked pie shells. Wet the edge of the crust and cover with a crust or latticed top. Bake for forty-five minutes to one hour in a 375–400-degree (F.) oven. If the peaches lack acidity, as is often the case as the season advances, a reduction in the amount of sugar may be necessary.

Total Weight: 17 lb. 4 oz.
Yield: 10 pies, 10¾ inches in diameter; amount of filling, approximately 1 lb. 11 oz. each.
Per Serving: Cost____ Selling Price____ Calories____

PINEAPPLE PIE

Ingredients	Amount	Weight	Multiple	Unit Cost	Total Cost
Crushed or grated pine-apple, #10 cans . . .	2				
Pineapple juice and water	6 qt.				
Sugar		6 lb. 4 oz.			
Cornstarch		7 oz.			
Flour		1 lb. 2 oz.			
Egg yolks	2⅔ c.				
Salt	4 tsp.				
Lemon juice	¼ c.				
Fat		1 lb.			
Pie shells, 10¾-inch . .	14				

Pour the pineapple into a colander to drain. Measure the juice and add water to make six quarts. Bring the juice and water to a boil. Mix the sugar, flour and cornstarch thoroughly and add to the rapidly boiling juice and water, stirring constantly. Cook seven to ten minutes. Add the well-beaten egg yolks mixed with a small amount of the thickened mixture. Cook for a few minutes. Remove from the fire and add the salt, lemon juice, fat and pineapple. Fill 10¾-inch pie shells, using three and one half cups of filling per pie. Cover with meringue and bake in a moderate oven until brown. See page 304 for recipe for meringue.

Total Weight: 28 lb.
Yield: Fourteen 10¾-inch pies, approximately 3½ c. filling or 2 lb. filling per pie.
Per Serving: Cost____   Selling Price____   Calories____

PLUM PIE

Ingredients	Amount	Weight	Multiple	Unit Cost	Total Cost
Seeded plums		10 lb.			
Sugar		6 lb.			
Cornstarch		4 oz.			
Cinnamon	2 tsp.				
Fat, melted		12 oz.			
Salt	1 tbsp.				

Quarter the fresh seeded plums. Mix all of the dry ingredients together and add to the plums. Add the melted fat. Divide between the uncooked pie shells, wet the edge of the crust and cover with crust or latticed top and bake in a 375–400-degree (F.) oven for forty-five minutes to one hour.

Total Weight: 16 lb. 12 oz.

Yield: Ten 10¾-inch pies; amount of filling, approximately 1 lb. 10 oz. each.

Per Serving: Cost____   Selling Price____   Calories____

PUMPKIN PIE

Ingredients	Amount	Weight	Multiple	Unit Cost	Total Cost
Sugar		4 lb. 6 oz.			
Salt	2¼ tbsp.				
Flour		6 oz.			
Cinnamon	2 tbsp.				
Ginger	3¾ tsp.				
Nutmeg	2 tbsp.				
Cloves	¼ tsp.				
Allspice	¼ tsp.				
Pumpkin	4 qt.				
Eggs, whole	14				
Milk, hot	4¼ qt.				

Mix the sugar, salt, flour and spices together and add to the pumpkin. Beat the eggs until light and add. Combine the pumpkin mixture with the hot milk. Put four cups of filling in each pie shell. The edge of the shell should be crimped to make a high standing rim in order to hold the four cups of filling. Bake in a 350-degree (F.) oven until firm, about one hour.

Total Weight: 23 lb.
Yield: Ten 10¾-inch pies, 4 cups of filling per pie.
Per Serving: Cost_____ Selling Price_____ Calories_____

RAISIN PIE

Ingredients	Amount	Weight	Multiple	Unit Cost	Total Cost
Raisins, seeded		4 lb. 4 oz.			
Water	4¼ qt.				
Brown sugar		1 lb. 4 oz.			
White sugar . . .		1 lb. 6 oz.			
Cornstarch . . .		3 oz.			
Salt	2 tsp.				
Cinnamon	½ tsp.				
Ground cloves . . .	¼ tsp.				
Fat		8 oz.			
Lemon juice	1½ c.				

The raisins may be soaked in the water overnight. Drain and bring the water in which they have been soaked to the boiling point. Add the well-mixed dry ingredients to the boiling liquid, stirring rapidly with a wire whip. Cook five to seven minutes. Add the fat and lemon juice and remove from the fire. Using three and one half cups or two pounds of filling, fill the unbaked bottom crust of a 10¾-inch pie tin. Wet the edges and cover with a top crust, pressing the edges firmly. Bake forty-five minutes in a 400-degree (F.) oven until the crust is brown and cooked.

Total Weight: 16 lb.
Yield: Eight 10¾-inch pies, 2 lb. filling per pie.
Per Serving: Cost_____ Selling Price_____ Calories_____

FRESH RHUBARB PIE

Ingredients	Amount	Weight	Multiple	Unit Cost	Total Cost
Fresh rhubarb		11 lb. 3 oz.			
Flour		1 lb. 3 oz.			
Sugar		7 lb.			
Fat		10 oz.			

Wash and cut the rhubarb in three-quarter-inch lengths. Mix the flour and the sugar thoroughly and add to the rhubarb. This is filling for ten pies, ten and three fourths inches in diameter. Spread out the pie shells and fill with the above mixture, putting one ounce of fat on the filling of each pie. Cover with a lattice top and bake in a 400-degree (F.) oven until the rhubarb is done. If the rhubarb is very juicy, the edges of the crust should be built up as high as possible to hold in the juice. The acidity and water content of the rhubarb varies considerably during the season, and it may be necessary to adjust the sugar and flour, changing it to meet this condition.

Total Weight: 20 lb.
Yield: Ten 10¾-inch pies, approximately 3½ c. filling or 2 lb. filling per pie.
Per Serving: Cost____   Selling Price____   Calories____

CHAPTER XV

Beverages — Coffee Making

The Essentials in Making Good Coffee Involve the Following: attention to the blend; freshness; temperature of the water; accuracy in measuring and care and frequency of making; cleanliness and adequacy of the equipment. These are discussed in further detail below.

The Blend of Coffee Selected Must Satisfy Patrons. What is considered a "good coffee" may vary slightly among various classes, nationalities or parts of the country; therefore, not only the blend but the strength of the brew must be suited to the majority of the consumers. This is important, for an institution may become known for its good or poor coffee as quickly as for any other single item of food.

It Is Important to Have Coffee Freshly Ground. To insure the maximum of freshness some roasters now pack institution and hotel grind coffee in vacuum cans to be opened and used as needed. Overpurchasing of coffee is in all cases to be avoided, except when purchased in airtight cans, and even in such cases roasters prefer that their customers buy in amounts suited to their immediate needs. Practically, coffee should be received two or three times a week. Standing orders should be placed for coffee to obviate thought on the part of the buyer and insure a constant supply.

The Water for Making Coffee Must Be Boiling. Water which is only hot, not actually boiling, is a frequent cause of poor coffee. The urn itself should be maintained at an even temperature, as cooling down and heating up again affects coffee quality adversely.

Measurements Must Be Accurate. Six to eight ounces of coffee per gallon of water is the accepted standard, but this depends upon the quality of the coffee purchased and the strength of coffee desired. Since coffee is difficult to measure accurately, it should always be weighed. The worker who is to make the coffee must be careful. The same person should have the responsibility for the care of the equipment and the making of the coffee from day to day. Poor coffee is traceable very frequently not to the grade of the coffee purchased and the equipment used but to the haphazard method of making the brew and caring for the equipment.

Coffee Should Be Made Frequently. More coffee should not be made than will be used up in one and one half to two hours, since that is the maximum time during which quality can be maintained. If any remains at the end of this time, it should be thrown away.

All Equipment Must Be Kept Perfectly Clean. The urn must be thoroughly rinsed after each using and cleaned thoroughly each day. Baking soda is commonly used but should be rinsed out carefully to avoid affecting the taste of the coffee. There are a number of "urn cleaners" on the market which remove rancid coffee oils from gauge glasses, faucets and drain pipes, as well as the inside of the urn, perhaps better than soda. These should be used daily. There are brushes available for cleaning faucets and gauge glasses. After cleaning, rinse urns, faucets and gauges well with clear water and dry the inside of the urn with a clean white cloth, which will automatically testify to the cleanliness of the urn. Leave covers open when not in use to permit circulation of fresh air.

The Equipment for Coffee Making Must Fit the Needs of the Institution. Where small amounts of fresh coffee are needed over long periods, the "Silex" type of equipment is satisfactory. In school lunchrooms, cafeterias, banquet service or other institutions where a large volume must be ready at one time for peak service, the urn type of equipment is more desirable.

URN COFFEE

Ingredients	Amount	Weight	Multiple	Unit Cost	Total Cost
Coffee, urn grind . . .		1 lb.			
Water	2½ gal.				

To Make Coffee in an Urn :

Be sure the urn is clean and the water boiling.

Take a clean urn bag from the cold water in which it is kept immersed and place ground coffee in it and put in the urn.

Pour or flow the water over at a uniform, moderate speed. When pouring by hand, pour slowly, moving the stream over the entire surface of the ground coffee.

Repour the coffee. With some urns repouring approximately one half of the coffee is sufficient. Other equipment demands more. The amount of repouring will depend on how fast or slowly the water goes over in the first place; to what degree the first pouring has removed the strength from the grind; and the strength of the brew desired. It will be necessary to establish the procedure for repouring according to the kind of coffee and the equipment to be used.

Remove the urn bag when the brew is finished and before starting to serve.

This process varies slightly when other forms of equipment are substituted for the cloth urn bags.

Yield: 2 gallons coffee; 48 servings, ⅔ c. each.
Per Serving: Cost——   Selling Price——   Calories——

HOT COCOA

Ingredients	Amount	Weight	Multiple	Unit Cost	Total Cost
Sugar		1 lb. 12 oz.			
Cocoa		1 lb. 2 oz.			
Salt	1½ tsp.				
Boiling water	2¼ qt.				
Milk	3 gal.				
Vanilla	2 tbsp.				

Mix the sugar, cocoa and salt and add to the boiling water, stirring vigorously. Cook ten to fifteen minutes to develop flavor. Add the hot milk. Add the vanilla and just before serving one half teaspoon of cinnamon may be added for flavor, if desired. Serve with whipped cream. This may be cooled and poured over ice cubes and served as iced cocoa. A spoonful of whipped cream should be added to the top of each glass.

Total Volume: 14 qt.
Yield: 56 servings, 1 c. each.
Per Serving: Cost____ Selling Price____ Calories____

HOT CHOCOLATE

Ingredients	Amount	Weight	Multiple	Unit Cost	Total Cost
Chocolate		1 lb.			
Sugar		1 lb. 12 oz.			
Salt	1½ tsp.				
Water, boiling	2¼ qt.				
Milk	3 gal.				
Vanilla	2 tbsp.				

Melt the chocolate over hot water and add the sugar and salt. When well blended add the boiling water gradually and cook ten to fifteen minutes or until smooth, stirring frequently. Add the hot milk and the vanilla. Serve hot with whipped cream. This drink may be chilled and served over ice cubes as iced chocolate, in which case the glass may be garnished with whipped cream or whipped cream and grated nutmeg.

Total Volume: 14 qt.
Yield: 56 servings, 1 c. each.
Per Serving: Cost___   Selling Price___   Calories___

LEMONADE

INGREDIENTS	AMOUNT	WEIGHT	MULTIPLE	UNIT COST	TOTAL COST
Sugar		7 lb. 8 oz.			
Water	2 qt.				
Lemon juice	3 qt.				
Ice water	6 qt.				

Make a syrup of the sugar and the two quarts of water and let cool. Mix with the lemon juice and the ice water. While the syrup is cooling mint leaves may be added if mint-flavored lemonade is desired, in which case they should be strained out before the syrup is added to the water and lemon juice. To serve, fill a glass half full of ice and add the lemonade.

Total Volume: 12½ qt.
Yield: 50 servings, 1 c. each.
Per Serving: Cost___   Selling Price___   Calories___

GINGER ALE LEMONADE

INGREDIENTS	AMOUNT	WEIGHT	MULTIPLE	UNIT COST	TOTAL COST
Lemon juice	3 qt.				
Sugar		7 lb. 8 oz.			
Water	2 qt.				
Ice water	3 qt.				
Ginger ale	3 qt.				
Mint leaves	1 c.				

Make a syrup of the sugar and water and while it is cooling add the mint leaves. Combine the cold syrup, lemon juice, ginger ale and water and strain out the mint leaves. All ingredients should be as cold as possible to prevent too great dilution from the melting ice when the drink is served. Pour into glasses half filled with ice.

Total Volume: 12½ qt.
Yield: 50 servings, 1 c. each.
Per Serving: Cost____ Selling Price____ Calories____

CHAPTER XVI

Table of Weights and Their Approximate Measures

TABLE OF WEIGHTS AND THEIR APPROXIMATE MEASURES

Food Materials	Weight	Approximate Measure
Almond paste	1 lb.	1½ c.
Apples, A.P.,* fresh	6 oz.	1 apple, 100 size box
Diced, half-inch cubes	1 lb.	4⅓ c.
Apricots, dried, A.P.*	1 lb.	3 c.
1 lb. apricots soaked and cooked equals, without juice . . .		4½ c.
1 lb. apricots after soaking and cooking weighs, without juice	2½ lb.	
Bacon, cooked and cut fine . . .	1 lb.	3⅓ c.
Bacon, sliced, rind trimmed . . .	1 lb.	20–28 slices
Baking powder	1 lb.	2⅛ c.
Bananas, 1 average size	5–6 oz.	
Diced ½-inch cubes	1 lb.	3 c.
Barley, pearl	1 lb.	2⅓ c.
Beans, dried Lima beans, uncooked	1 lb.	2⅔ c.
1 lb. dried Lima beans soaked and cooked equals		6½ c.
1 lb. dried Lima beans after soaking and cooking weighs . . .	2 lb. 9 oz.	
Beans, kidney, A.P.*	1 lb.	2⅔ c.
1 lb. kidney beans soaked and cooked equals		7 c.
1 lb. kidney beans after soaking and cooking weighs	2 lb. 6 oz.	
Beans, navy, A.P.*	1 lb.	2⅓ c.
1 lb. navy beans soaked and cooked equals		6 c.
1 lb. navy beans after soaking and cooking weighs	2 lb. 3 oz.	

* A.P. = As Purchased.

TABLE OF WEIGHTS AND MEASURES (*Continued*)

Food Materials	Weight	Approximate Measure
Beets, diced, cooked	1 lb.	$2\frac{1}{2}$ c.
Blueberries	1 lb.	4 c.
Bran	1 lb.	$10\frac{1}{2}$ c.
Bread, soft, broken	1 lb.	9 c.
Broken, stale	1 lb.	9 c.
Butter	1 lb.	2 c.
Cabbage, shredded	1 lb.	$5\frac{1}{2}$ c.
Carrots, diced	1 lb.	4 c.
Catsup	1 lb.	$1\frac{3}{4}$ c.
Celery, $\frac{1}{2}$-inch pieces	1 lb.	$4\frac{1}{2}$ c.
$\frac{1}{4}$-inch pieces	1 lb.	4 c.
Cherries, candied	1 lb.	$2\frac{1}{2}$ c.
Cheese, cottage, A.P.,* unmixed .	1 lb.	$2\frac{2}{3}$ c.
Nippy, cubed, $\frac{1}{4}$-inch	1 lb.	$3\frac{1}{4}$ c.
Nippy, ground	1 lb.	$3\frac{1}{2}$ c.
Chicken, cooked and cubed . . .	1 lb.	3 c.
Chicken fat	1 lb.	$2\frac{1}{8}$ c.
Chocolate, cut fine	1 lb.	4 c.
Melted	1 lb.	$1\frac{3}{4}$ c.
Cocoa	1 lb.	4 c.
Cocoanut, fancy, loose pack . . .	1 lb.	8 c.
Short	1 lb.	7 c.
Coffee	1 lb.	5–$5\frac{1}{2}$ c.
Corn, canned . . . . · . . .	1 lb.	$1\frac{3}{4}$ c.
Corn meal	1 lb.	3 c.
Cornstarch	1 lb.	$3\frac{1}{8}$ c.
Corn syrup	1 lb.	$1\frac{1}{3}$ c.
Crackers, soda, whole	1 lb.	120 crackers
Broken	1 lb.	$10\frac{2}{3}$ c.
Crumbs	1 lb.	$4\frac{1}{2}$ c.
Cranberries, uncooked	1 lb.	5 c.
Cream of tartar	1 lb.	3 c.
Crumbs, light bread, unsifted . .	1 lb.	4 c.
Dark bread, unsifted . . .	1 lb.	$3\frac{2}{3}$ c.
Light, sweet, unsifted	1 lb.	$3\frac{1}{2}$ c.
Dark, sweet, unsifted	1 lb.	$3\frac{2}{3}$ c.
Currants	1 lb.	$3\frac{3}{8}$ c.
Dates, seeded, cut fine	1 lb.	2–$2\frac{1}{2}$ c.

* A.P. = As Purchased.

TABLE OF WEIGHTS AND MEASURES (*Continued*)

Food Materials	Weight	Approximate Measure
Eggs, hard-cooked	1 lb.	8 eggs
Hard-cooked and chopped . .	1 lb.	$3\frac{1}{4}$ c.
Eggs, whole in shell	1 lb.	8 eggs
Egg whites	$\frac{1}{2}$ lb.	8 whites = 1 c.
Egg yolks	$\frac{1}{2}$ lb.	12 yolks = 1 c.
Farina, uncooked	1 lb.	$2\frac{2}{3}$ c.
1 lb. farina when cooked equals .		3 qt.
Figs, layer, whole	1 lb.	$2\frac{1}{2}$ c.
Flour, graham, unsifted . . .	1 lb.	4 c.
Pastry, unsifted	1 lb.	4 c.
Rye, unsifted	1 lb.	$4\frac{1}{2}$–5 c.
Bread (all purpose) unsifted . .	1 lb.	$3\frac{2}{3}$ c.
French dressing	1 lb.	2 c.
Gelatin	1 lb.	3 c.
Giblets, cooked, trimmed and cubed	1 lb.	$2\frac{1}{4}$–$2\frac{1}{2}$ c.
Glucose	1 lb.	$1\frac{1}{3}$ c.
Grapenuts	1 lb.	$3\frac{7}{8}$ c.
Grapes, cut and seeded as for salad	1 lb.	$2\frac{3}{4}$ c.
Green peppers	1 lb.	7 medium
Chopped	1 lb.	$3\frac{1}{2}$ c.
One	3 oz.	1 large pepper
Ham, ground, cooked	1 lb.	$2\frac{1}{2}$ c.
Hamburg steak, raw	1 lb.	2 c.
Hominy, pearl	1 lb.	$2\frac{1}{2}$ c.
Honey, strained	1 lb.	$1\frac{1}{3}$ c.
Lard or compound	1 lb.	$2\frac{1}{8}$–$2\frac{1}{2}$ c.
Lemons, 300 size	1 lb.	4 lemons
Lemon juice	1 lb.	2 c.
		4–5 lemons = 1 c.
Lettuce (5 dozen per crate), 1 head trimmed	12–16 oz.	1 head = 12–16 leaves for salad
Macaroni, broken $1\frac{1}{2}$-inch pieces .	1 lb.	5 c.
1 lb. macaroni when cooked equals		3 qt.
Marshmallows	1 lb.	2 qt. or 102 whole marshmallows
Mayonnaise	1 lb.	$2\frac{1}{8}$ c.
Meat, cooked, cubed, $\frac{1}{2}$-inch pieces	1 lb.	$3\frac{2}{3}$ c.

TABLE OF WEIGHTS AND MEASURES (*Continued*)

Food Materials	Weight	Approximate Measure
Milk	1 lb.	2 c.
Molasses	1 lb.	1⅓ c.
Mushrooms, sliced, fresh	1 lb.	5¾ c.
Noodles, uncooked, broken . . .	1 lb.	8 c.
Nuts: Almonds, sliced	1 lb.	3¾ c.
Almonds, whole, blanched . .	1 lb.	3 c.
Brazil nuts, sliced	1 lb.	4 c.
English walnuts, chopped . . .	1 lb.	4 c.
English walnuts, whole . . .	1 lb.	4½–5 c.
Filberts, sliced	1 lb.	4–4½ c.
Peanuts, whole	1 lb.	3 c.
Pecans, chopped	1 lb.	4 c.
Pecans, whole	1 lb.	4¼ c.
Oats, rolled, A.P.*	1 lb.	5½ c.
1 lb. oats when cooked equals .		2⅓ qt.
Oil, cotton-seed	1 lb.	2⅕ c.
Onion, chopped	1 lb.	3 c.
Oranges, cut in ½-inch cubes . .	1 lb.	2⅔ c.
Oysters: Standards		1 qt. 80–85 oysters
Selects		1 qt. 46–60 oysters
Counts		1 qt. 35–40 oysters
Peaches, dried, A.P.*	1 lb.	3 c.
1 lb. peaches soaked and cooked equals, without juice . . .		4½ c.
1 lb. peaches soaked and cooked weighs, without juice . . .	2½ lb.	
Peanut butter	1 lb.	1⅔ c.
Peas, canned, drained	1 lb.	2⅔ c.
Fresh, uncooked	1 lb.	3 c.
Split, A.P.*	1 lb.	2⅓ c.
Pickles, whole, sweet	1 lb.	16, 3-inch length 22, 2-inch length
Chopped	1 lb.	3 c.
Pickle relish	1 lb.	2¾ c.
Pimento, chopped	1 lb.	2 c.
Pineapple, grated	1 lb.	2 c.
Canned, broken pieces	1 lb.	2 c.
Fresh, A.P.* (average size) . .	2 lb. 8 oz.	1 pineapple

* A.P. = As Purchased.

TABLE OF WEIGHTS AND MEASURES (*Continued*)

Food Materials	Weight	Approximate Measure
Potatoes, unpeeled	1 lb. before peeling	$\frac{3}{4}$ lb. after peeling
Diced for creaming	1 lb. before peeling	$2\frac{1}{3}$ c. diced
Prunes, A.P.* (40–50 size) . . .	1 lb.	$2\frac{1}{2}$ c.
1 lb. prunes soaked and cooked equals, without juice . . .	1 lb. 10 oz.	4 c.
1 lb. prunes, soaked, cooked and pitted		$2\frac{1}{4}$ c.
Pumpkin, canned	1 lb.	$1\frac{3}{4}$ c.
Radishes, cleaned, medium-sized .	1 lb.	108 radishes
Raisins, seeded	1 lb.	$2\frac{1}{2}$ c.
Seedless	1 lb.	3 c.
White	1 lb.	3 c.
Rice, whole	1 lb.	$2\frac{1}{8}$ c.
1 lb. rice when cooked equals .		2 qt.
Salmon	1 lb.	2 c.
Salt	1 lb.	$2\frac{3}{8}$ c.
Sauerkraut	1 lb.	$2\frac{1}{8}$ c.
Shrimp, green, A.P.*	1 lb.	30–33 shrimp or 7–8 oz. after cleaning or $1\frac{2}{3}$ c.
Soda	1 lb.	2 c.
Spaghetti	1 lb.	5 c.
1 lb. spaghetti when cooked equals		$2\frac{3}{4}$ qt.
Spices: Allspice, ground	1 lb.	$4\frac{1}{4}$ c.
Whole	1 lb.	5 c.
Caraway seed	1 lb.	4 c.
Celery salt	1 lb.	$2\frac{3}{4}$ c.
Celery seed	1 lb.	4 c.
Chili powder	1 lb.	$3\frac{2}{3}$ c.
Cinnamon, ground	1 lb.	4 c.
Cloves, ground	1 lb.	$3\frac{3}{4}$ c.
Cloves, whole	1 lb.	5 c.
Curry powder	1 lb.	4 c.
Ginger, candied, cut $\frac{1}{4}$-inch . .	1 lb.	3 c.
Ginger, ground	1 lb.	$4\frac{1}{4}$ c.
Mace, ground	1 lb.	4 c.
Mace, whole	1 lb.	7 c.

* A.P. = As Purchased.

TABLE OF WEIGHTS AND MEASURES (*Continued*)

Food Materials	Weight	Approximate Measure
Spices, *continued*		
Mustard, ground	1 lb.	5 c.
Mustard, prepared	1 lb.	4¼ c.
Nutmeg	1 lb.	3½ c.
Paprika	1 lb.	3¾ c.
Pepper, black	1 lb.	3⅔ c.
Red	1 lb.	3⅔ c.
White	1 lb.	4½ c.
Peppercorns	1 lb.	3⅓ c.
Poppy seed	1 lb.	3 c.
Sage	1 lb.	5¾ c.
Spinach, washed, trimmed, un-		
cooked	1 lb.	3⅓ c.
Cooked	1 lb.	2 c.
Strawberries, hulled	1 lb. 2 oz.	1 qt.
1 qt. of strawberries when crushed		2¼ c.
String beans, canned	1 lb.	2 c.
Sweetbreads, A.P.*	1 lb.	1⅝ c. cooked
Sugar: Brown	1 lb.	2¾ c.
Granulated	1 lb.	2⅛ c.
Loaf	1 lb.	80–90 pieces
Powdered	1 lb.	2¾ c.
Suet, ground	1 lb.	3½ c.
Tapioca: Minute	1 lb.	2¾ c.
Pearl	1 lb.	3½ c.
1 lb. tapioca, soaked and cooked		7½ c.
Tea	1 lb.	8 c.
Tuna fish	1 lb.	2 c.
Vanilla	1 lb.	2 c.
Vinegar	1 lb.	2 c.
Yeast	1 lb.	32 individual cakes

* A.P. = As Purchased.

INDEX

Index